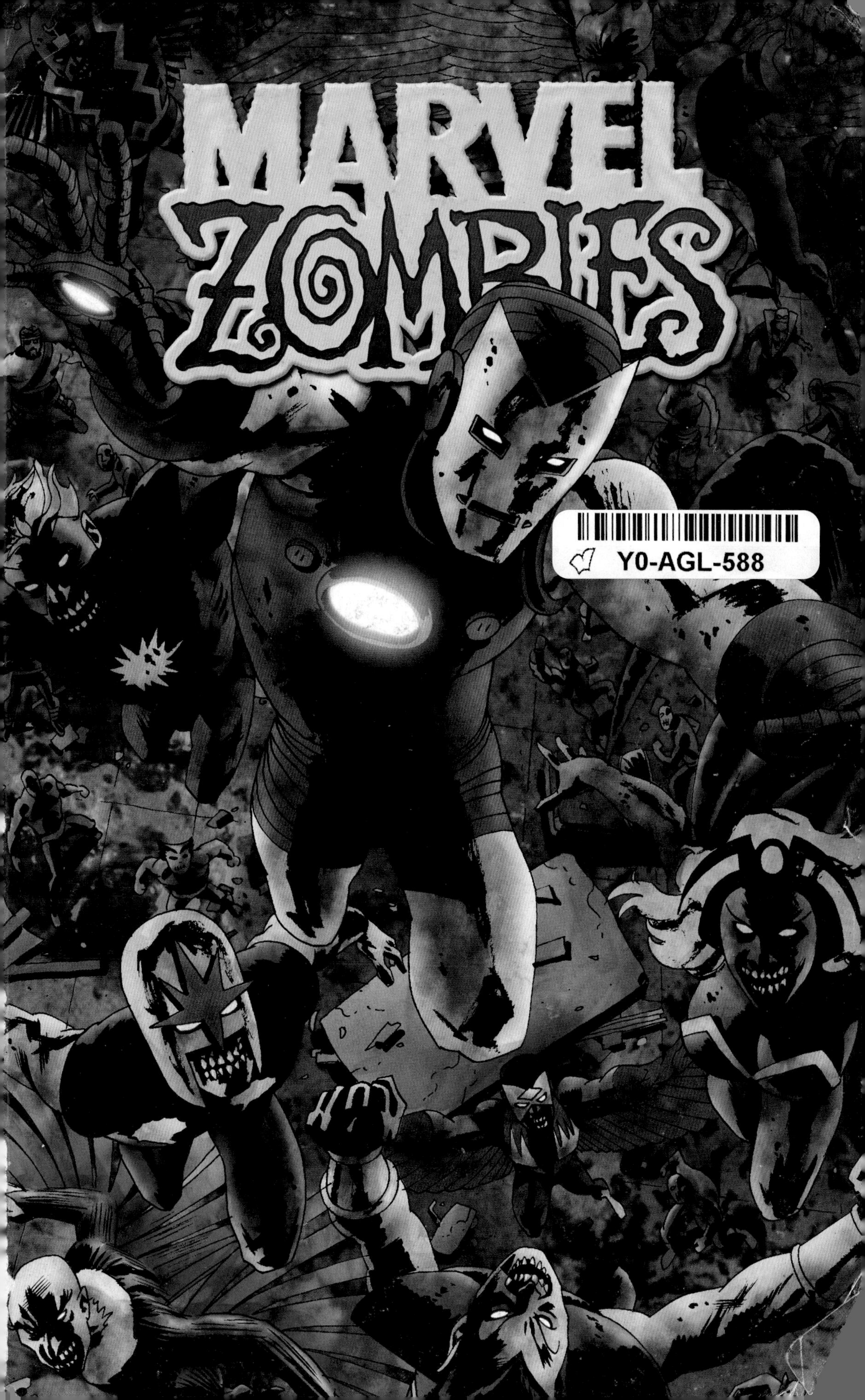
MARVEL
ZOMBIES

MARVEL ZOMBIES

WRITER: Robert Kirkman
ARTIST: Sean Phillips
COLORIST: June Chung
LETTERER: Virtual Calligraphy's Randy Gentile
COVER ARTIST: Arthur Suydam

ASSISTANT EDITORS: Nicole Boose & John Barber
EDITOR: Ralph Macchio

COLLECTION EDITOR: Mark D. Beazley
EDITORIAL ASSISTANT: Alex Starbuck
ASSISTANT EDITORS: John Denning & Cory Levine
EDITOR, SPECIAL PROJECTS: Jennifer Grünwald
SENIOR EDITOR, SPECIAL PROJECTS: Jeff Youngquist
VICE PRESIDENT OF SALES: David Gabriel
PRODUCTION: Jerry Kalinowski
BOOK DESIGNER: Patrick McGrath
VICE PRESIDENT OF CREATIVE: Tom Marvelli
EDITOR IN CHIEF: Joe Quesada
PUBLISHER: Dan Buckley

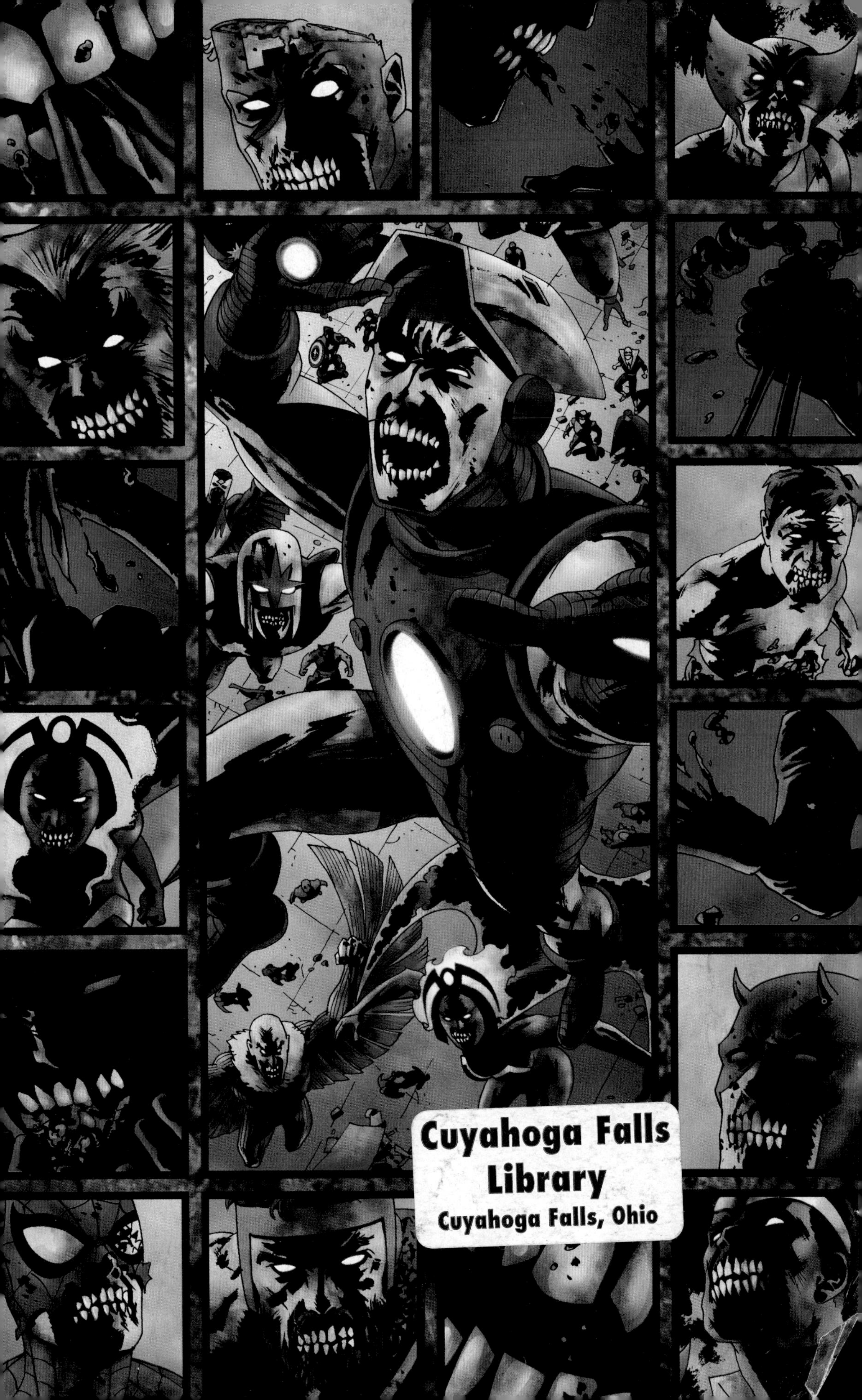

MARVELOUS ZOMBIES

I didn't even really want to do this book. No, seriously. Aside from the plethora of marvelous Marvel Comics I do on a monthly basis, I keep my toe firmly dipped into the creator-owned pool of the comics industry. I do two other books, *Invincible* and *The Walking Dead*, the latter of which (as the title would indicate) is a zombie book.

I love zombies—zombie movies, zombie comics, zombie lunch boxes, zombie toothpaste—I love it all. But the thing is, *The Walking Dead* pretty much scratches that itch. And it's *very* easy in this business I like to call comics to get labeled as something. You can be the "talking animal guy" or the "crappy ending guy" or the "way too much dialogue guy" after just one or two high-profile projects.

I didn't want to be the "zombie guy" not that I think there's anything wrong with that—it's just that I've always prided myself on the diversity of the work I produce. I didn't want to suddenly look like a one-trick pony. Especially because the bulk of my work aside from *The Walking Dead* is super hero stuff...so a zombie super hero book seemed a bit too, I don't know...easy.

So when Ralph Macchio (of *Karate Kid* fame, I don't know if anybody knows that), the editor of this fine book, called me up, I was stunned. After I got over the initial shock of receiving a phone call from cinema's Karate Kid, I started to listen to what he was saying, things like:

"Zombie Marvel Universe."

"Ultimate Fantastic Four."

"Mark Millar's idea."

"Would you want in?"

Turns out ol' Mark Millar created some kooky zombie-filled Marvel Universe that was to be discovered by the Ultimate Fantastic Four in the opening arc of his new run on that book. Marvel, being the brilliant company they are, decided to do a mini-series spinning off from that world. Since I was quickly becoming the "zombie guy" due to my other zombie book...I got the call.

I thought about it, and ultimately I accepted. You just don't turn down The Karate Kid.

It's not wise.

Nor do you ignore the words of wisdom from the Kid's cohorts—Associate Editors John Barber and Nicole Boose. Both of whom contributed mightily to the direction this series finally took. Couldn't have done it without them. Thanks, guys!

So then came the fun part...what do we actually do in this mini-series? A lot of ideas were thrown about. One involved Hawkeye escaping in a Quinjet to the Arctic and trying to live there—until the zombies found him and he had to go on the run again. Kinda boring, I know...we didn't do it after all.

Another idea I had was "Luke Cage: last man on Earth!" For that idea Luke Cage would be finding pockets of civilization, normal humans in hiding...and he would be leading the hordes of Marvel Zombies *to them*. He'd be working for the zombies because the child he had with Jessica Jones was being held prisoner, and the zombies agreed to not eat her—as long as Cage provided them something *else* to eat. I thought it was kinda cool. Maybe a little obscure...it relied heavily on a plot-line from *The Pulse* and could have been confusing, but it would have been cool, Cage forming an army, figuring out how to take out the zombies...stuff like that.

Thankfully, Karate Kid drop-kicked that idea right into the trash. In a very "paint fence wash windows" kinda moment, he suggested maybe we just focus on the zombies as the main characters. That guy's a freaking Zen master or something.

It had never even occurred to me that we could do that. I wasn't really thinking outside of the box. I thought we'd need someone for the reader to relate to...someone to see the world through their eyes...it couldn't all just be *zombies*.. but actually...it *could*.

My mind began to race with possibilities. I mean, five full issues with just zombies.. running around, doing whatever? Could that work? Could that be entertaining? I thought it could...but there was a catch.

I called Ralph up one day while I was plotting the book out. I had realized that doing a book with an entirely zombie cast had one major problem...*they were zombies*. "Ralph," I said, "I don't really know how I can do this. These guys are rotting and falling apart, losing body parts and eating whatever they can find...this book is going to be *gross*, bloody and *gross*." To which he replied, "Yeah?" I was shocked...I said to him, I said, "*Ralph*, for the love of Pete, this is a *Marvel comic*." And he said back to me, "So? I think it'll be fine. Go *crazy!*"

And I did. I got off the phone and over the next three weeks I put my heart and soul into the first issue of this book you now hold in your hands. I won't ruin anything for you here but it was nasty, *really* nasty...way nastier than it had any right to be. There were severed arms and swollen legs and chewed intestines and all kinds of gross gore stuff that every zombie story should be chock-full of.

I actually *liked* it. I don't usually get done with a script and think "hey, that was pretty good." Usually it's "Man, I hope they like it." Because I have no idea how to judge my own work. But this, I thought, was cool. I emailed it into the editorial office (which is how we do things here in the future). A buddy of mine called, an "industry pro" as I like to call them, I won't drop names (oh, it was Steven Spielberg, who am I kidding?). He asked what I was up to. I said, well, I just turned in the first script for *Marvel Zombies* and Steve said, *really*? Wow what's it like? I then went on to tell him about all the nastiness inside, in great detail, and as I went on I got more and more excited.

"And then this happens! And then this! And then

this! It's *crazy!!*"

And I paused. The phone was silent. Steven was stunned. He replied back to me, "This is a Marvel book, right? You did *what?!*" I came to a startling realization—I had made a huge mistake! I immediately hung up on Spielberg (which immediately shot me out of the running to write *Indiana Jones 4*) and I started to sweat buckets!

I was going to be fired. I couldn't believe I was *stupid* enough to put the things I'd put in *Marvel Zombies #1* in an actual honest-to-god *Marvel Comic*. I thought for sure they would read the script and think I was playing a prank on them—that I had put that stuff in there just to mess with them...I thought they would be outraged. Which sucked because now that my screenwriting career was in the toilet I *needed* this job!

The phone rang. The caller I.D. clearly read "*Karate Kid.*"

Reluctantly, I answered the phone. "*Yes?*" Only to hear, "Robert, it's Ralph calling. I read the script to *Marvel Zombies #1*." Stunned as I was that he hadn't yet started yelling, I asked, "*and?*" To which he said, "Looks great. I'm sending it on to Sean the artist, I'll get to him in a minute or two." I was *stunned*. Everything seemed to be fine. He was letting it go, letting the book be bloody, nasty, and gory.

Up until that point, I had no idea how this book would sell. I thought, "it's kind of a spin-off from *Ultimate Fantastic Four*, it might do okay." I didn't think in a million years it would be the success it ultimately became, but from that point on, when I knew they were going to let it be gory...I knew it was something special, something people couldn't get somewhere else.

I knew it had a chance.

So for the next four issues, with every script, I tried my hardest to come up with *something, anything* that would be so horrible, so disgusting they would make me change it...and it *never* happened. Every disgusting thing the zombies did was kept in. Nothing was changed, nothing was altered...it was just bizarre, and frustrating...I thought I was one sick puppy, but I couldn't come up with anything they balked at.

I don't think it was only the gore or the shock value that drew attention to the book, because Ralph and his crack team of ninja editors assembled a fine creative team (aside from me). Sean Phillips was picked as the artist...Sean is well known for his work on dozens of other books, most recently *Sleeper* with Ed Brubaker. He did a fantastic job on this book, as you'll soon see. He made the book a real treat to work on. Sean is a great guy.

It'd be a huge oversight to go without mentioning Arthur Suydam as well. His covers (all 75 of them) for this series were a real driving force behind the sales success. They were just so wacky and off the wall...when you saw a copy of *Marvel Zombies* on the shelf, you knew it couldn't be anything else.

Kudos to Marvel Editor in Chief Joe Quesada for suggesting the idea of using classic Marvel covers as the template for the *Zombies* covers. Also, it was talent coordinator Chris Allo who came up with the name "Arthur Suydam" as a potential cover artist. Great ideas both!

And the book was a success.

The first issue quickly sold out and went into multiple printings, a trend that continued with each successive issue. People seemed to enjoy the book, Marvel was happy with its success and all that led to the Hardcover that you now hold in your hot little hands.

So while at first I was reluctant to accept the job, I'm glad I did...I had a blast on this series and I can't wait to do it all over again!

I'll see you then!

ROBERT "THE ZOMBIE GUY" KIRKMAN
Backwoods, Kentucky
June 2006

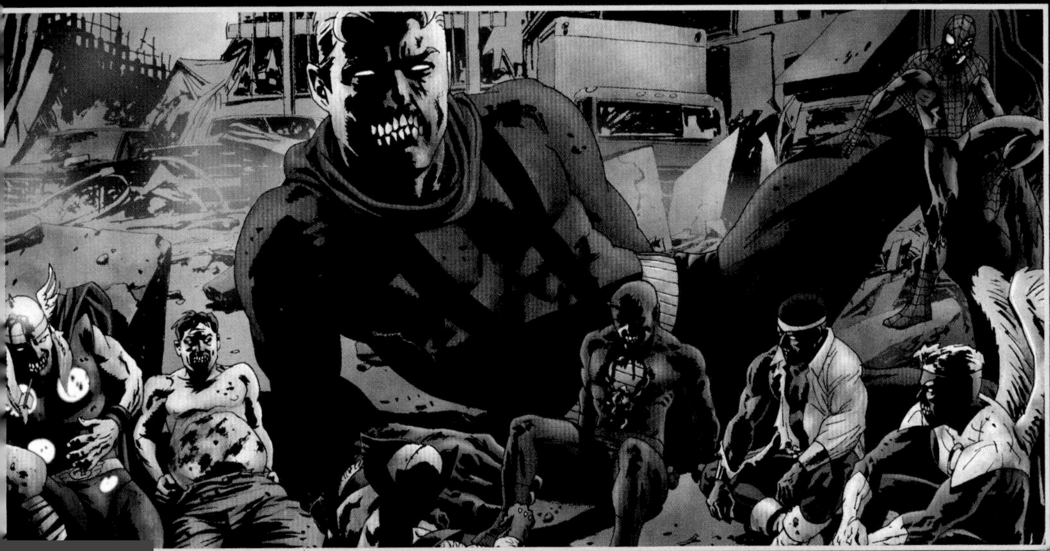

It started with a flash in the sky, and a ripple through the clouds. The hunger is what brought it here — and feed it did, until the Marvel Heroes were no more.

They were replaced by soulless monsters, driven only by an insatiable hunger for human flesh.

After they ran out of food, Reed Richards devised a plan to lure his counterpart from another dimension into a deadly trap. Thanks to Magneto, who had managed to stay uninfected, Reed's plan failed, leaving him and the rest of the Fantastic Four stranded in another dimension.

Magneto has destroyed the machine that allowed their passage to that dimension — and is left to carry on with his life. He does not expect to live long.

This is no world of Marvel Heroes.

This is the world of...

MARVEL ZOMBIES

PART 1 OF 5

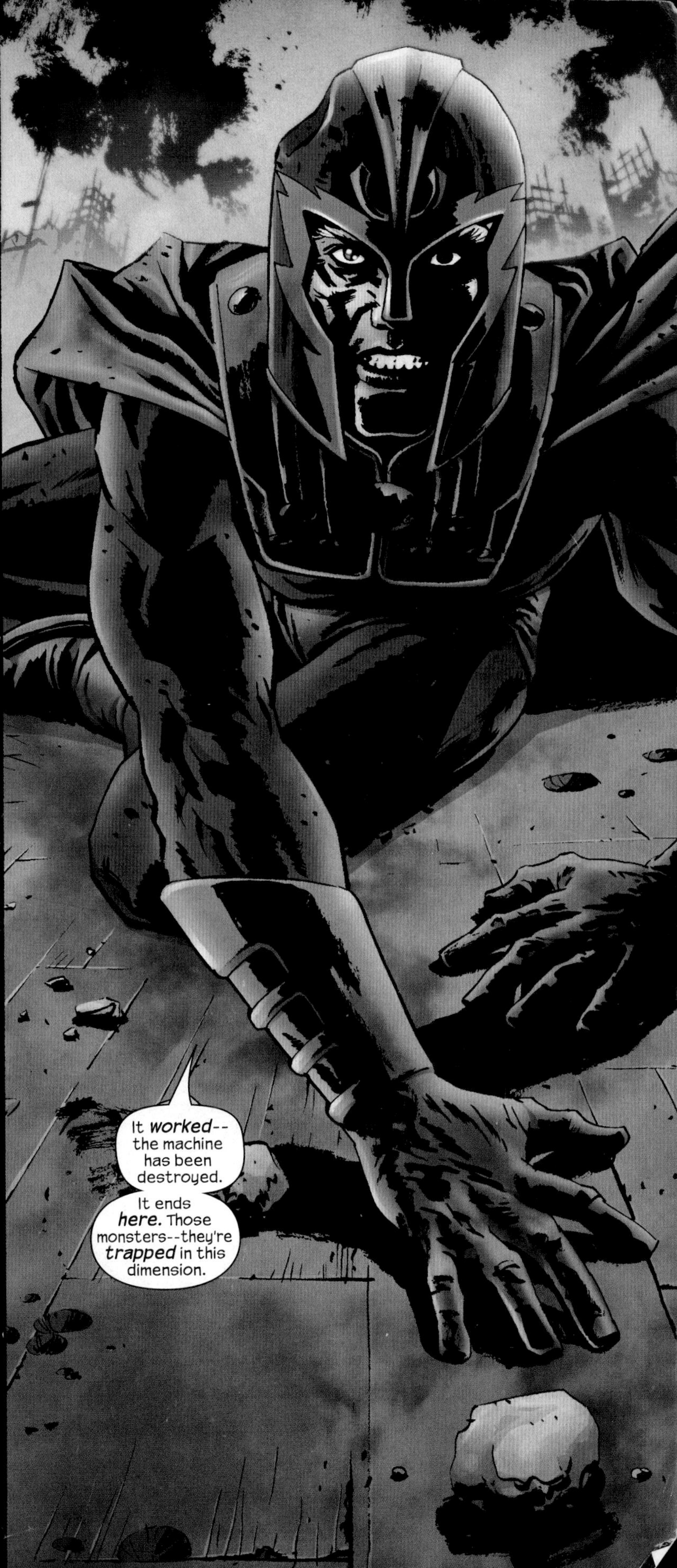

It *worked*--the machine has been destroyed.
It ends *here.* Those monsters--they're *trapped* in this dimension.

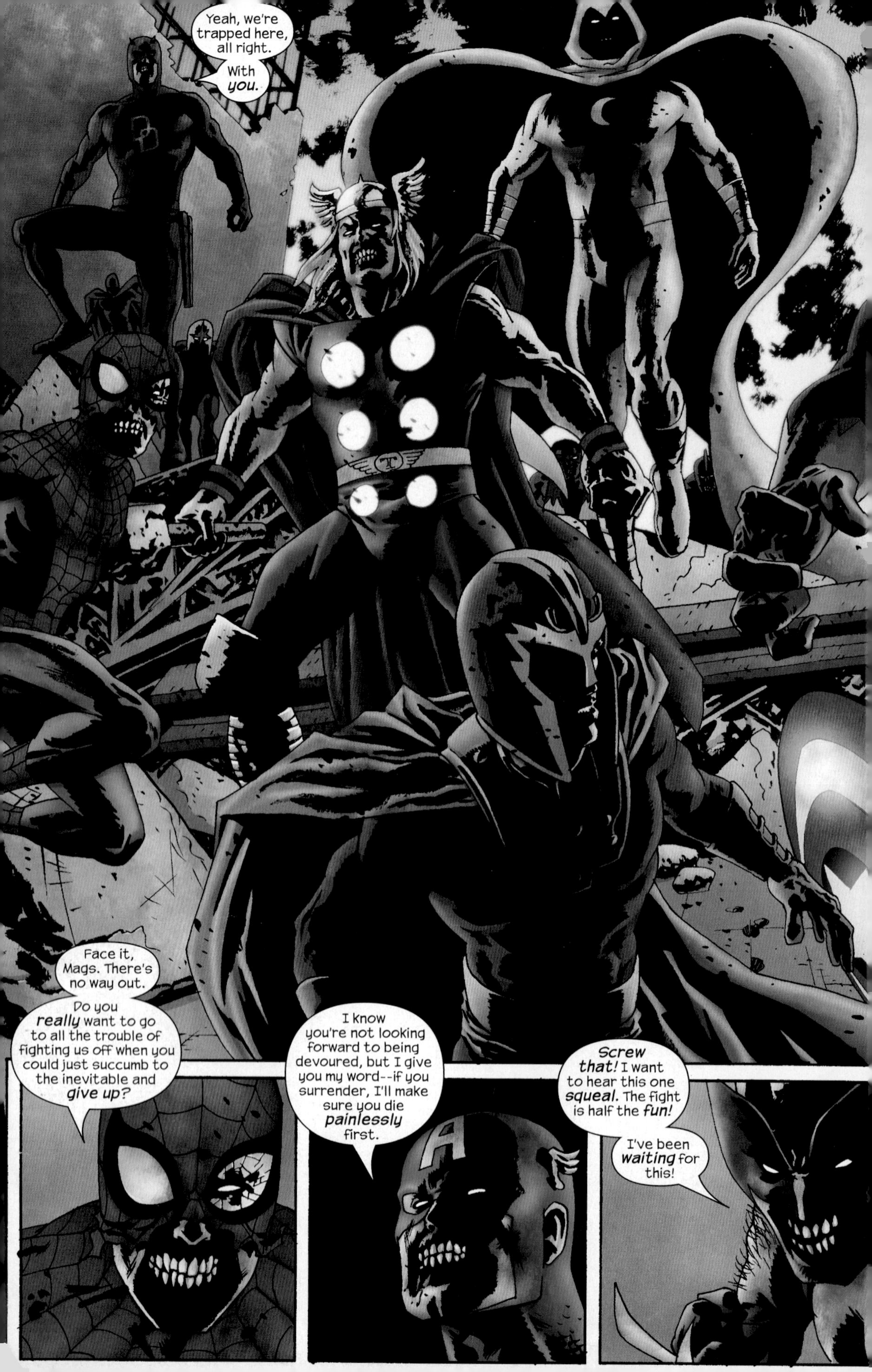
Yeah, we're trapped here, all right.
With *you*.
Face it, Mags. There's no way out.
Do you ***really*** want to go to all the trouble of fighting us off when you could just succumb to the inevitable and ***give up***?
I know you're not looking forward to being devoured, but I give you my word--if you surrender, I'll make sure you die ***painlessly*** first.
Screw that! I want to hear this one ***squeal.*** The fight is half the ***fun!***
I've been ***waiting*** for this!

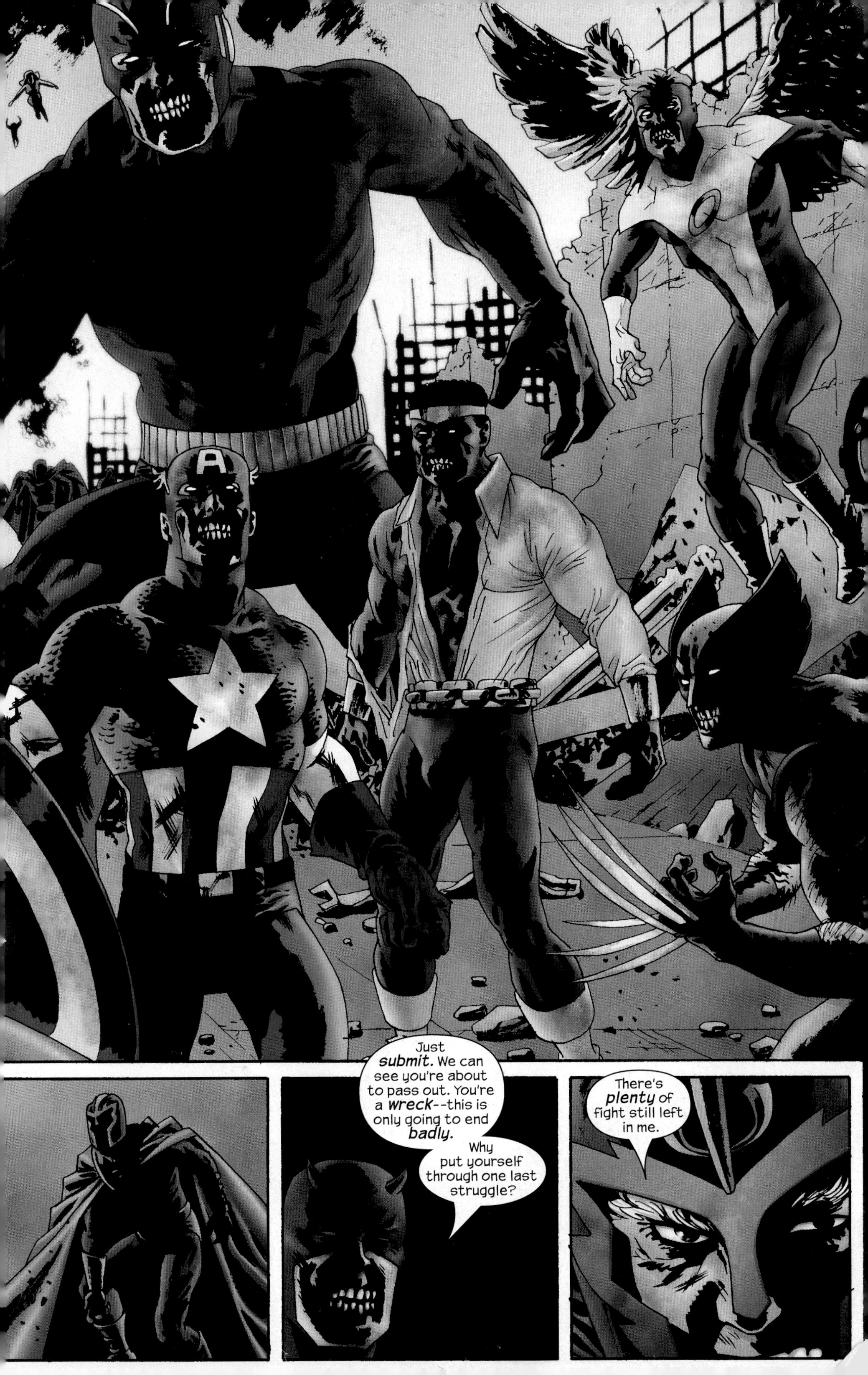
Just submit. We can see you're about to pass out. You're a wreck--this is only going to end badly.
Why put yourself through one last struggle?
There's plenty of fight still left in me.

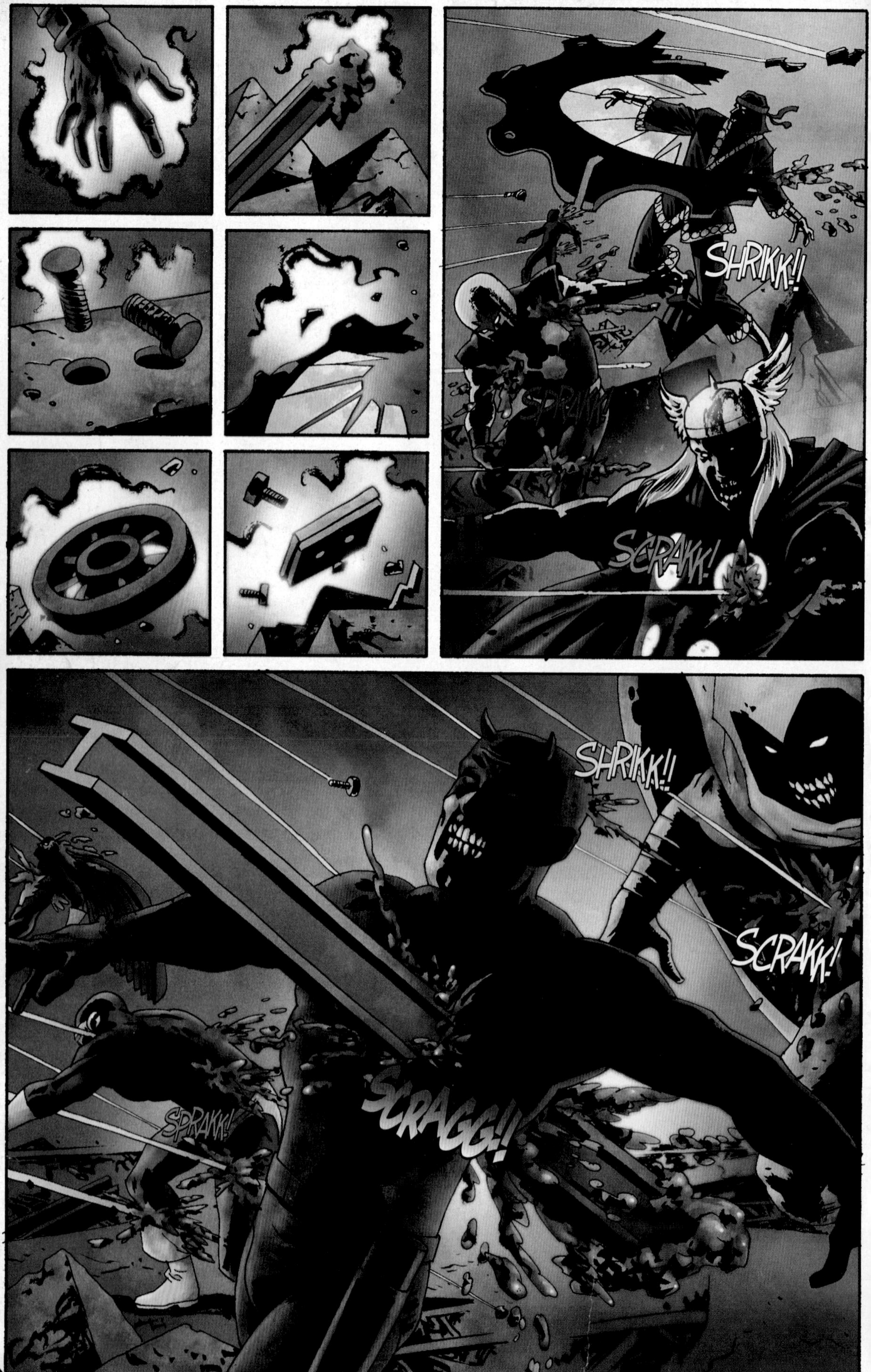
SHRIKK!!
SPRAKK
SCRAKK!
SHRIKK!!
SCRAKK!
SPRAKK!
SCRAGG!!

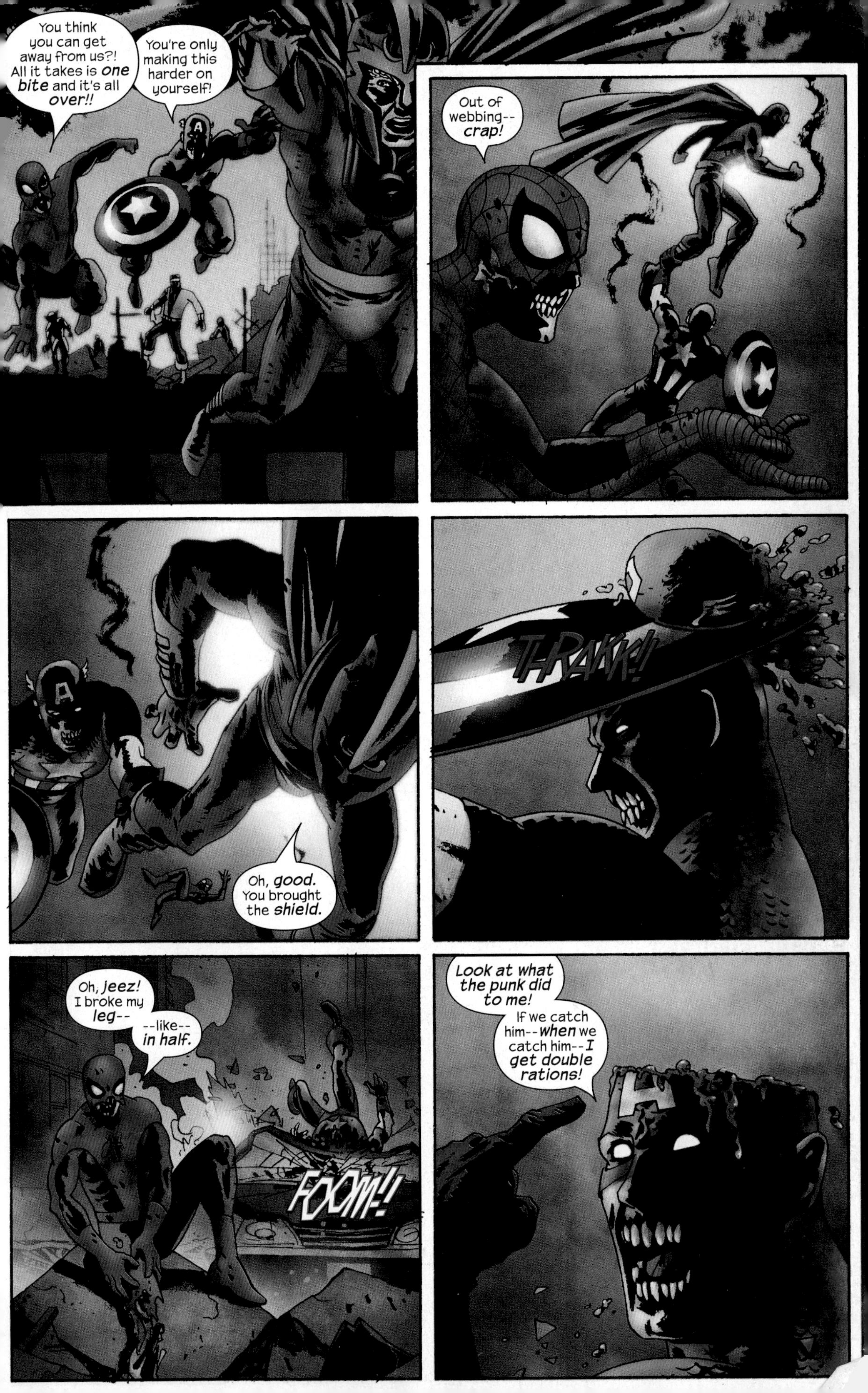
You think you can get away from us?! All it takes is *one bite* and it's all *over!!*
You're only making this harder on yourself!
Out of webbing-- *crap!*
Oh, *good.* You brought the *shield.*
THRAKK!
Oh, *jeez!* I broke my *leg*--
--like-- *in half.*
FOOM!!
Look at what the punk did to me!
If we catch him--*when* we catch him--*I get double rations!*

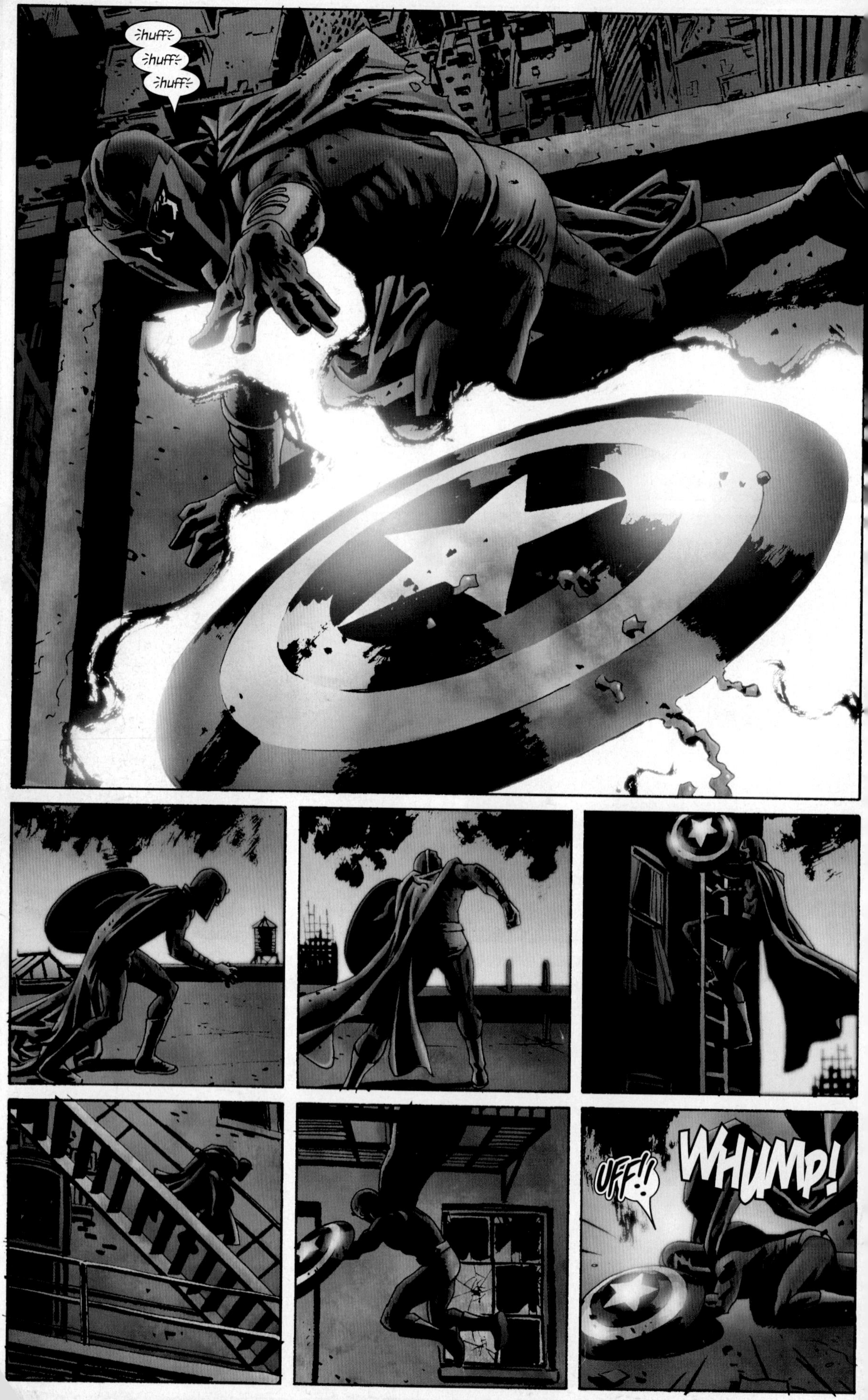
huff
huff
huff
UFF!!
WHUMP!

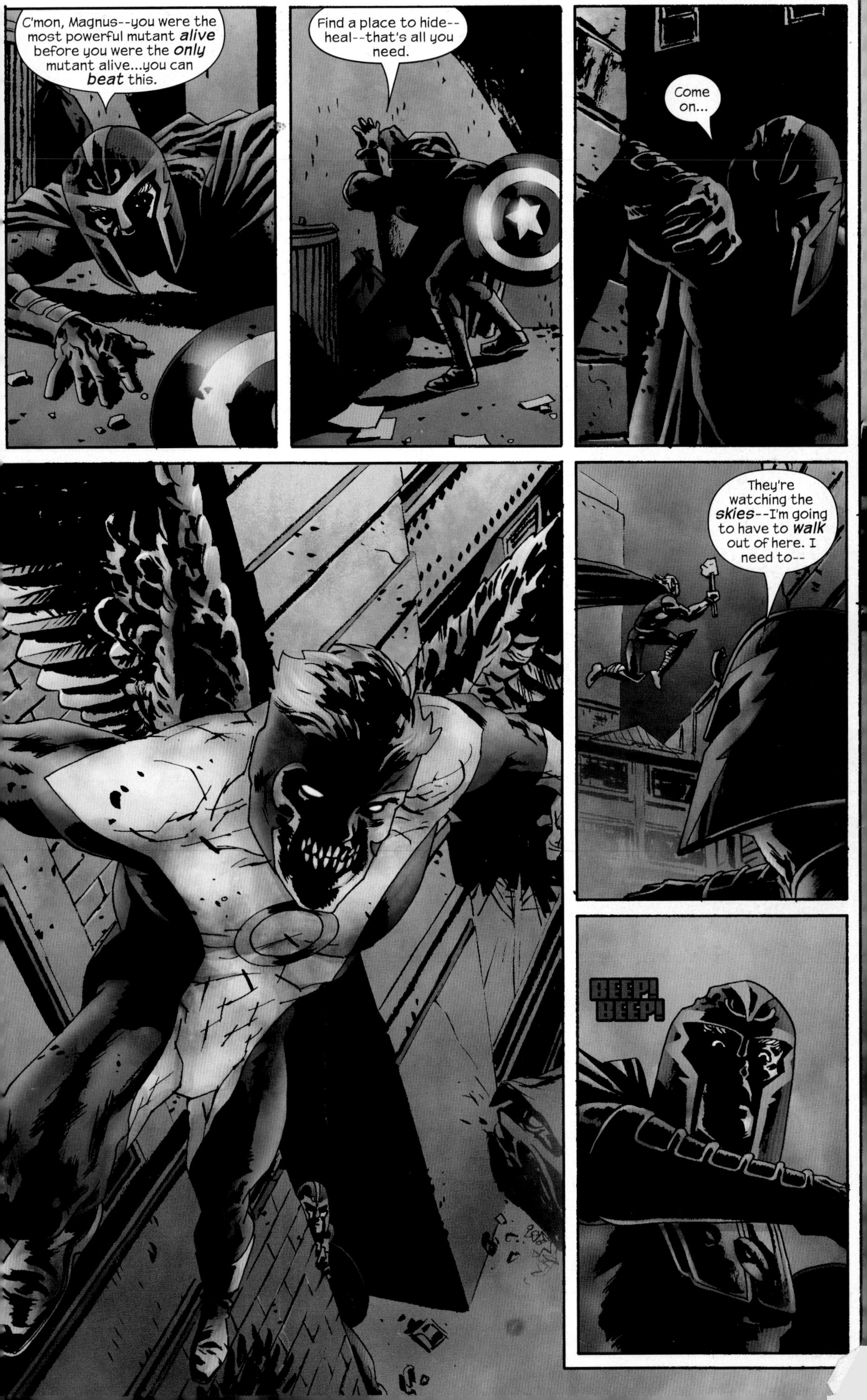
C'mon, Magnus--you were the most powerful mutant alive before you were the only mutant alive...you can beat this.
Find a place to hide--heal--that's all you need.
Come on...
They're watching the skies--I'm going to have to walk out of here. I need to--
BEEP! BEEP!

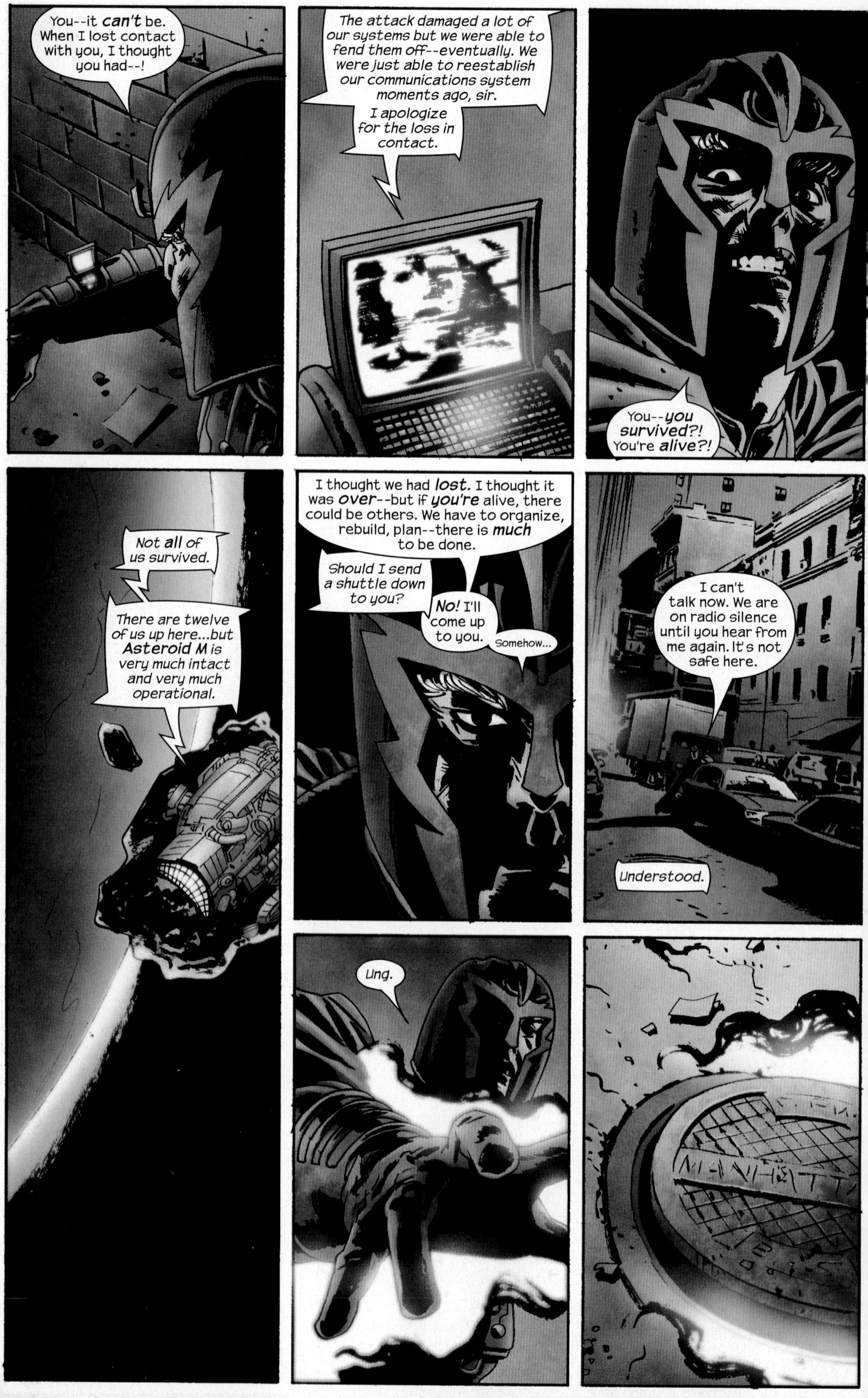
You--it can't be. When I lost contact with you, I thought you had--!
The attack damaged a lot of our systems but we were able to fend them off--eventually. We were just able to reestablish our communications system moments ago, sir.
I apologize for the loss in contact.
You--you survived?! You're alive?!
Not all of us survived.
There are twelve of us up here...but Asteroid M is very much intact and very much operational.
I thought we had lost. I thought it was over--but if you're alive, there could be others. We have to organize, rebuild, plan--there is much to be done.
Should I send a shuttle down to you?
No! I'll come up to you.
Somehow...
I can't talk now. We are on radio silence until you hear from me again. It's not safe here.
Understood.
Ung.

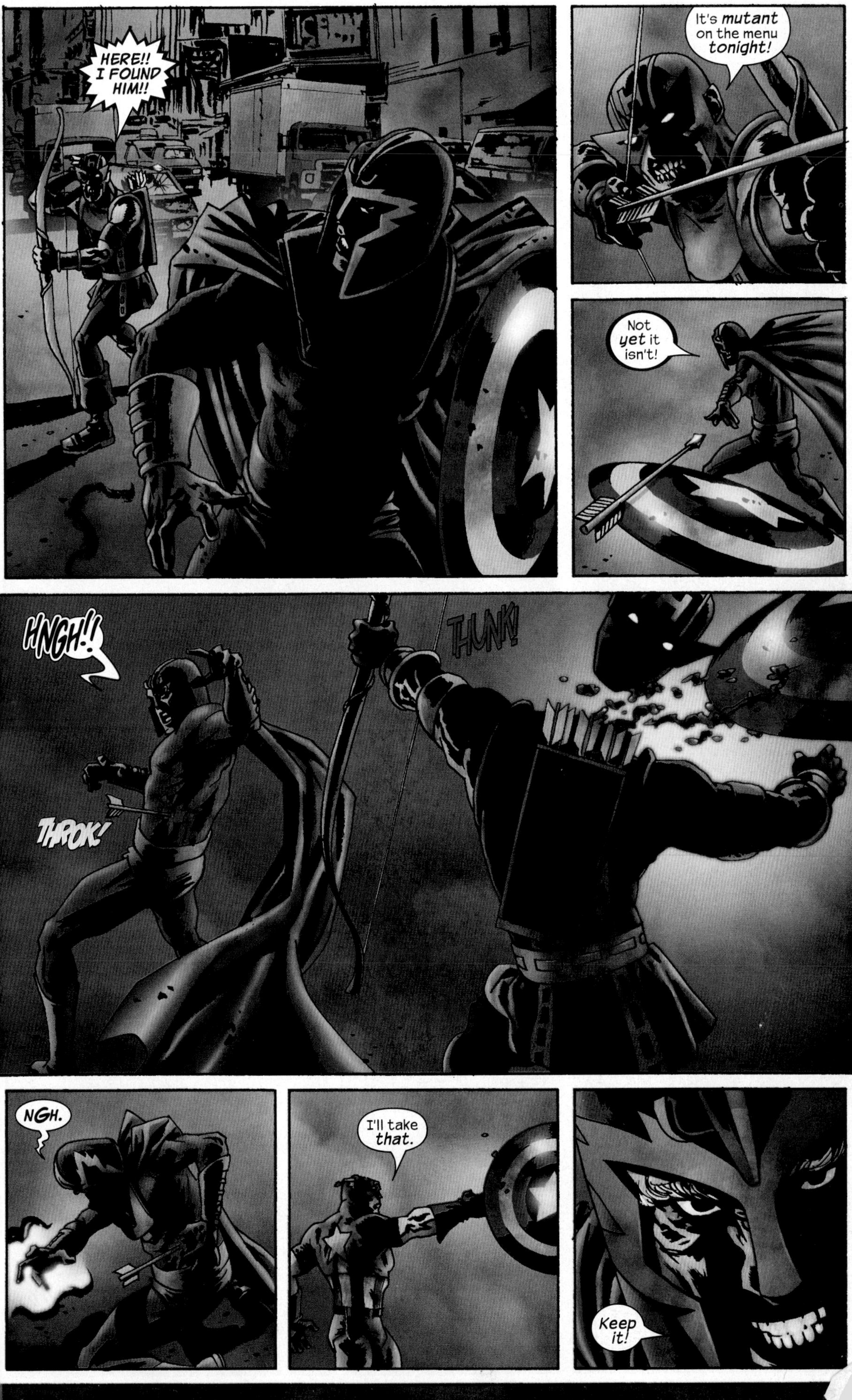
HERE!! I FOUND HIM!!
It's mutant on the menu tonight!
Not yet it isn't!
HNGH!!
THUNK!
THROK!
NGH.
I'll take that.
Keep it!

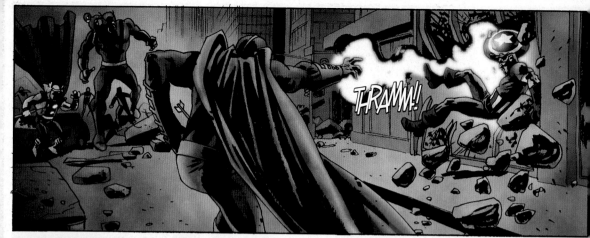

THRAMM!!

Why, Magneto? Why put yourself *through* all this?

It is clear to me, mutant, that thou dost not know when thou art defeated.

I could--say the same--
--about *you*.

GAK!

THUNK!

ULP!

If-- I can-- --only...

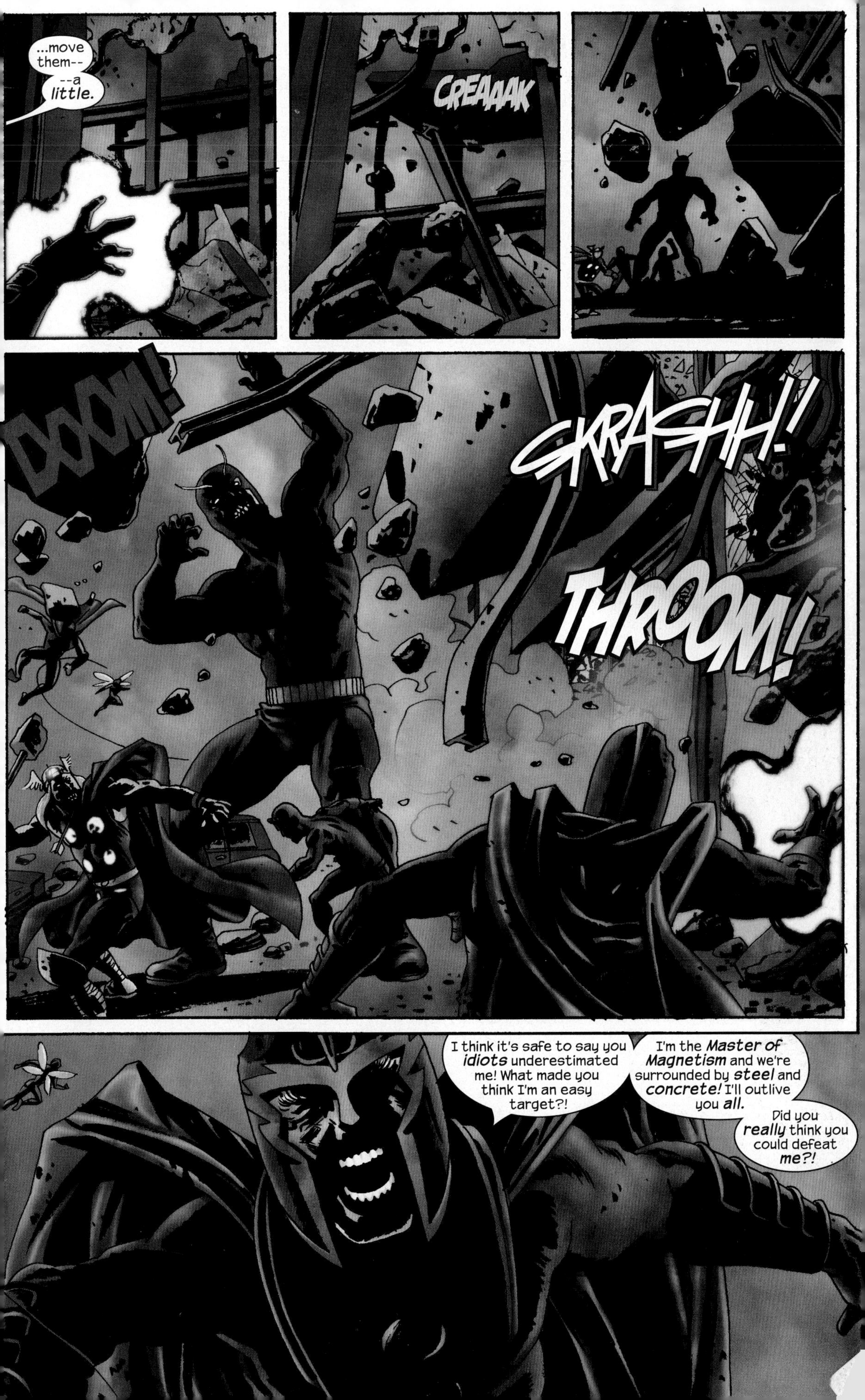
...move them--
--a little.
CREAAAK
DOOM!
SKRASHH!
THROOM!
I think it's safe to say you idiots underestimated me! What made you think I'm an easy target?!
I'm the Master of Magnetism and we're surrounded by steel and concrete! I'll outlive you all.
Did you really think you could defeat me?!

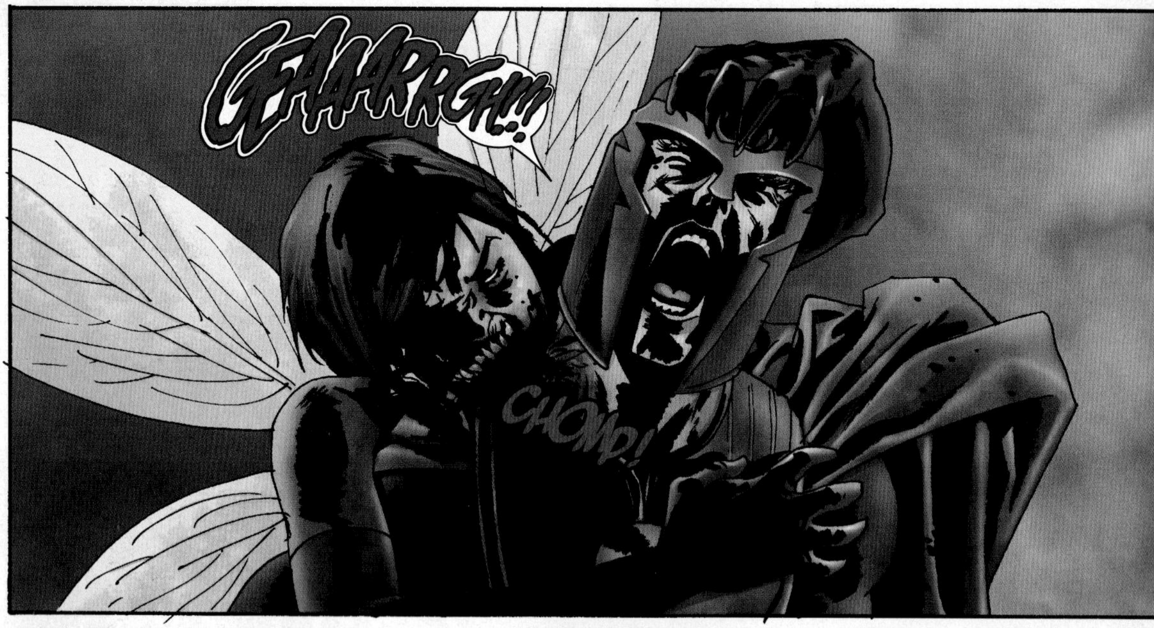
GEAAARRGH!!!
CHOMP!

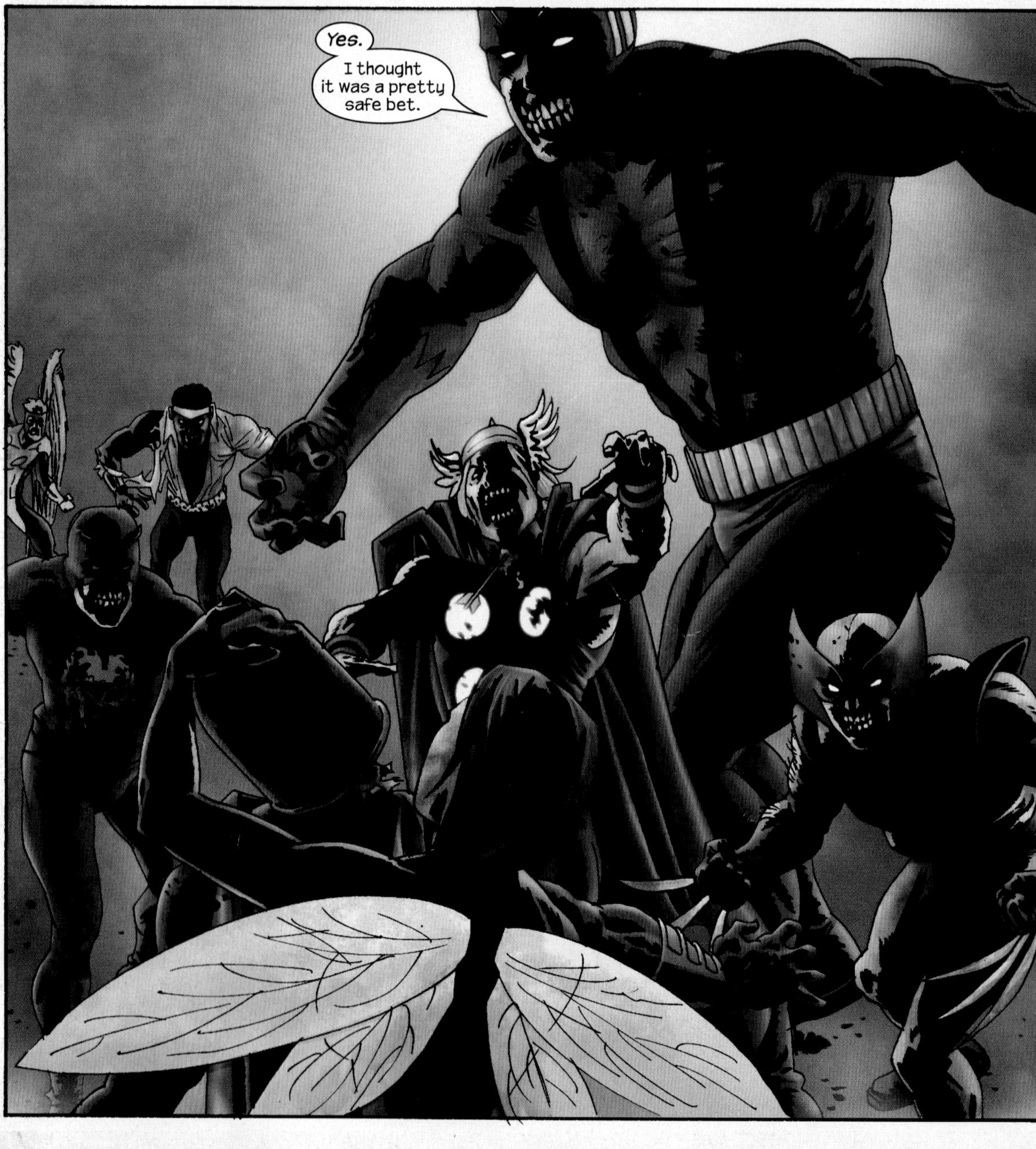
Yes.
I thought it was a pretty safe bet.

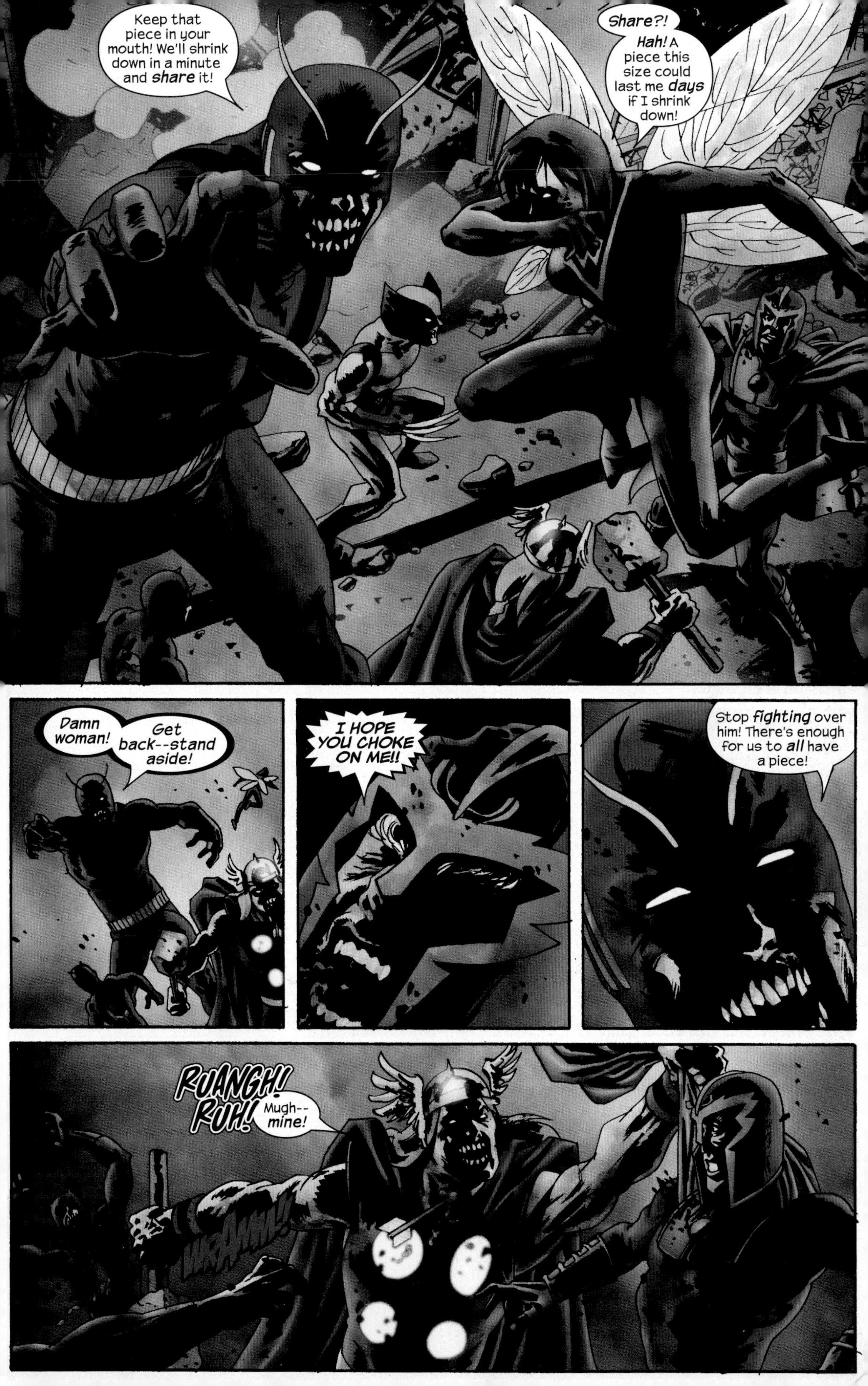
Keep that piece in your mouth! We'll shrink down in a minute and *share* it!
Share?!
Hah! A piece this size could last me *days* if I shrink down!
Damn woman!
Get back--stand aside!
I HOPE YOU CHOKE ON ME!!
Stop *fighting* over him! There's enough for us to *all* have a piece!
RUANGH! RUH!
Mugh-- mine!

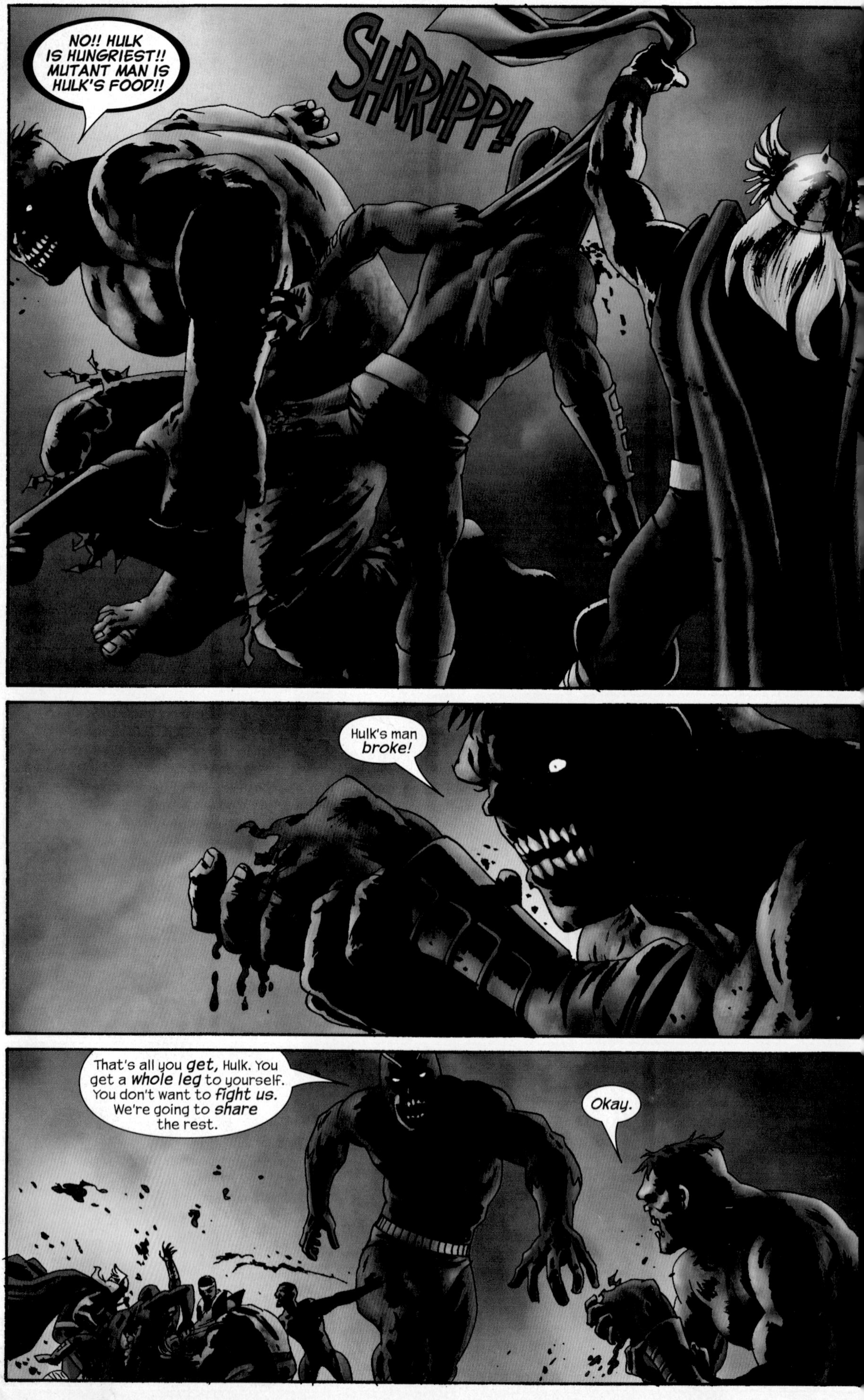
NO!! HULK IS HUNGRIEST!! MUTANT MAN IS HULK'S FOOD!!
SHRRIPP!!
Hulk's man broke!
That's all you get, Hulk. You get a whole leg to yourself. You don't want to fight us. We're going to share the rest.
Okay.

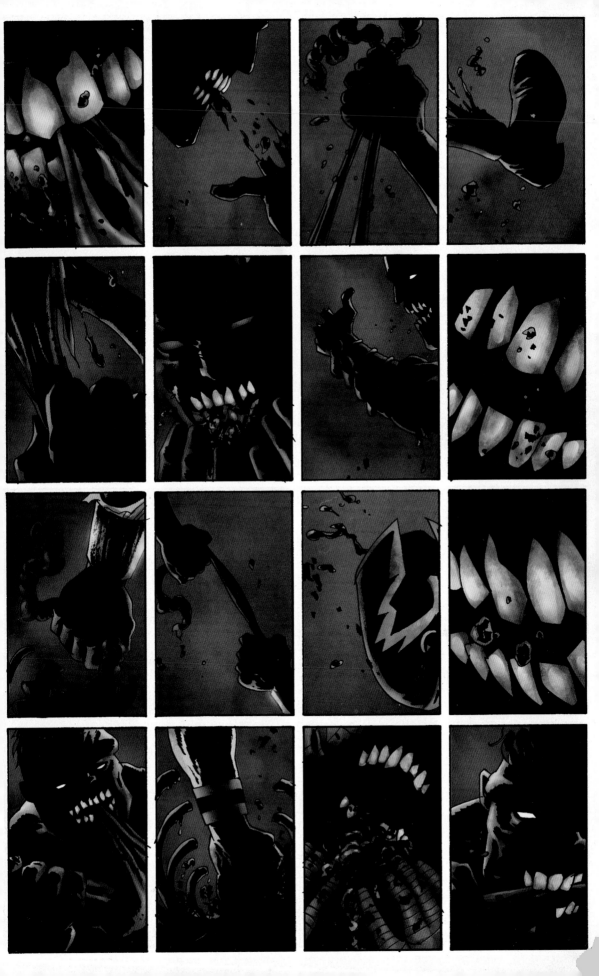

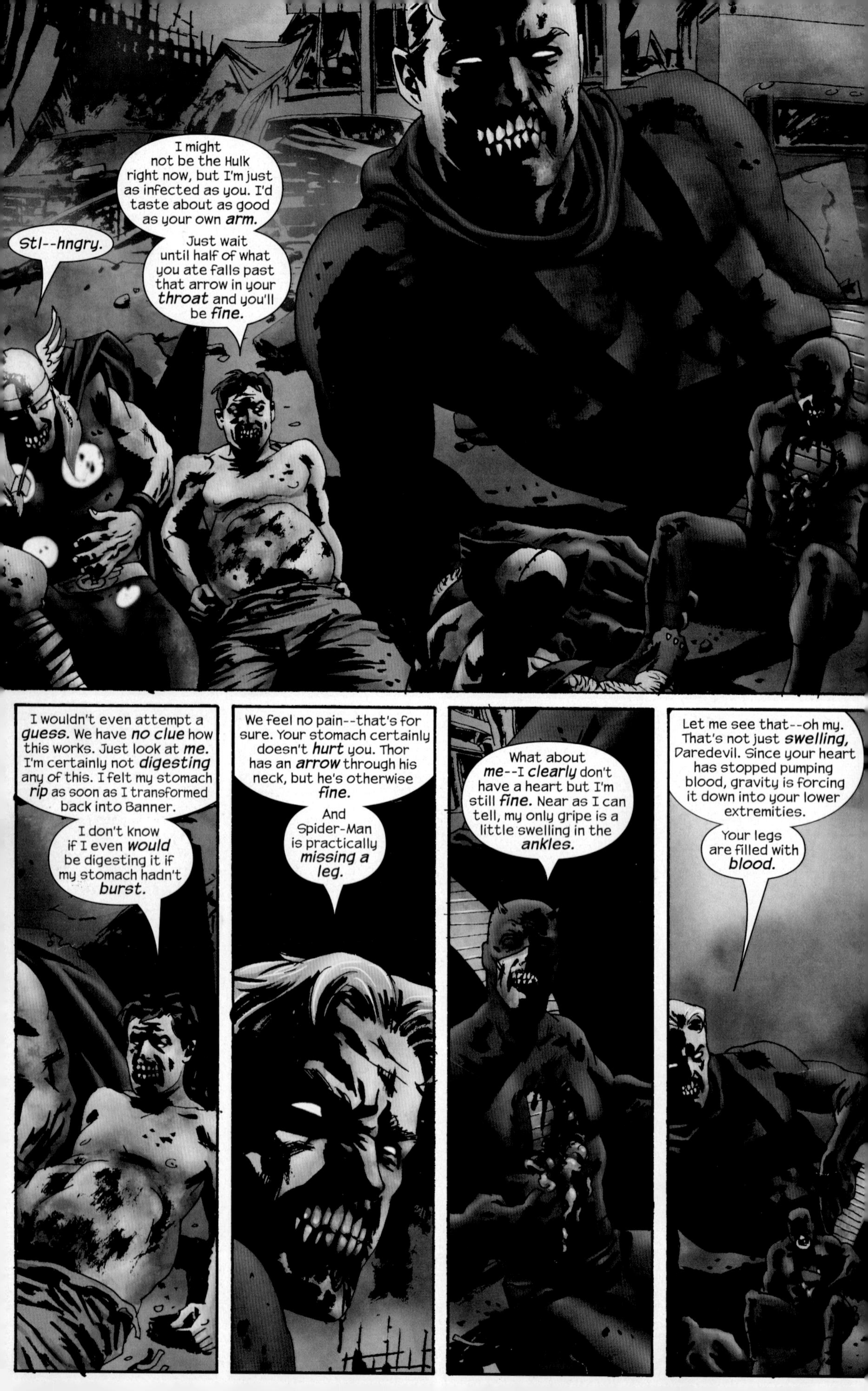
I might not be the Hulk right now, but I'm just as infected as you. I'd taste about as good as your own arm.
Stl--hngry.
Just wait until half of what you ate falls past that arrow in your throat and you'll be fine.
I wouldn't even attempt a guess. We have no clue how this works. Just look at me. I'm certainly not digesting any of this. I felt my stomach rip as soon as I transformed back into Banner.
I don't know if I even would be digesting it if my stomach hadn't burst.
We feel no pain--that's for sure. Your stomach certainly doesn't hurt you. Thor has an arrow through his neck, but he's otherwise fine.
And Spider-Man is practically missing a leg.
What about me--I clearly don't have a heart but I'm still fine. Near as I can tell, my only gripe is a little swelling in the ankles.
Let me see that--oh my. That's not just swelling, Daredevil. Since your heart has stopped pumping blood, gravity is forcing it down into your lower extremities.
Your legs are filled with blood.

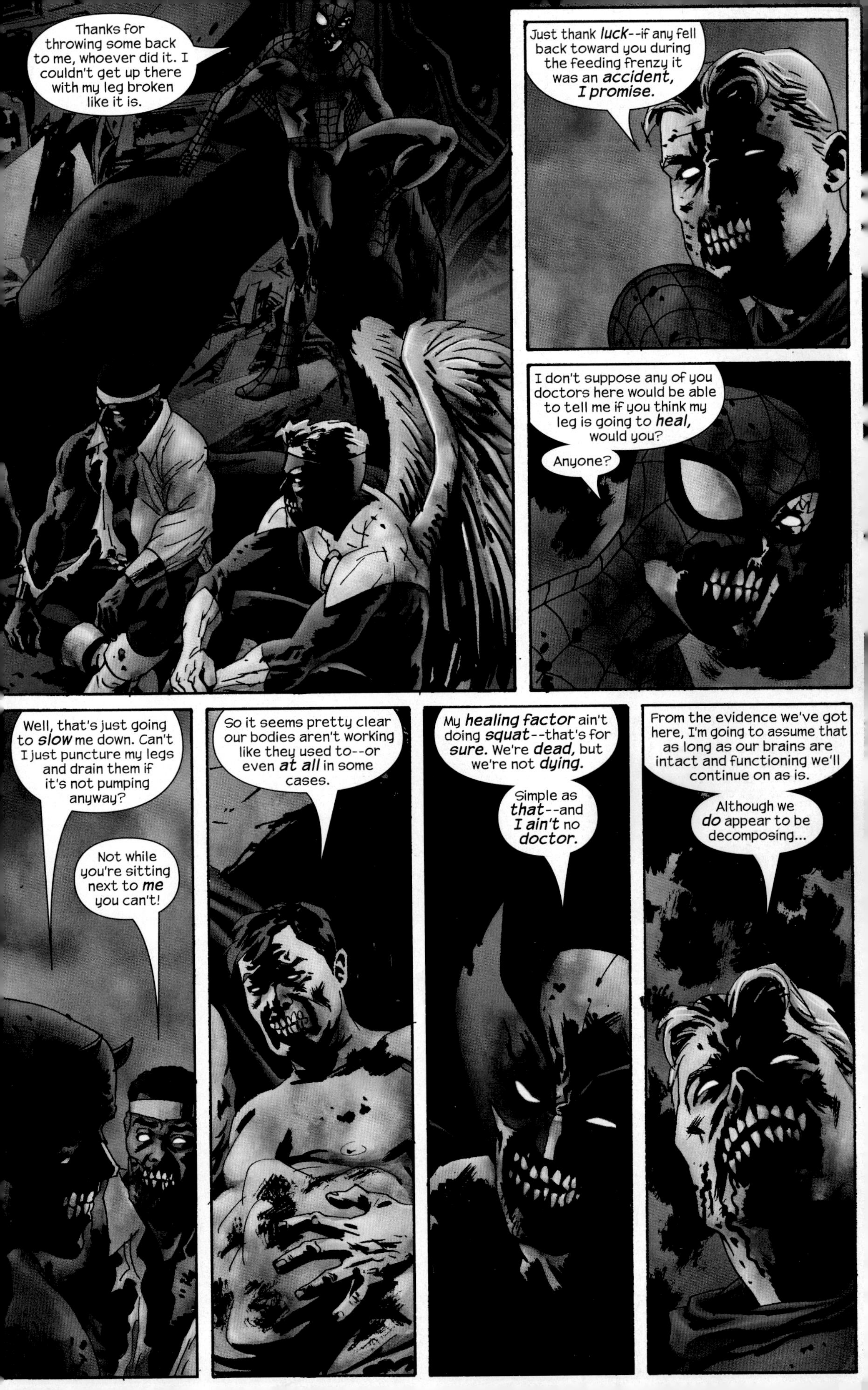
Thanks for throwing some back to me, whoever did it. I couldn't get up there with my leg broken like it is.
Just thank *luck*--if any fell back toward you during the feeding frenzy it was an *accident, I promise.*
I don't suppose any of you doctors here would be able to tell me if you think my leg is going to *heal,* would you?
Anyone?
Well, that's just going to *slow* me down. Can't I just puncture my legs and drain them if it's not pumping anyway?
Not while you're sitting next to *me* you can't!
So it seems pretty clear our bodies aren't working like they used to--or even *at all* in some cases.
My *healing factor* ain't doing *squat*--that's for *sure.* We're *dead,* but we're not *dying.*
Simple as *that*--and *I ain't* no *doctor.*
From the evidence we've got here, I'm going to assume that as long as our brains are intact and functioning we'll continue on as is.
Although we *do* appear to be decomposing...

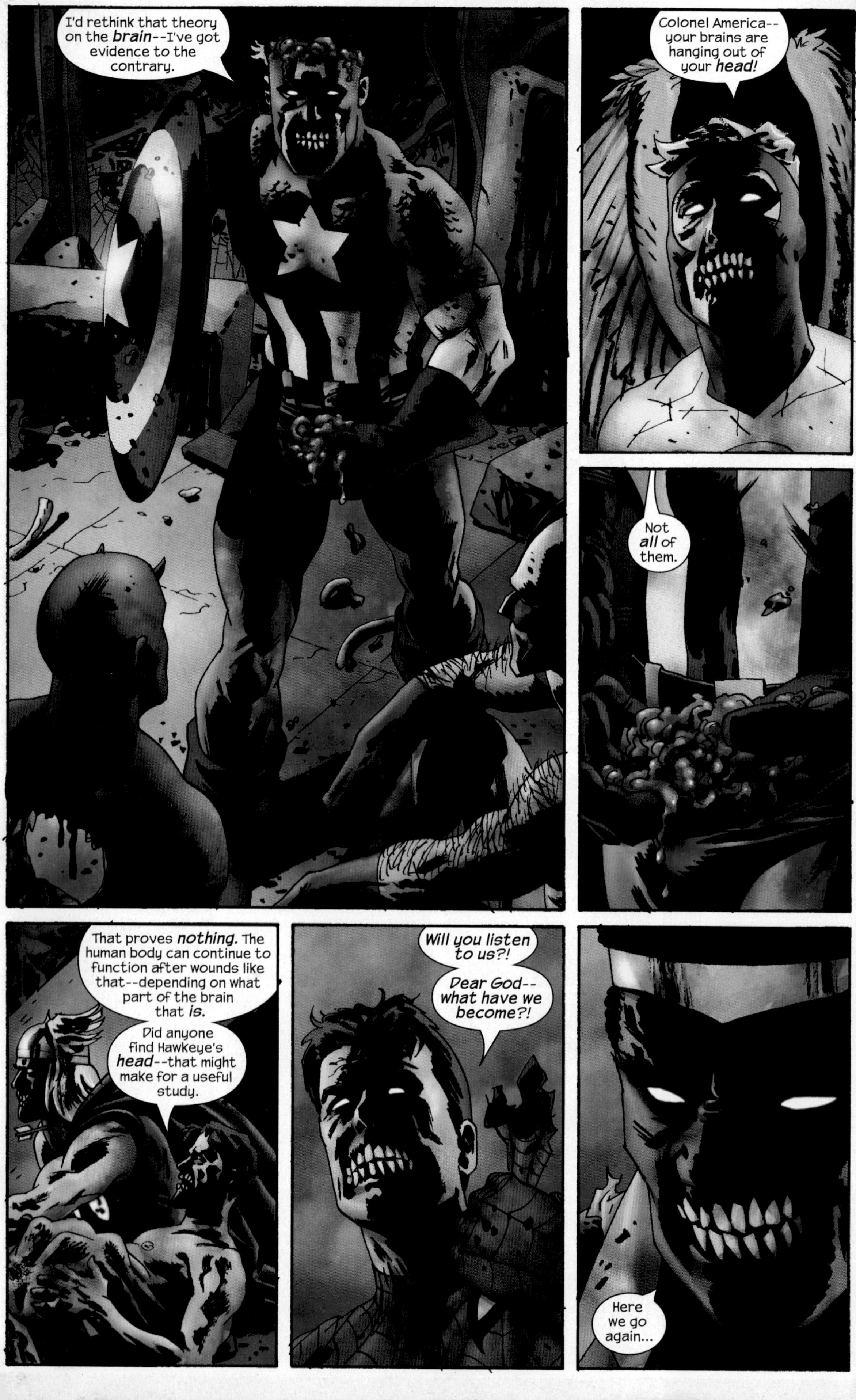
I'd rethink that theory on the brain--I've got evidence to the contrary.
Colonel America--your brains are hanging out of your head!
Not all of them.
That proves nothing. The human body can continue to function after wounds like that--depending on what part of the brain that is.
Did anyone find Hawkeye's head--that might make for a useful study.
Will you listen to us?!
Dear God--what have we become?!
Here we go again...

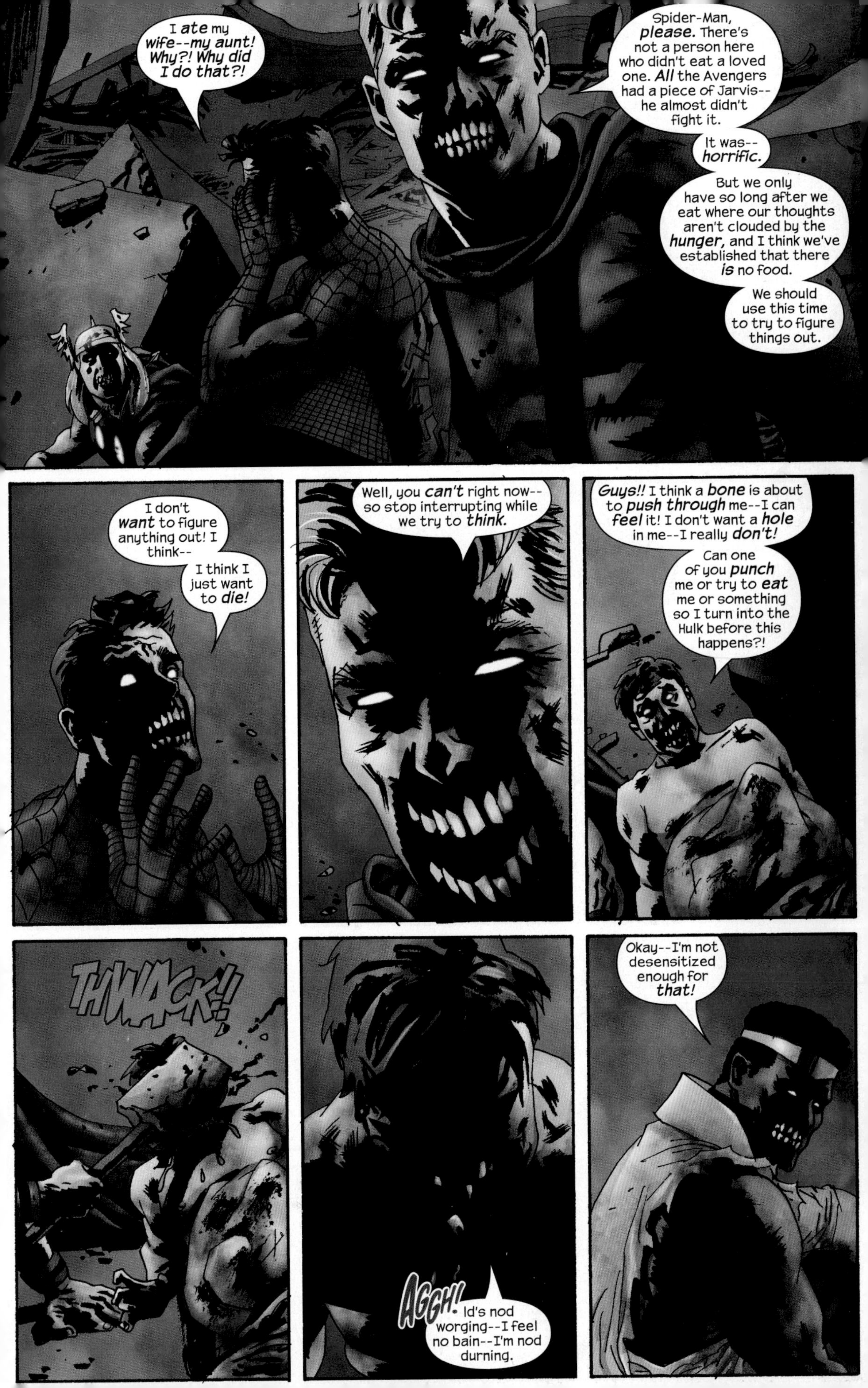
I ate my wife--my aunt! Why?! Why did I do that?!
Spider-Man, please. There's not a person here who didn't eat a loved one. All the Avengers had a piece of Jarvis--he almost didn't fight it.
It was--horrific.
But we only have so long after we eat where our thoughts aren't clouded by the hunger, and I think we've established that there is no food.
We should use this time to try to figure things out.
I don't want to figure anything out! I think--
I think I just want to die!
Well, you can't right now--so stop interrupting while we try to think.
Guys!! I think a bone is about to push through me--I can feel it! I don't want a hole in me--I really don't!
Can one of you punch me or try to eat me or something so I turn into the Hulk before this happens?!
THWACK!!
AGGH!
Id's nod worging--I feel no bain--I'm nod durning.
Okay--I'm not desensitized enough for that!

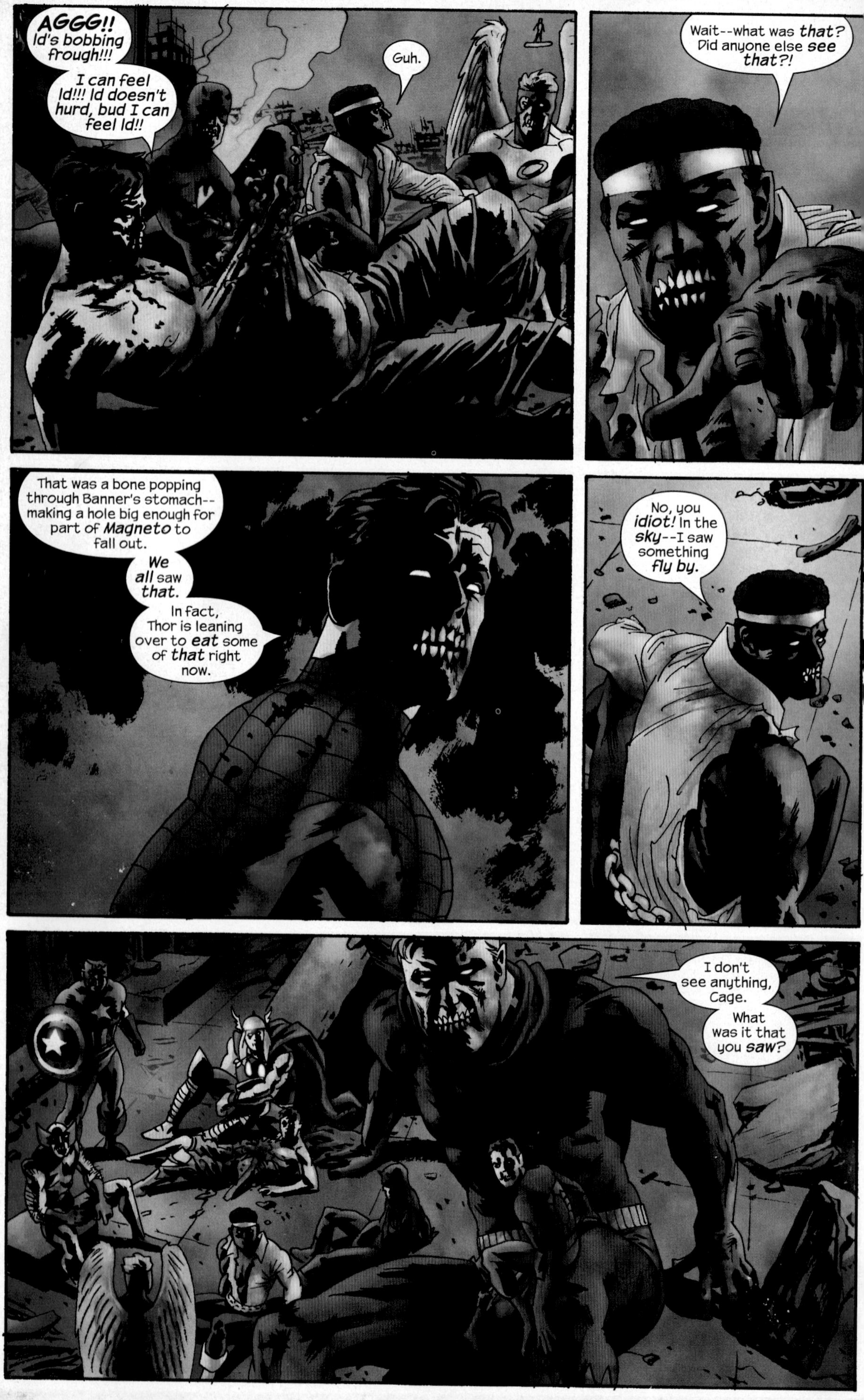
AGGG!! Id's bobbing frough!!!
I can feel Id!!! Id doesn't hurd, bud I can feel Id!!
Guh.
Wait--what was that? Did anyone else see that?!
That was a bone popping through Banner's stomach--making a hole big enough for part of Magneto to fall out.
We all saw that.
In fact, Thor is leaning over to eat some of that right now.
No, you idiot! In the sky--I saw something fly by.
I don't see anything, Cage.
What was it that you saw?

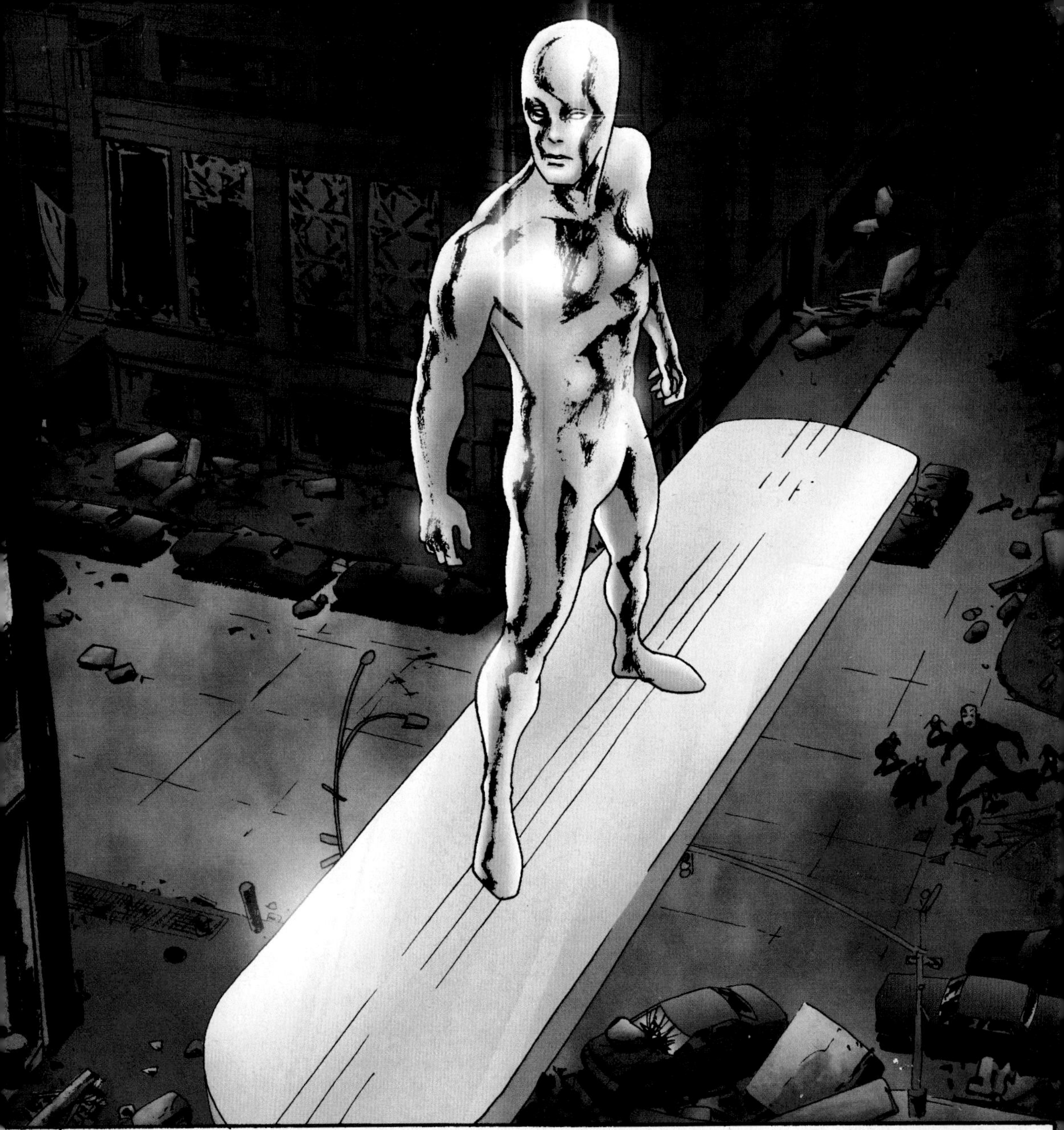

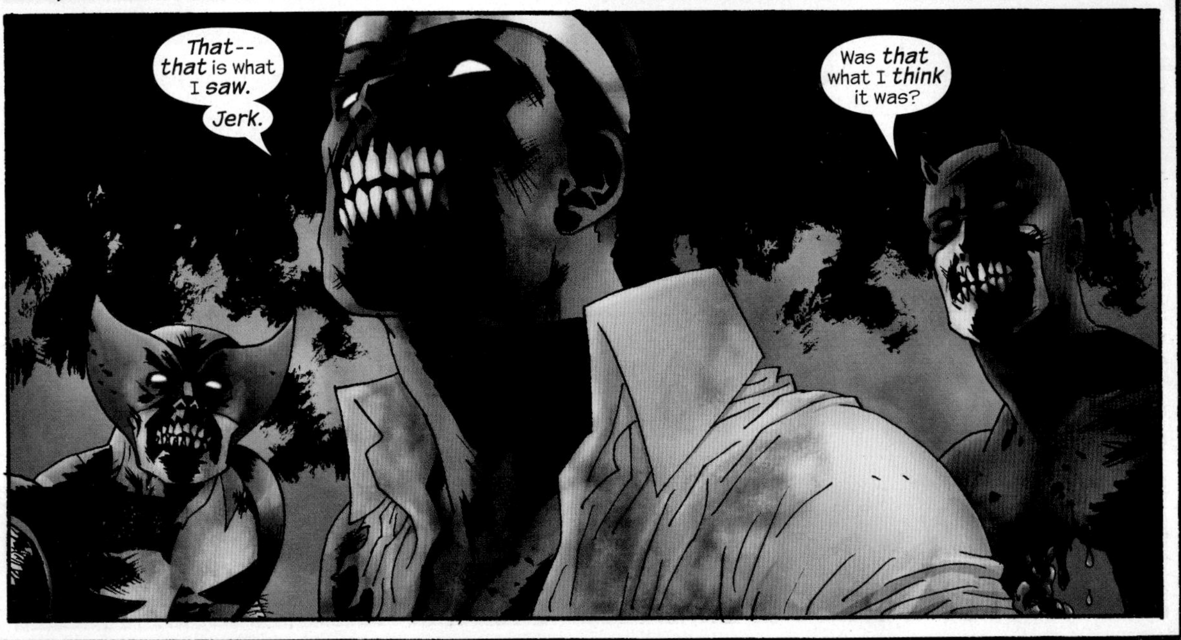
That--
that is what I saw.
Jerk.
Was that what I think it was?

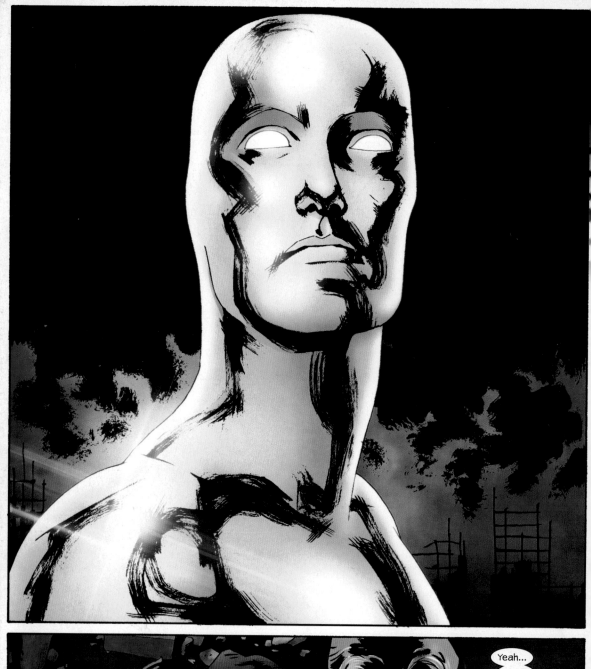

Yeah...
...more food.

MARVEL ZOMBIES

PART 2 OF 5

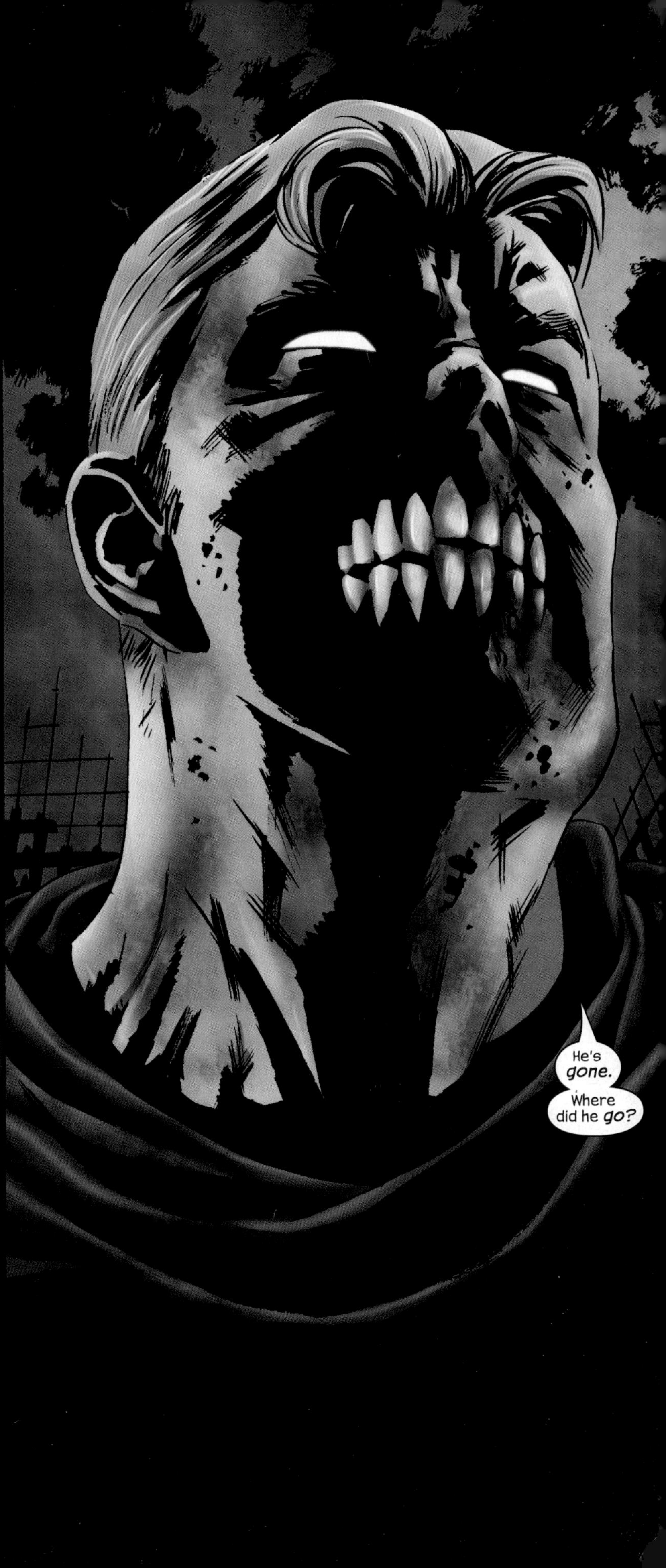
He's gone.
Where did he go?

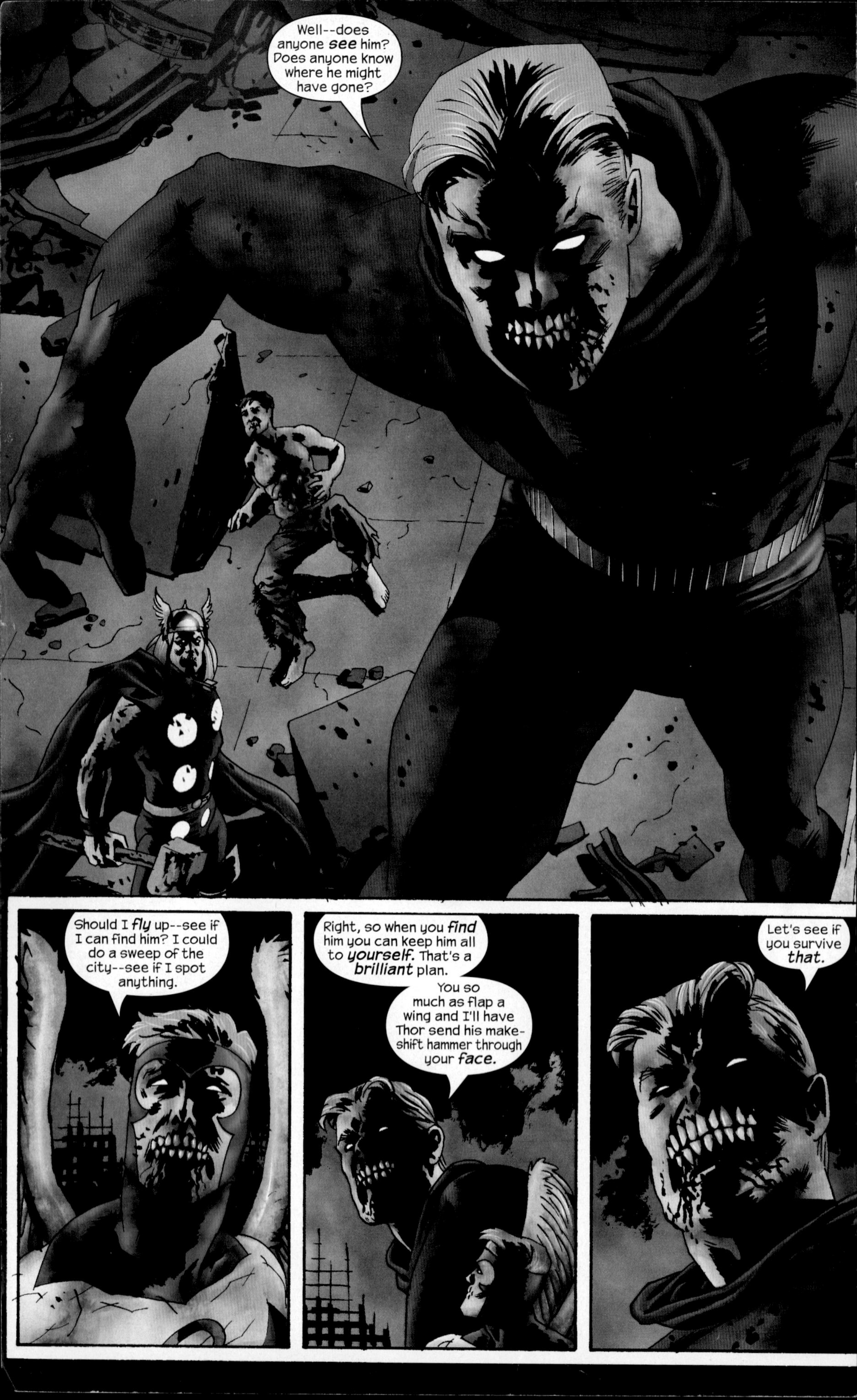
Well--does anyone see him? Does anyone know where he might have gone?
Should I fly up--see if I can find him? I could do a sweep of the city--see if I spot anything.
Right, so when you find him you can keep him all to yourself. That's a brilliant plan.
You so much as flap a wing and I'll have Thor send his make-shift hammer through your face.
Let's see if you survive that.

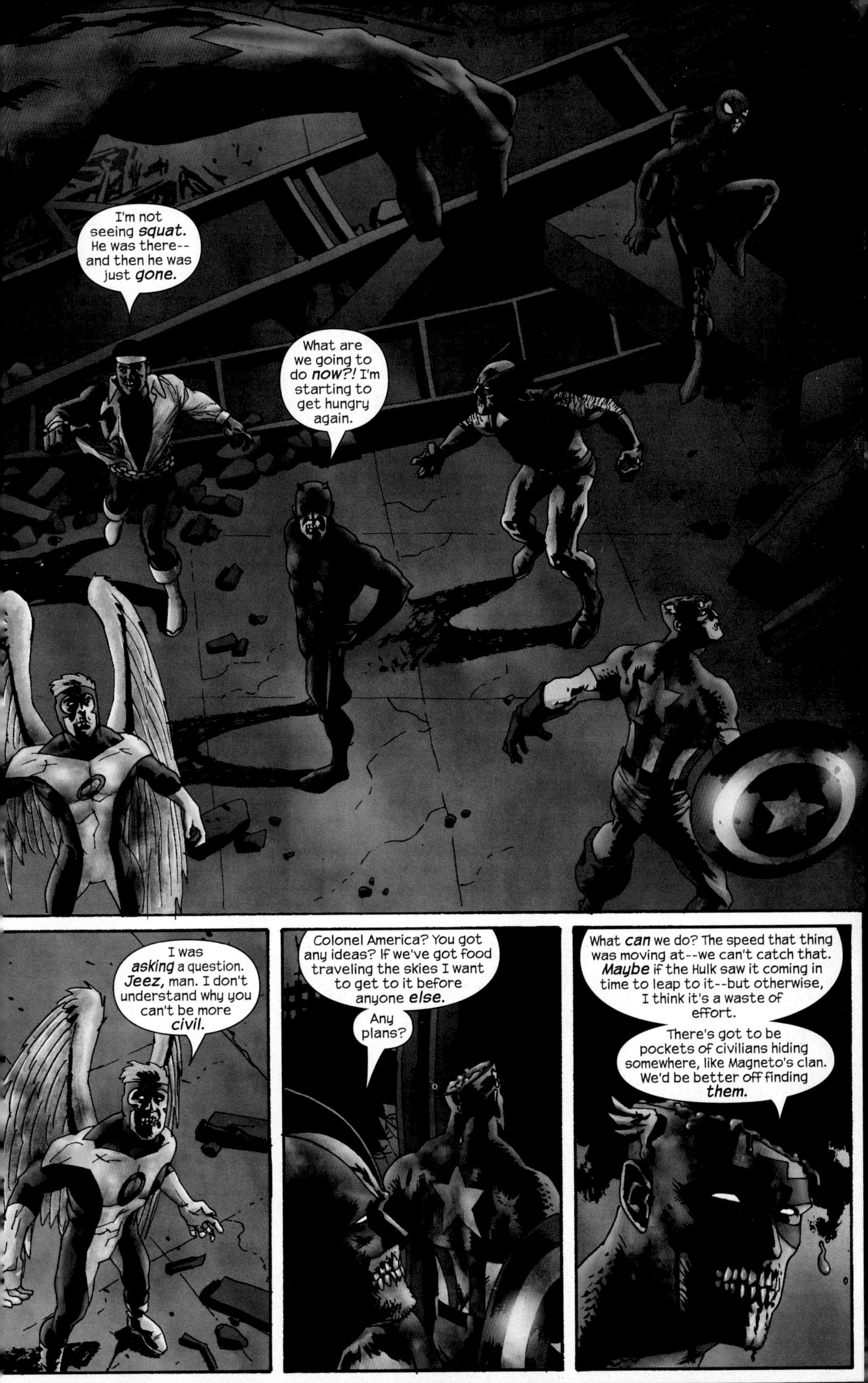
I'm not seeing squat. He was there-- and then he was just gone.
What are we going to do now?! I'm starting to get hungry again.
I was asking a question. Jeez, man. I don't understand why you can't be more civil.
Colonel America? You got any ideas? If we've got food traveling the skies I want to get to it before anyone else.
Any plans?
What can we do? The speed that thing was moving at--we can't catch that. Maybe if the Hulk saw it coming in time to leap to it--but otherwise, I think it's a waste of effort.
There's got to be pockets of civilians hiding somewhere, like Magneto's clan. We'd be better off finding them.

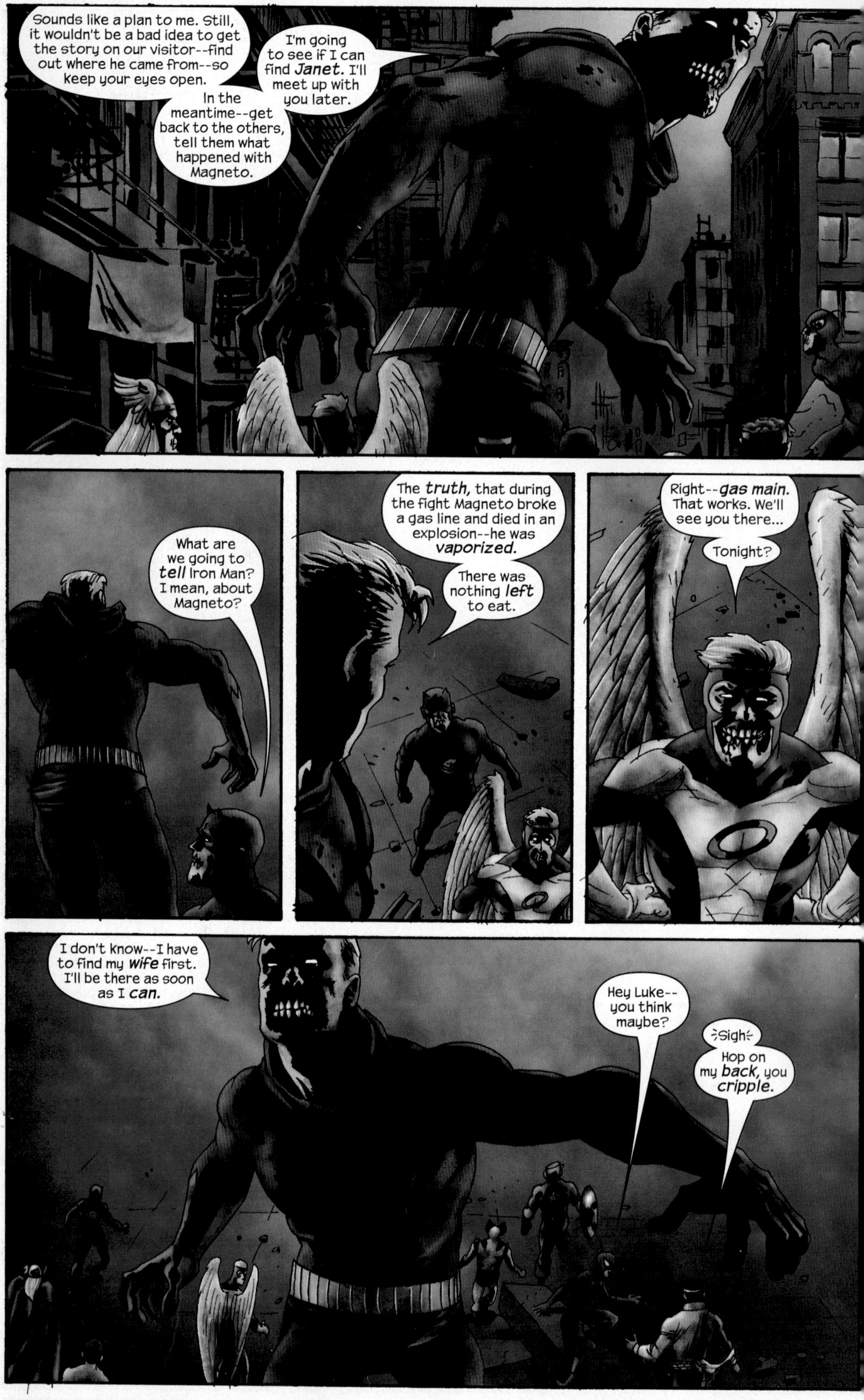

Sounds like a plan to me. Still, it wouldn't be a bad idea to get the story on our visitor--find out where he came from--so keep your eyes open.
I'm going to see if I can find Janet. I'll meet up with you later.
In the meantime--get back to the others, tell them what happened with Magneto.
What are we going to tell Iron Man? I mean, about Magneto?
The truth, that during the fight Magneto broke a gas line and died in an explosion--he was vaporized.
There was nothing left to eat.
Right--gas main. That works. We'll see you there...
Tonight?
I don't know--I have to find my wife first. I'll be there as soon as I can.
Hey Luke--you think maybe?
Sigh
Hop on my back, you cripple.

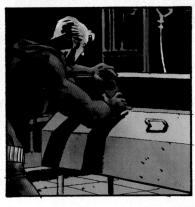

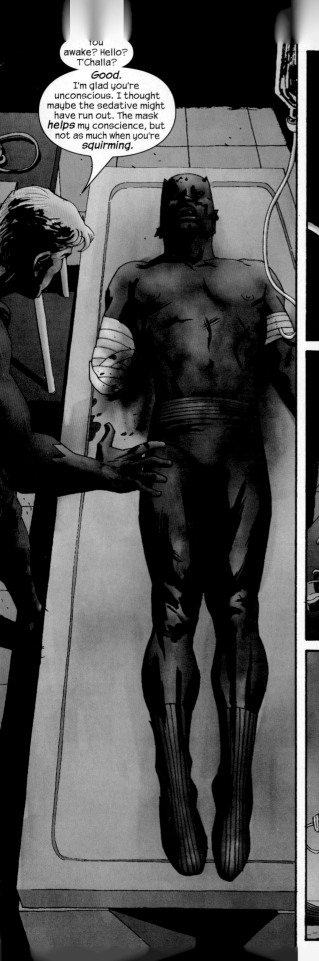

You awake? Hello? T'Challa?

Good. I'm glad you're unconscious. I thought maybe the sedative might have run out. The mask *helps* my conscience, but not as much when you're *squirming.*

I was going to do a little *work* today. See if I couldn't figure some things out.

Sadly, the meal I had earlier isn't going to last long enough for me to keep a clear head. Looks like I'm going to have to carve off another piece.

You don't have a preference, do you? I figured I'd start in on your legs before I finished off your arm.

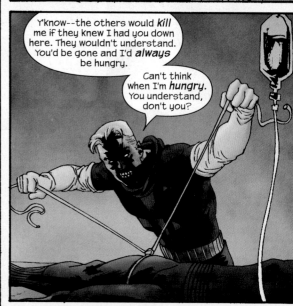

Y'know--the others would *kill* me if they knew I had you down here. They wouldn't understand. You'd be gone and I'd *always* be hungry.

Can't think when I'm *hungry.* You understand, don't you?

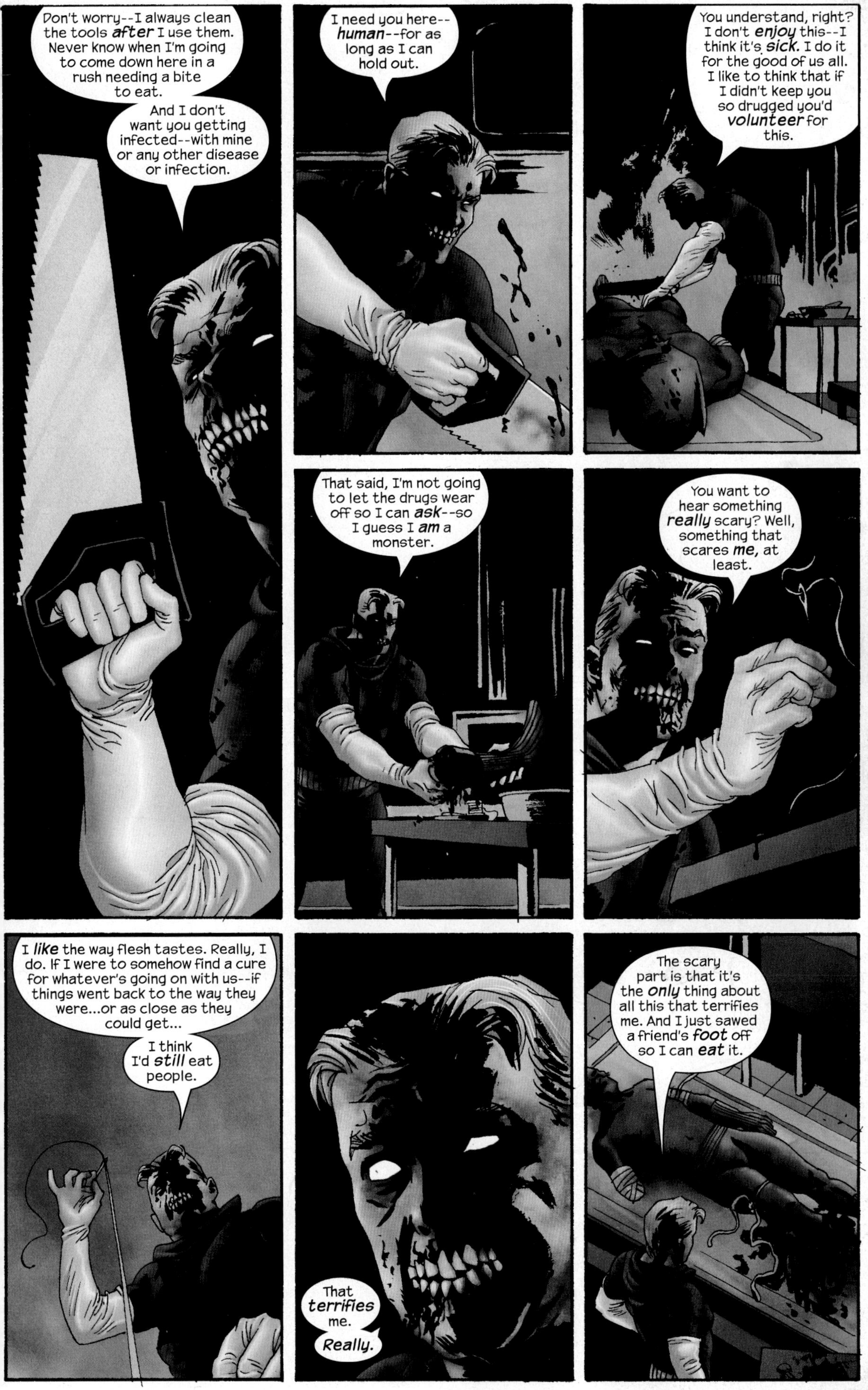
Don't worry--I always clean the tools *after* I use them. Never know when I'm going to come down here in a rush needing a bite to eat.
And I don't want you getting infected--with mine or any other disease or infection.
I need you here--*human*--for as long as I can hold out.
You understand, right? I don't *enjoy* this--I think it's *sick.* I do it for the good of us all. I like to think that if I didn't keep you so drugged you'd *volunteer* for this.
That said, I'm not going to let the drugs wear off so I can *ask*--so I guess I *am* a monster.
You want to hear something *really* scary? Well, something that scares *me,* at least.
I *like* the way flesh tastes. Really, I do. If I were to somehow find a cure for whatever's going on with us--if things went back to the way they were...or as close as they could get...
I think I'd *still* eat people.
That *terrifies* me.
Really.
The scary part is that it's the *only* thing about all this that terrifies me. And I just sawed a friend's *foot* off so I can *eat* it.

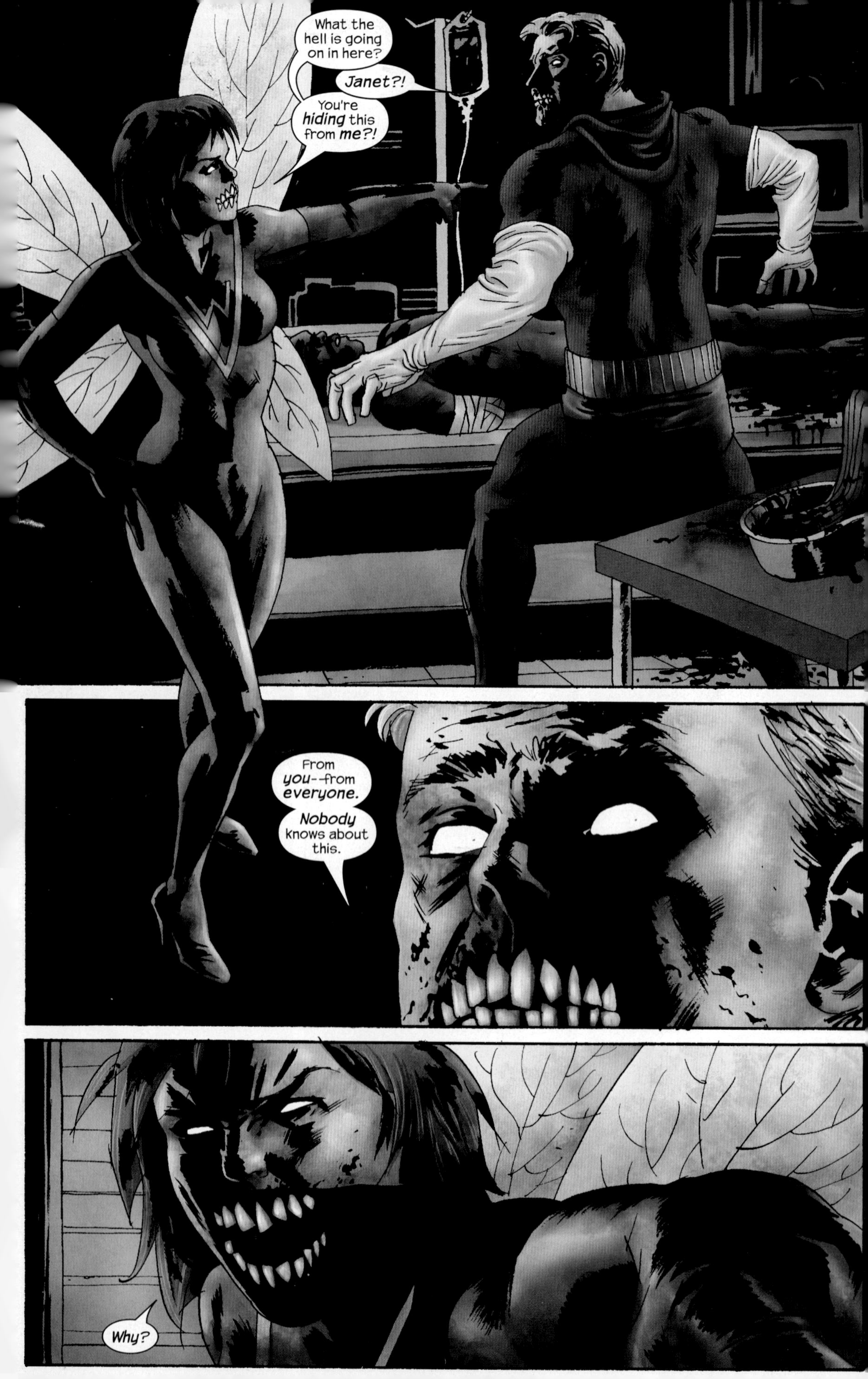
What the hell is going on in here?
Janet?!
You're hiding this from me?!
From you--from everyone.
Nobody knows about this.
Why?

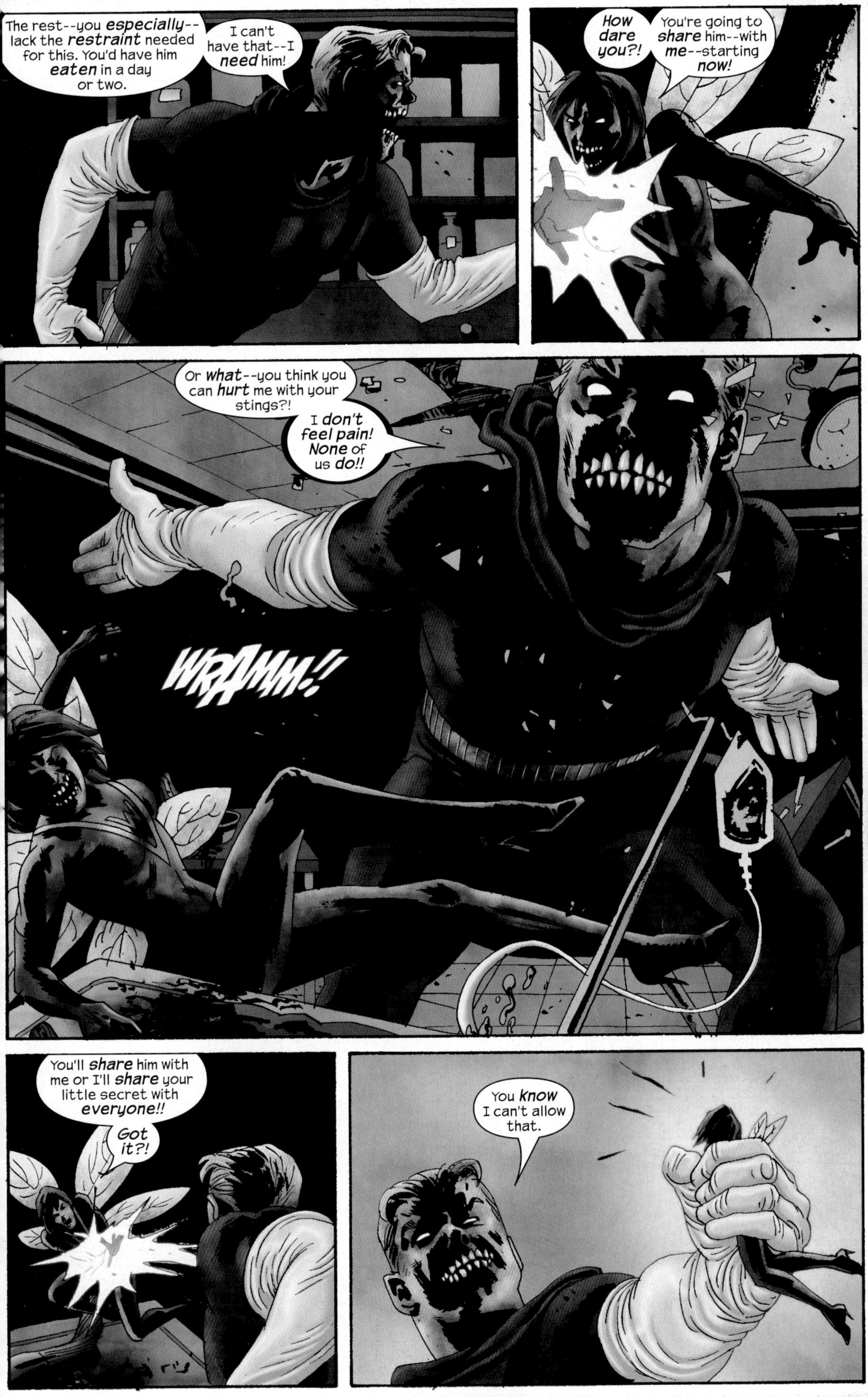
The rest--you especially--lack the restraint needed for this. You'd have him eaten in a day or two.
I can't have that--I need him!
How dare you?!
You're going to share him--with me--starting now!
Or what--you think you can hurt me with your stings?!
I don't feel pain! None of us do!!
WRAMM!!
You'll share him with me or I'll share your little secret with everyone!!
Got it?!
You know I can't allow that.

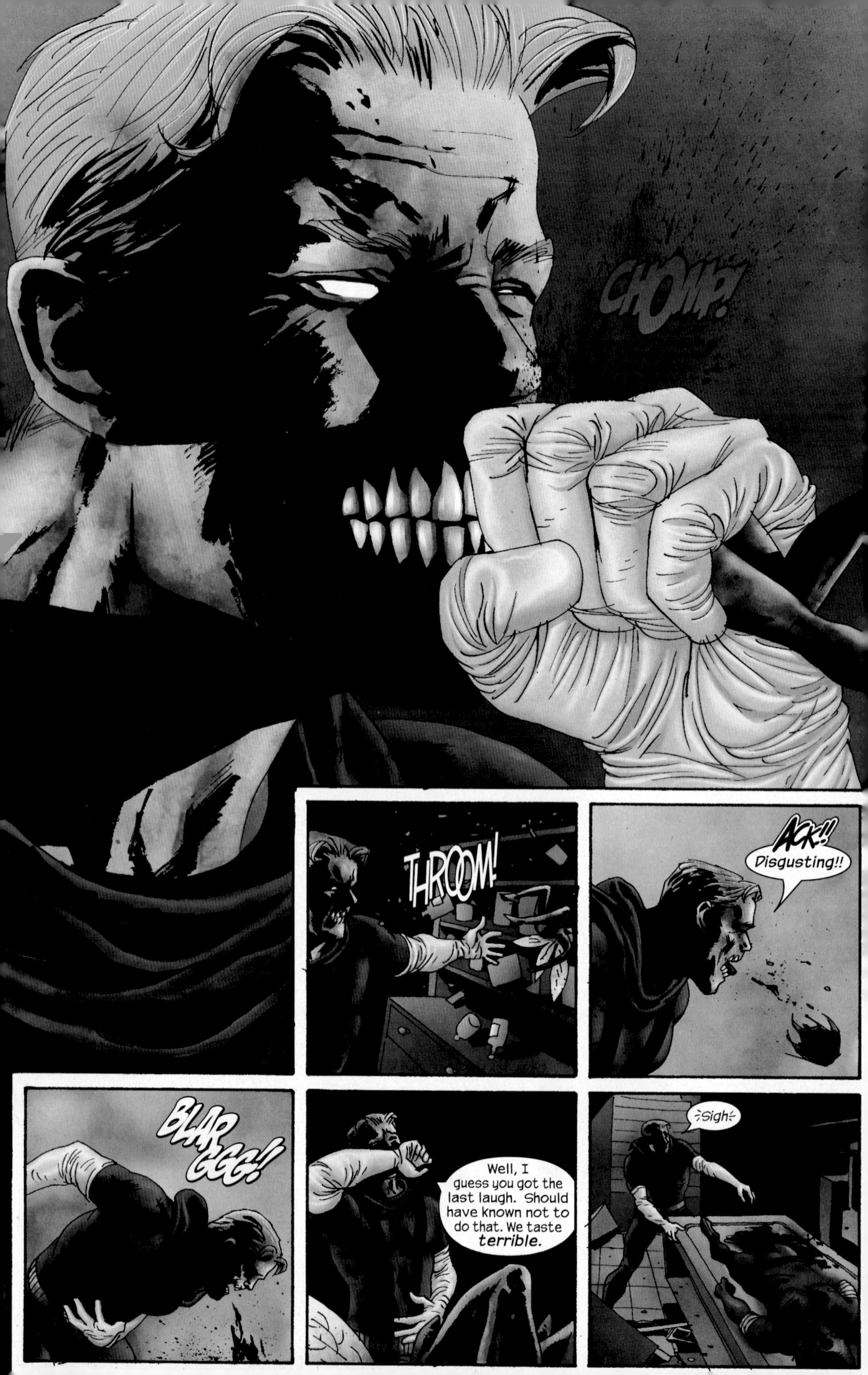
CHOMP!
THROOM!
ACK!!
Disgusting!!
BLARGGG!!
Well, I guess you got the last laugh. Should have known not to do that. We taste *terrible.*
Sigh

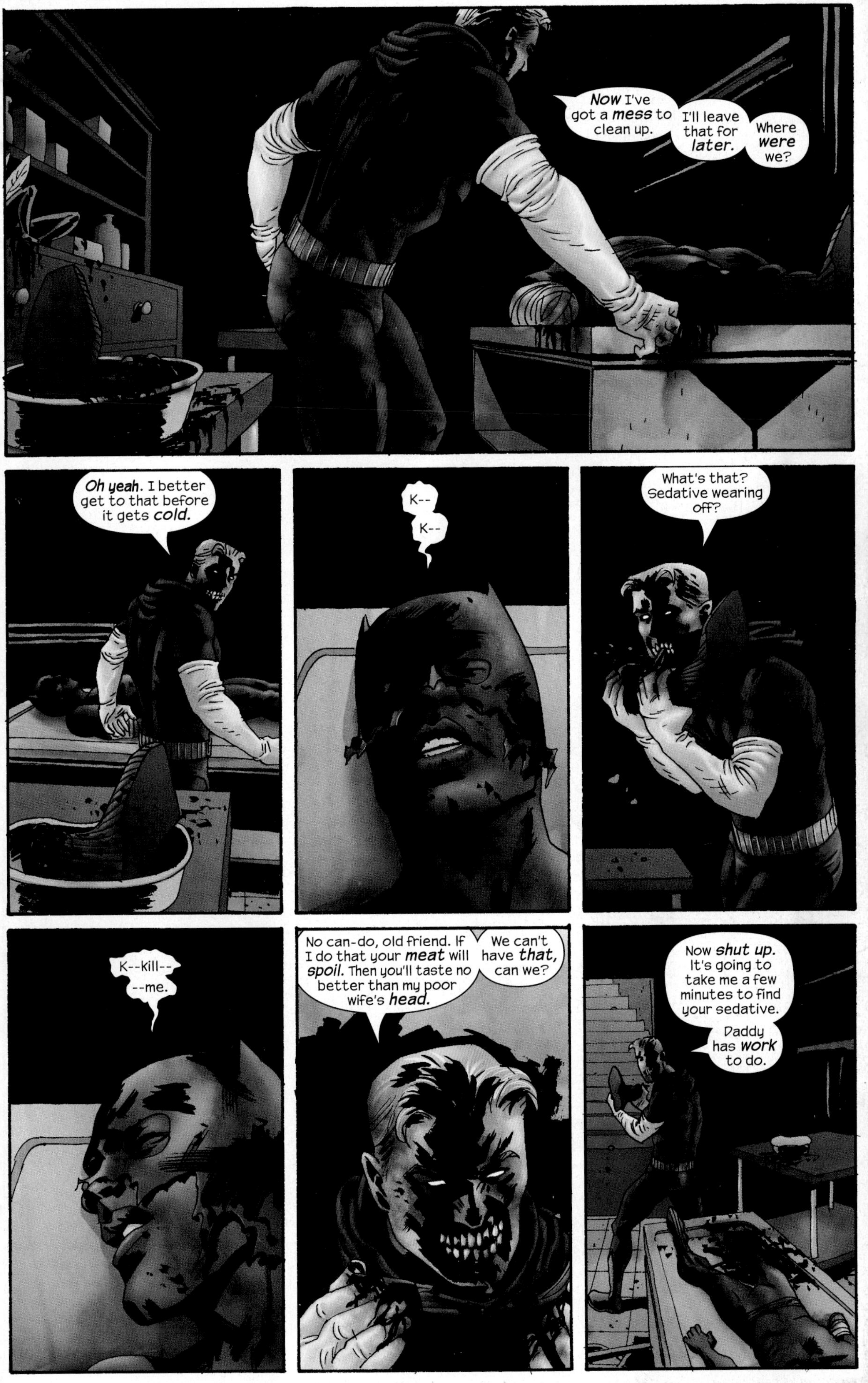
Now I've got a mess to clean up.
I'll leave that for later.
Where were we?
Oh yeah. I better get to that before it gets cold.
K--
K--
What's that? Sedative wearing off?
K--kill--
--me.
No can-do, old friend. If I do that your meat will spoil. Then you'll taste no better than my poor wife's head.
We can't have that, can we?
Now shut up. It's going to take me a few minutes to find your sedative.
Daddy has work to do.

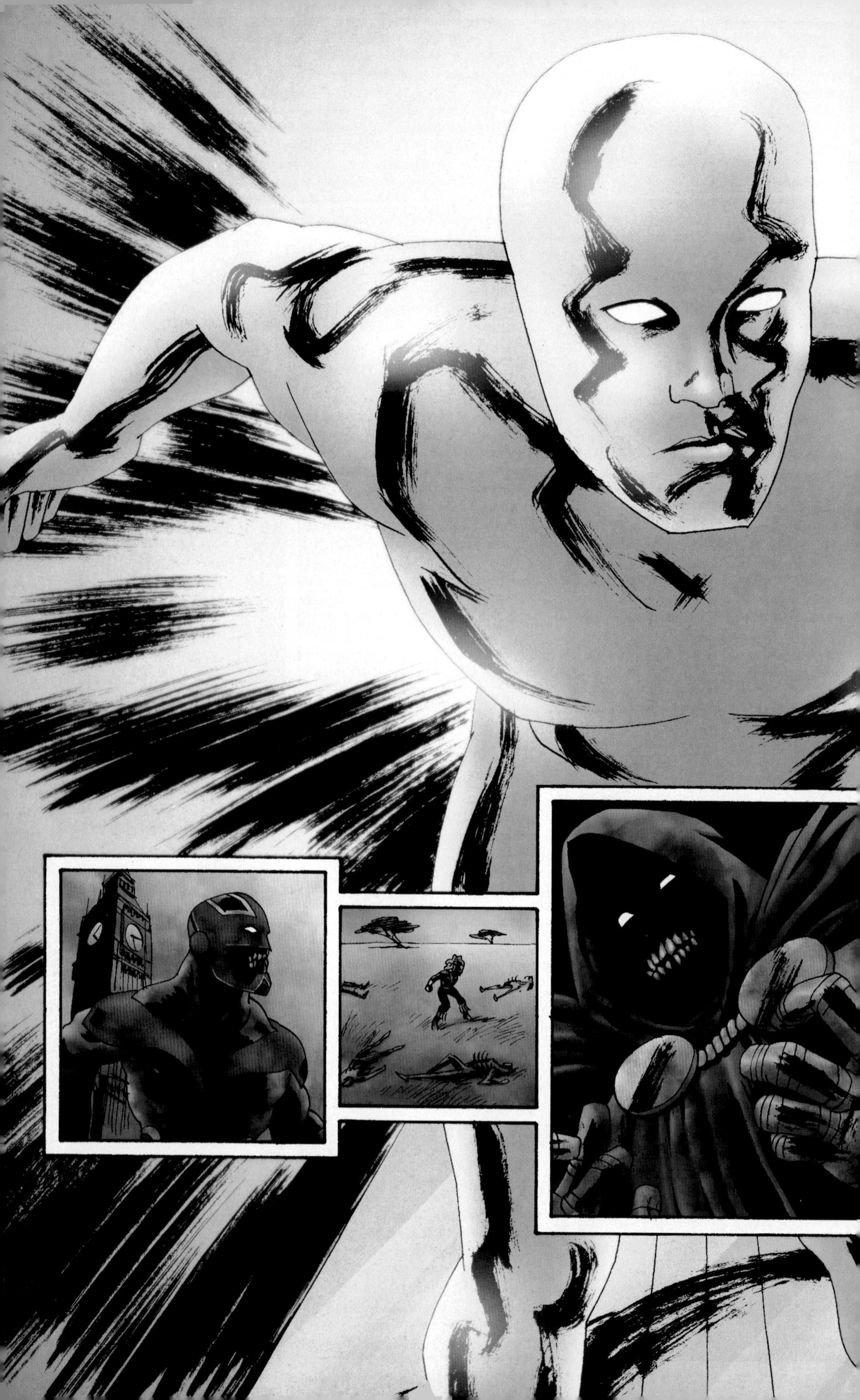

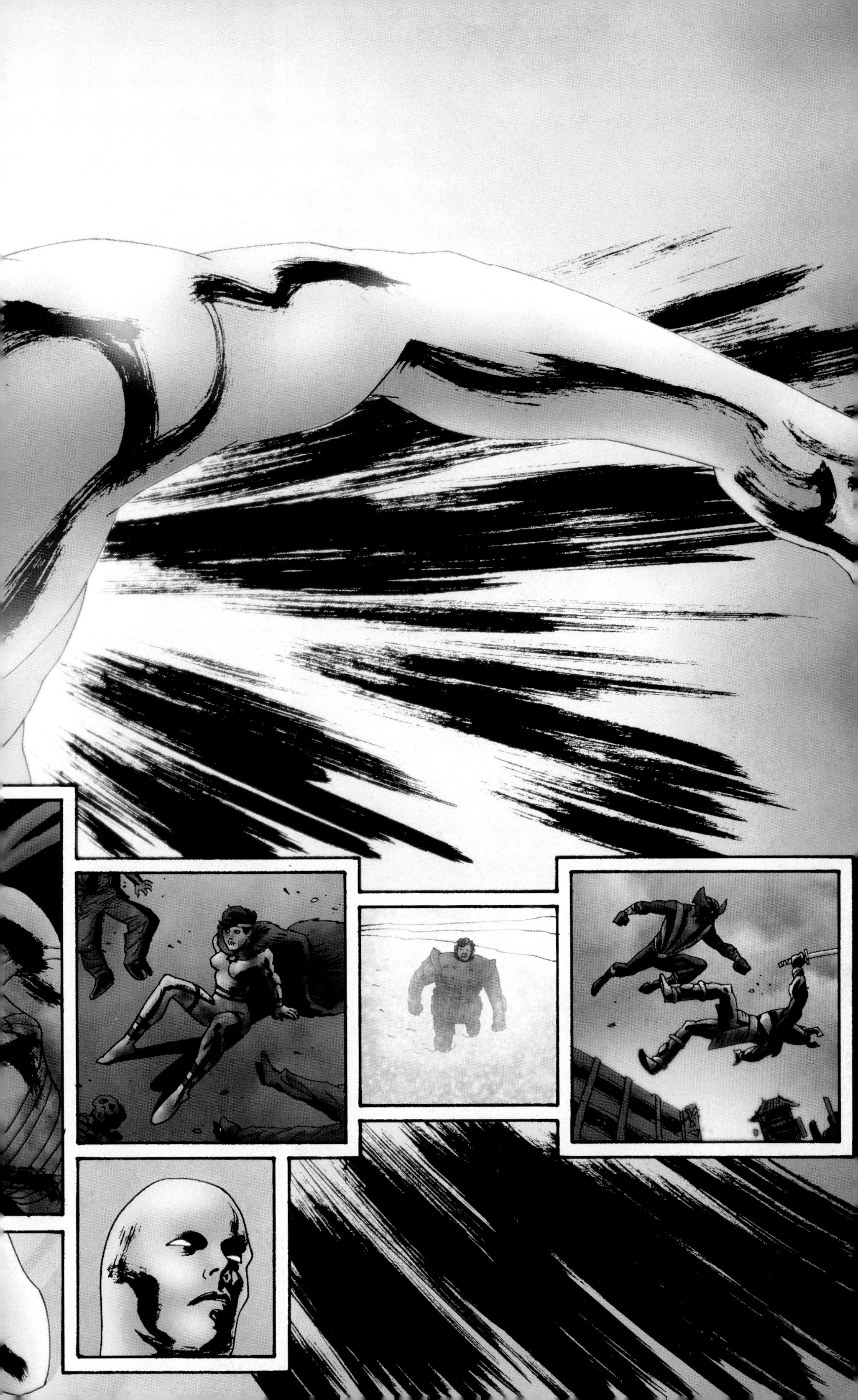

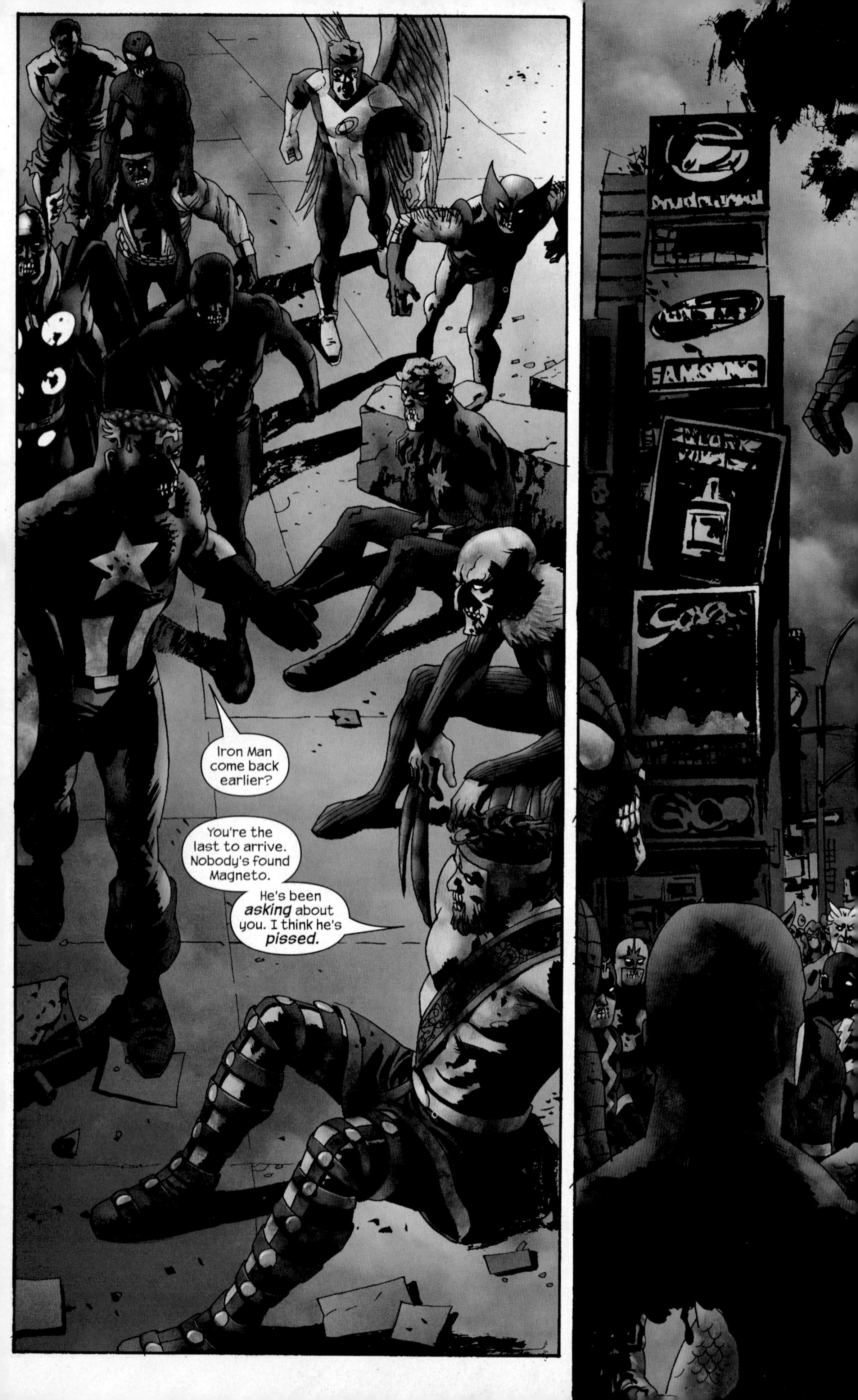
Iron Man come back earlier?
You're the last to arrive. Nobody's found Magneto.
He's been *asking* about you. I think he's *pissed.*

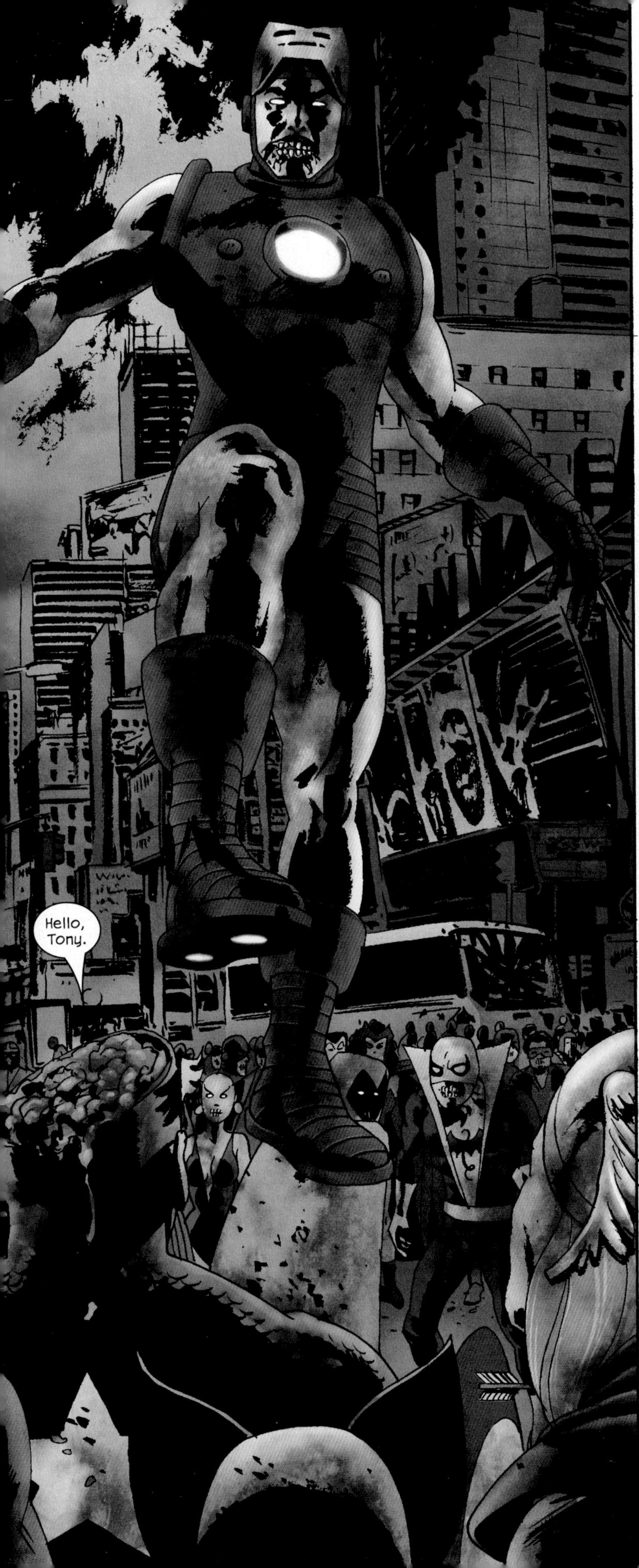
Hello, Tony.

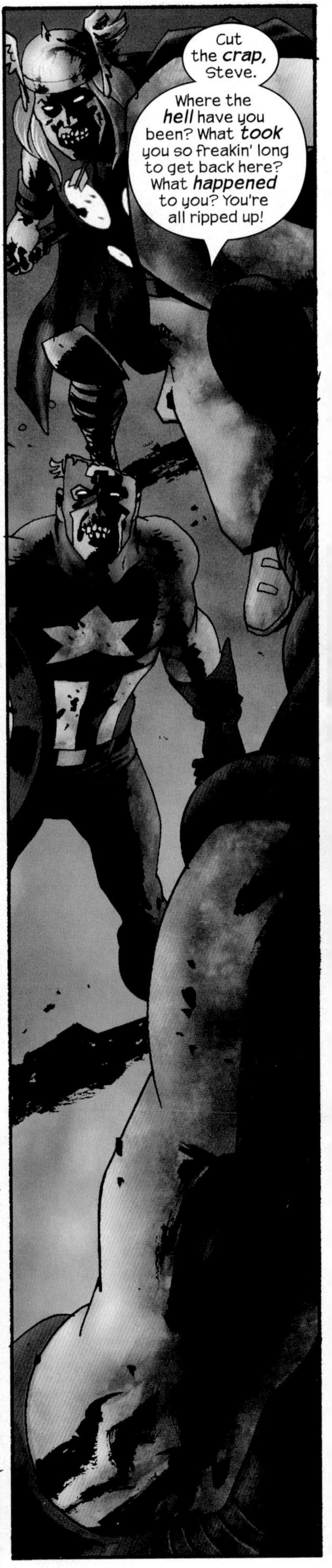
Cut the *crap,* Steve.
Where the *hell* have you been? What *took* you so freakin' long to get back here? What *happened* to you? You're all ripped up!

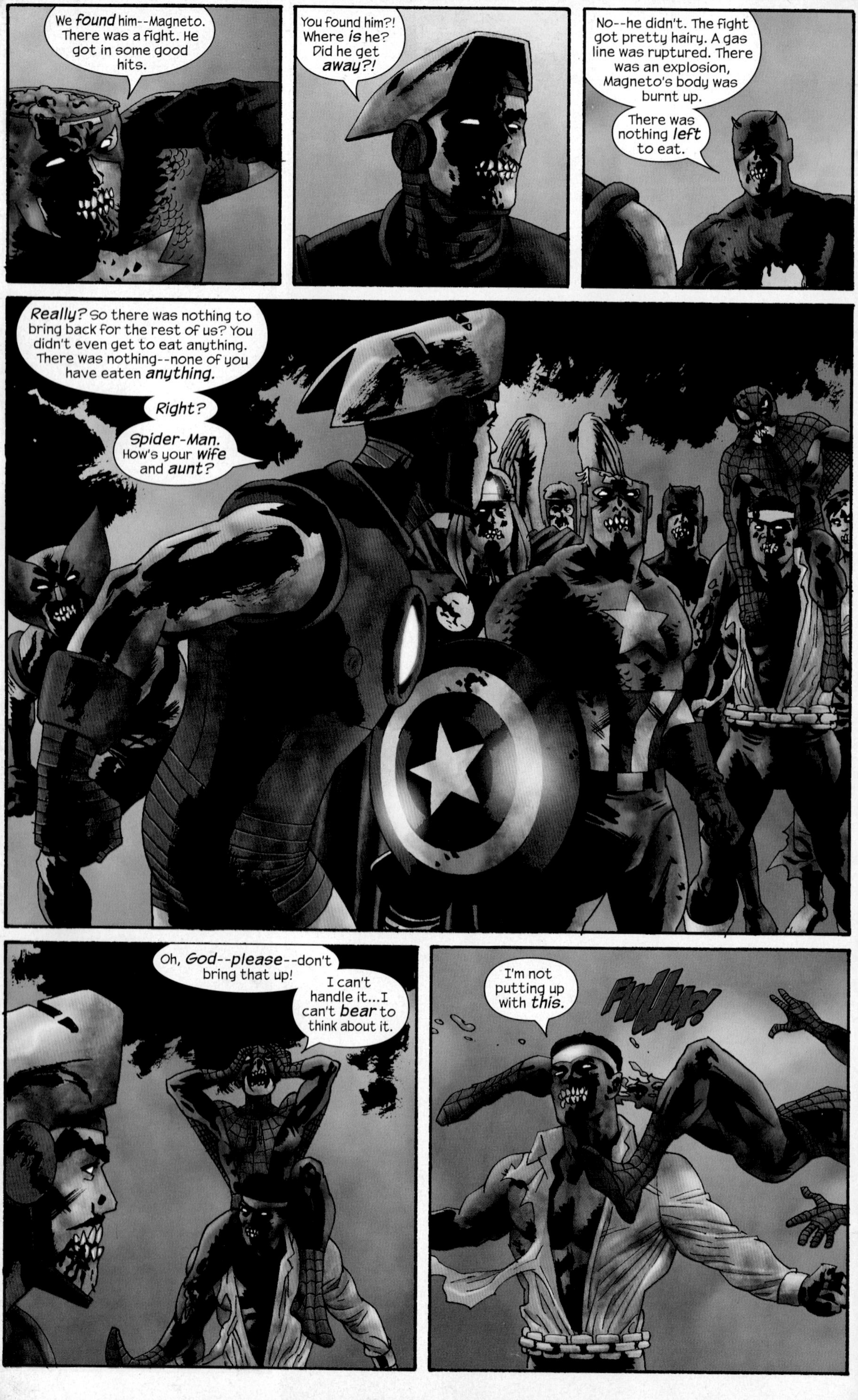

We found him--Magneto. There was a fight. He got in some good hits.
You found him?! Where is he? Did he get away?!
No--he didn't. The fight got pretty hairy. A gas line was ruptured. There was an explosion, Magneto's body was burnt up.
There was nothing left to eat.
Really? So there was nothing to bring back for the rest of us? You didn't even get to eat anything. There was nothing--none of you have eaten anything.
Right?
Spider-Man. How's your wife and aunt?
Oh, God--please--don't bring that up!
I can't handle it...I can't bear to think about it.
I'm not putting up with this.

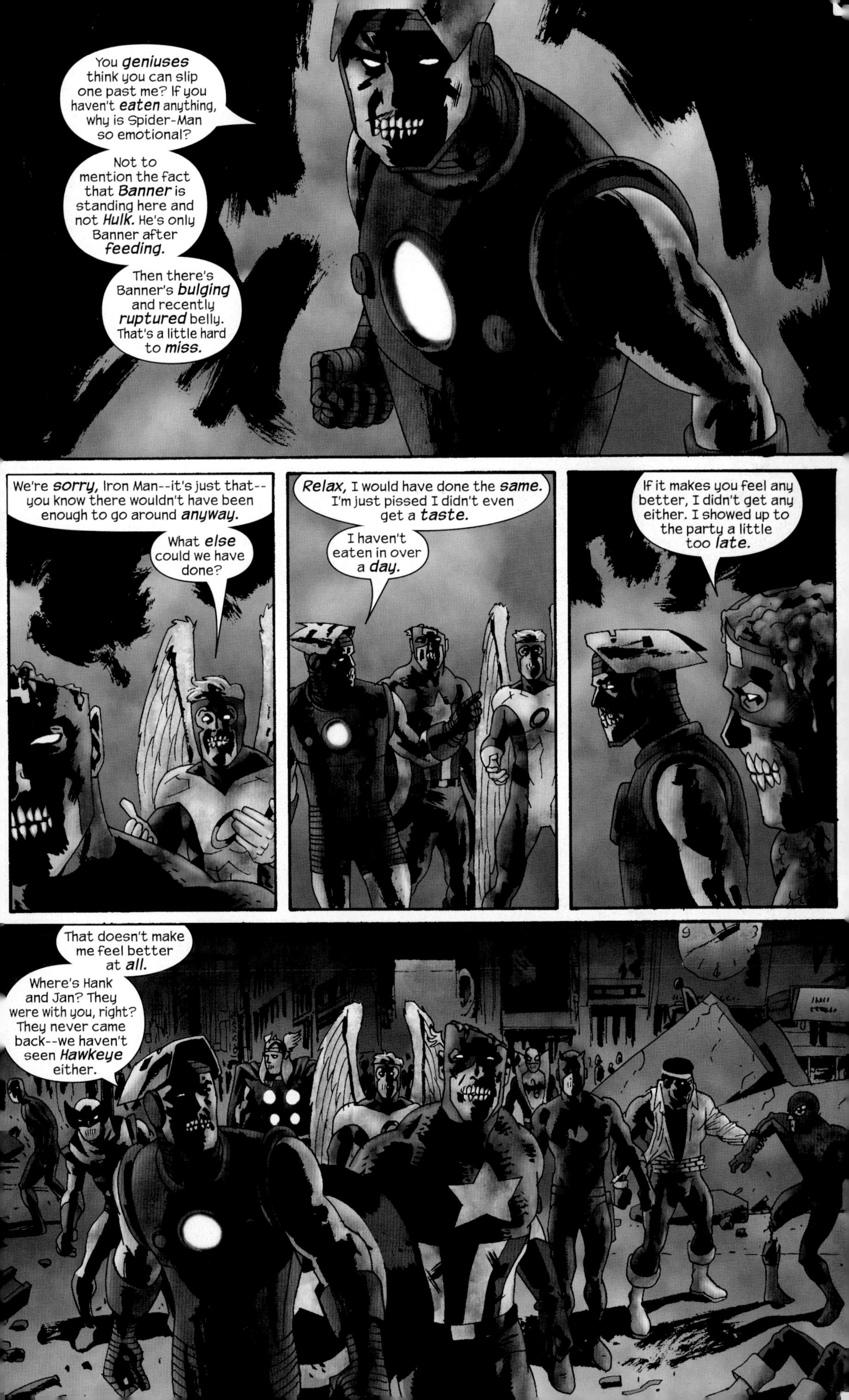
You geniuses think you can slip one past me? If you haven't eaten anything, why is Spider-Man so emotional?
Not to mention the fact that Banner is standing here and not Hulk. He's only Banner after feeding.
Then there's Banner's bulging and recently ruptured belly. That's a little hard to miss.
We're sorry, Iron Man--it's just that--you know there wouldn't have been enough to go around anyway.
What else could we have done?
Relax, I would have done the same. I'm just pissed I didn't even get a taste.
I haven't eaten in over a day.
If it makes you feel any better, I didn't get any either. I showed up to the party a little too late.
That doesn't make me feel better at all.
Where's Hank and Jan? They were with you, right? They never came back--we haven't seen Hawkeye either.

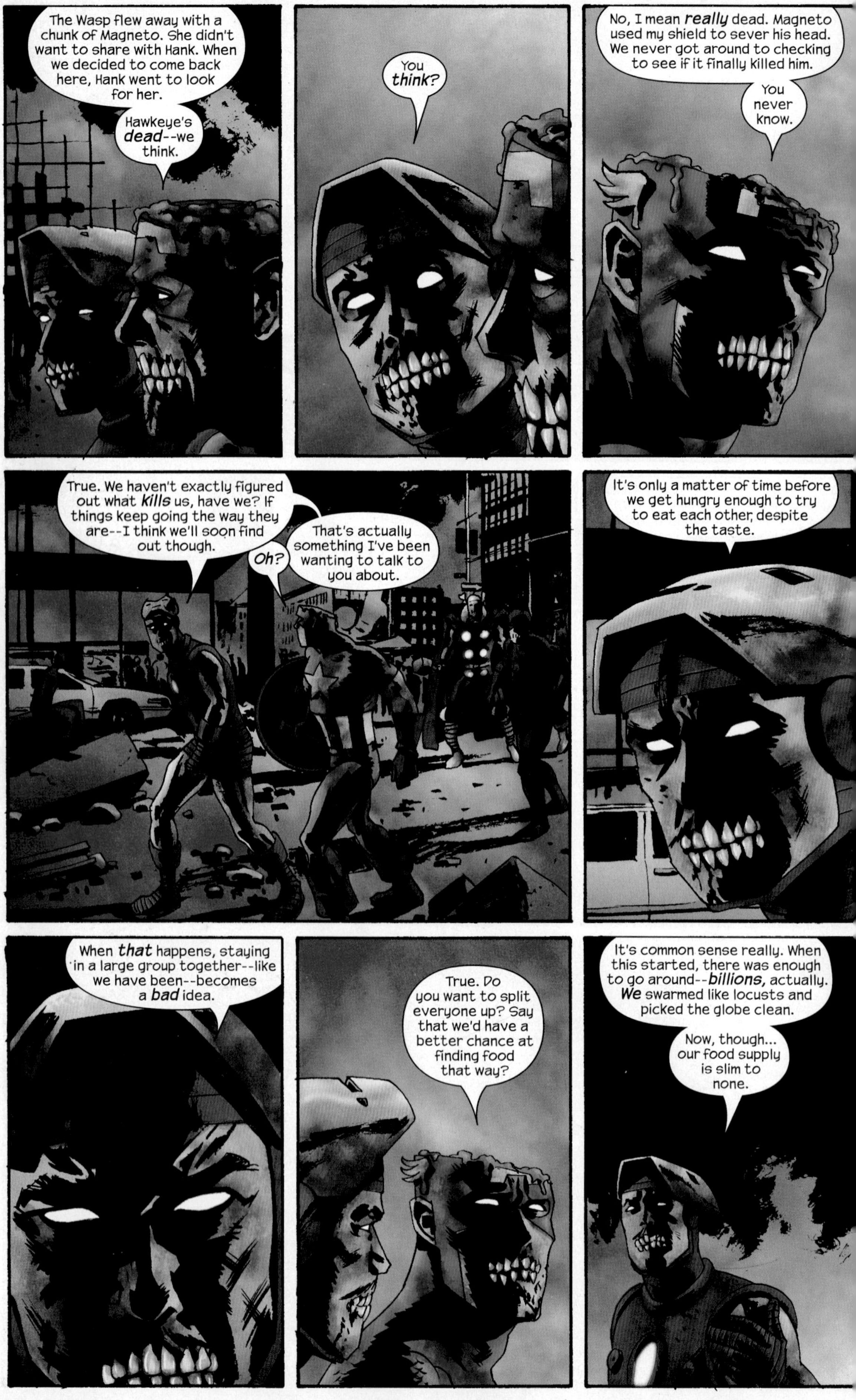
The Wasp flew away with a chunk of Magneto. She didn't want to share with Hank. When we decided to come back here, Hank went to look for her.
Hawkeye's dead--we think.
You think?
No, I mean really dead. Magneto used my shield to sever his head. We never got around to checking to see if it finally killed him.
You never know.
True. We haven't exactly figured out what kills us, have we? If things keep going the way they are--I think we'll soon find out though.
Oh?
That's actually something I've been wanting to talk to you about.
It's only a matter of time before we get hungry enough to try to eat each other, despite the taste.
When that happens, staying in a large group together--like we have been--becomes a bad idea.
True. Do you want to split everyone up? Say that we'd have a better chance at finding food that way?
It's common sense really. When this started, there was enough to go around--billions, actually. We swarmed like locusts and picked the globe clean.
Now, though... our food supply is slim to none.

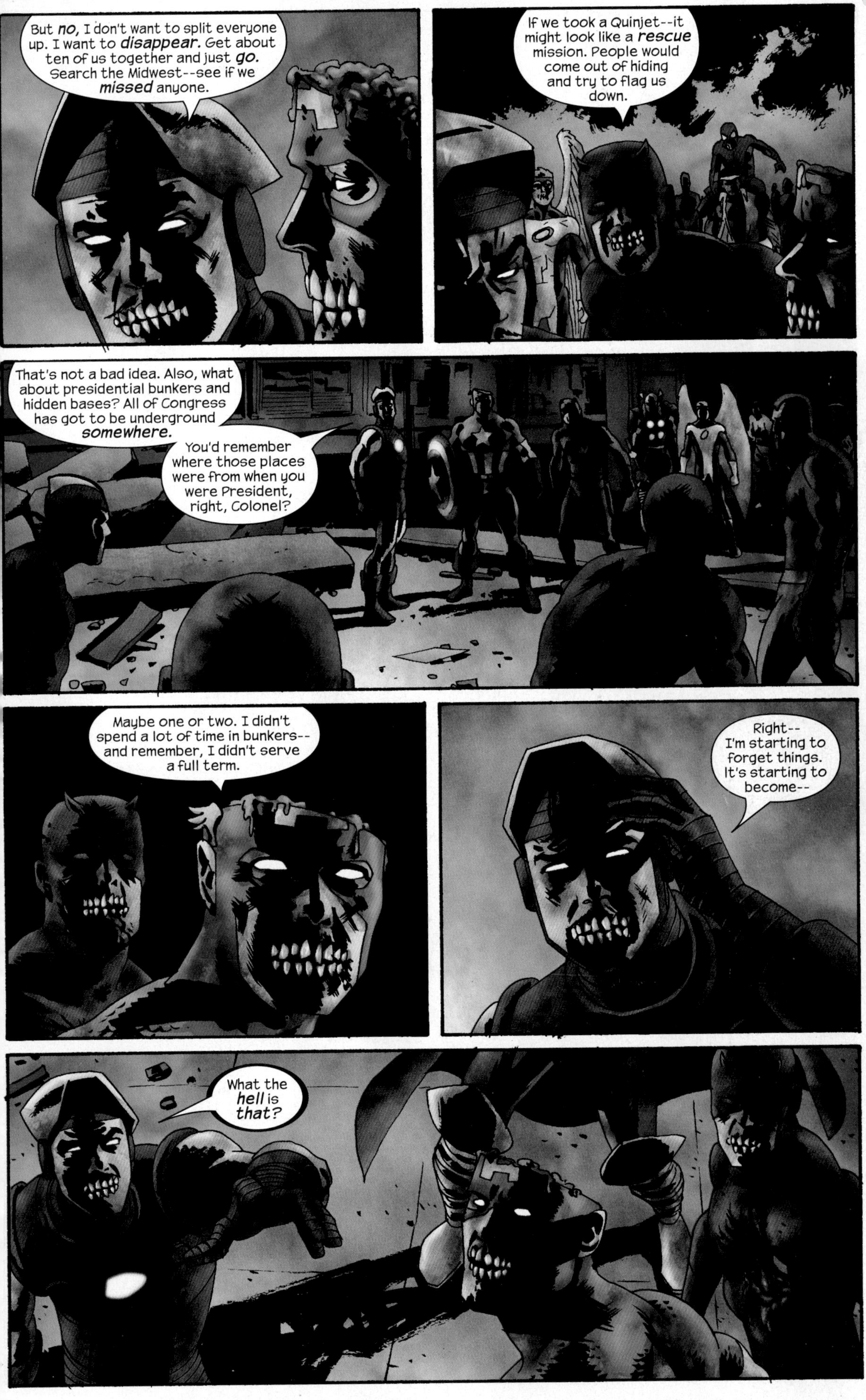
But no, I don't want to split everyone up. I want to disappear. Get about ten of us together and just go. Search the Midwest--see if we missed anyone.
If we took a Quinjet--it might look like a rescue mission. People would come out of hiding and try to flag us down.
That's not a bad idea. Also, what about presidential bunkers and hidden bases? All of Congress has got to be underground somewhere.
You'd remember where those places were from when you were President, right, Colonel?
Maybe one or two. I didn't spend a lot of time in bunkers--and remember, I didn't serve a full term.
Right--I'm starting to forget things. It's starting to become--
What the hell is that?

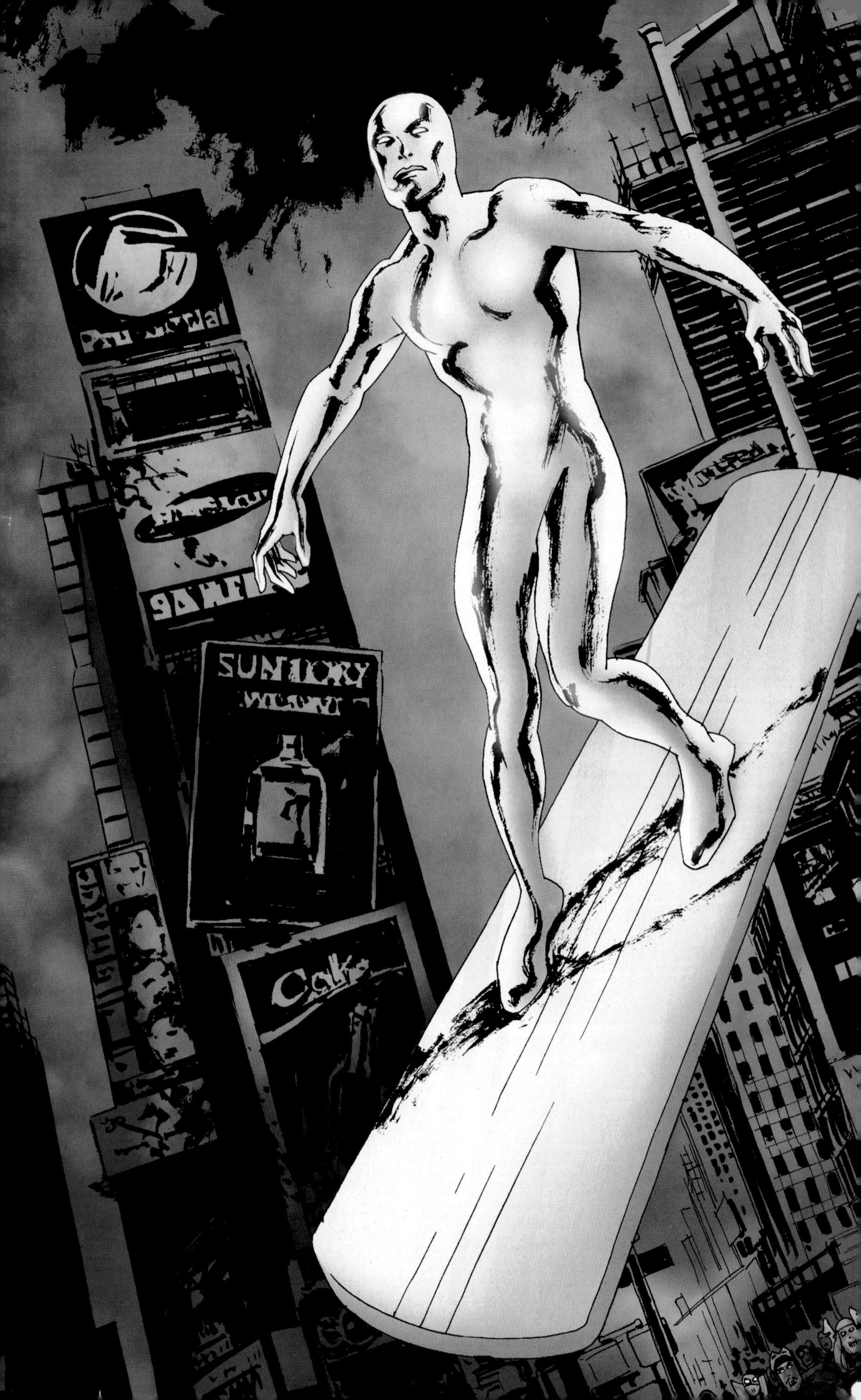
SUNTORY

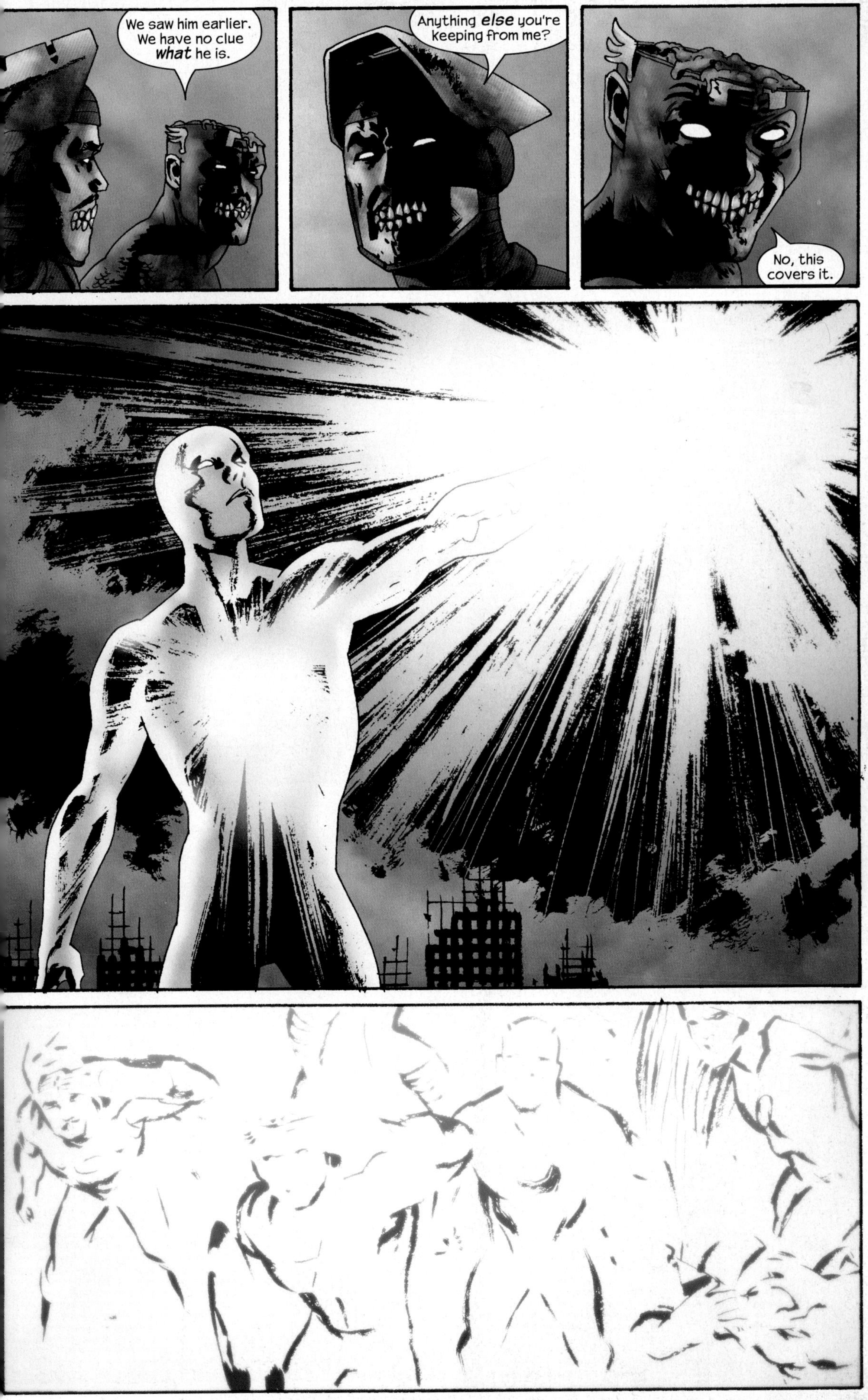
We saw him earlier. We have no clue *what* he is.
Anything *else* you're keeping from me?
No, this covers it.

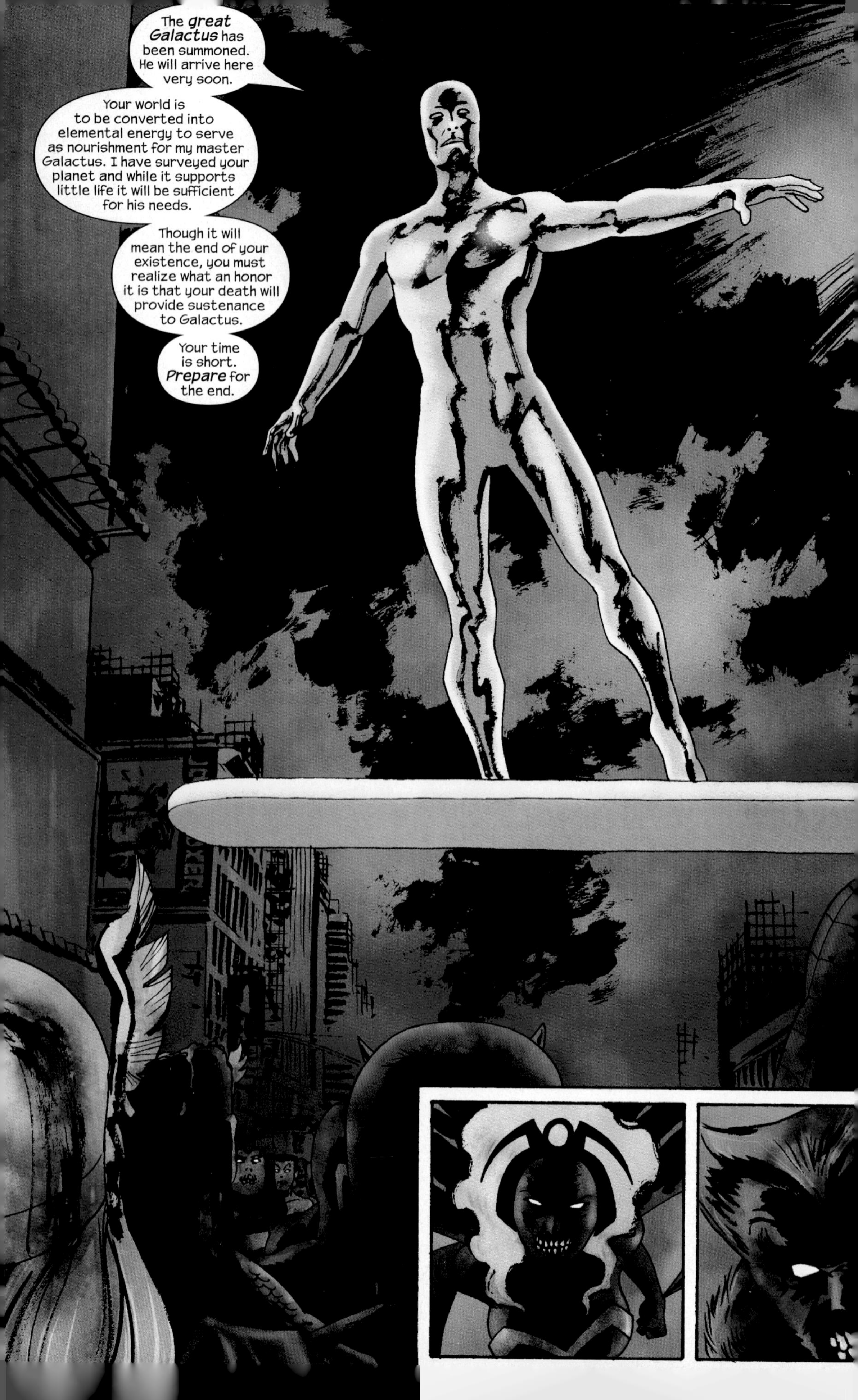
The *great* *Galactus* has been summoned. He will arrive here very soon.
Your world is to be converted into elemental energy to serve as nourishment for my master Galactus. I have surveyed your planet and while it supports little life it will be sufficient for his needs.
Though it will mean the end of your existence, you must realize what an honor it is that your death will provide sustenance to Galactus.
Your time is short. *Prepare* for the end.

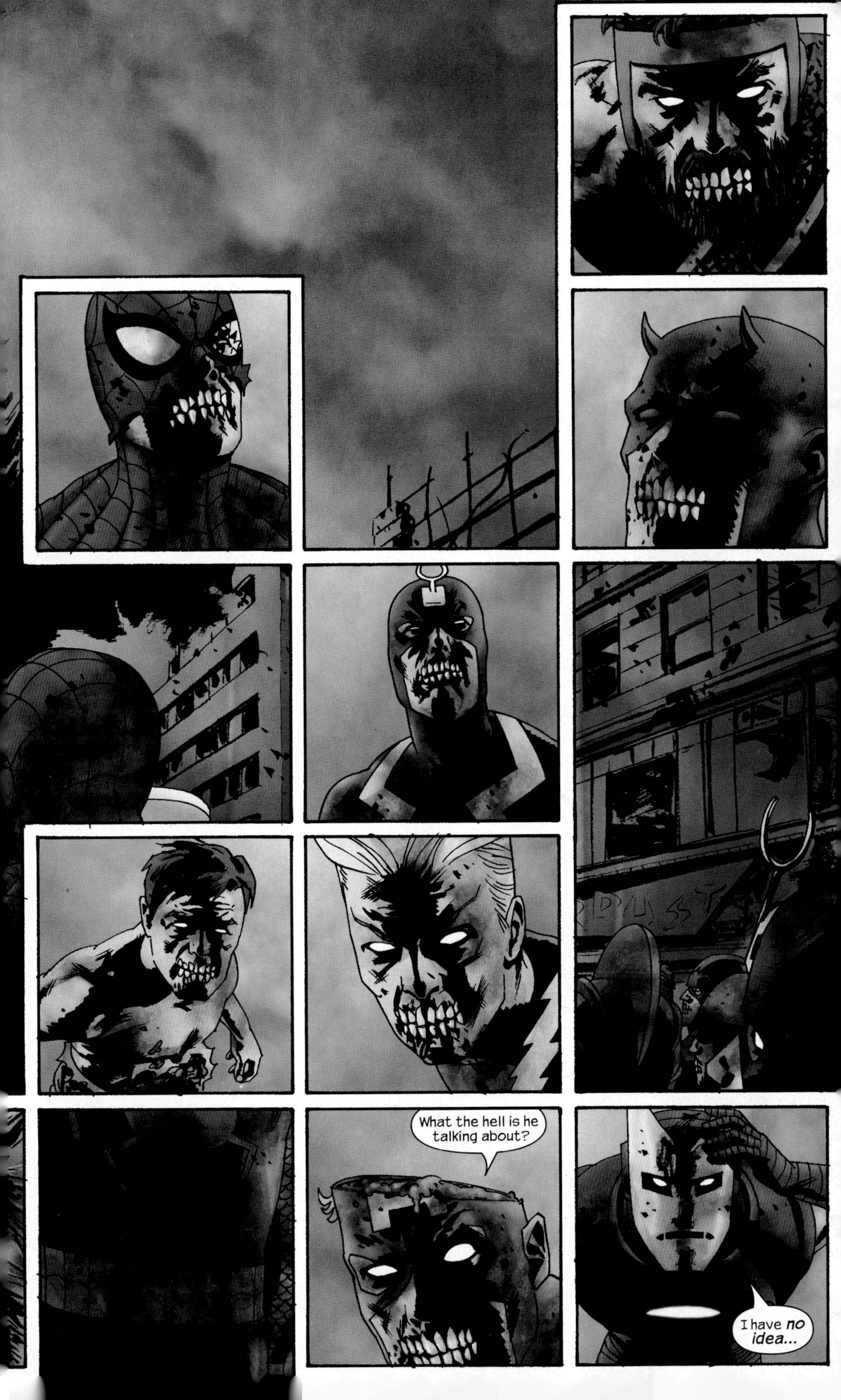
What the hell is he talking about?
I have no idea...

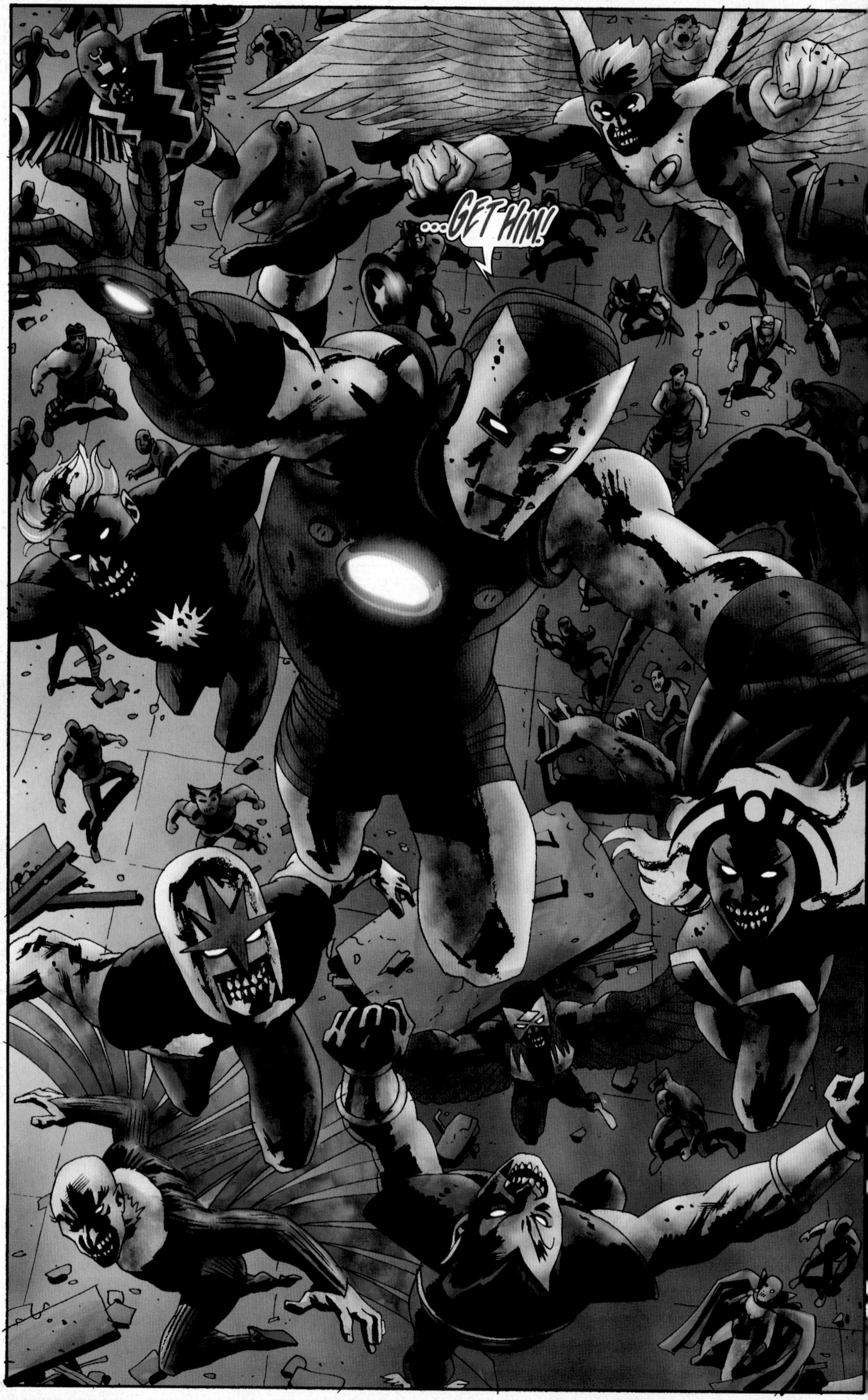
...GET HIM!

MARVEL ZOMBIES

PART 3 OF 5

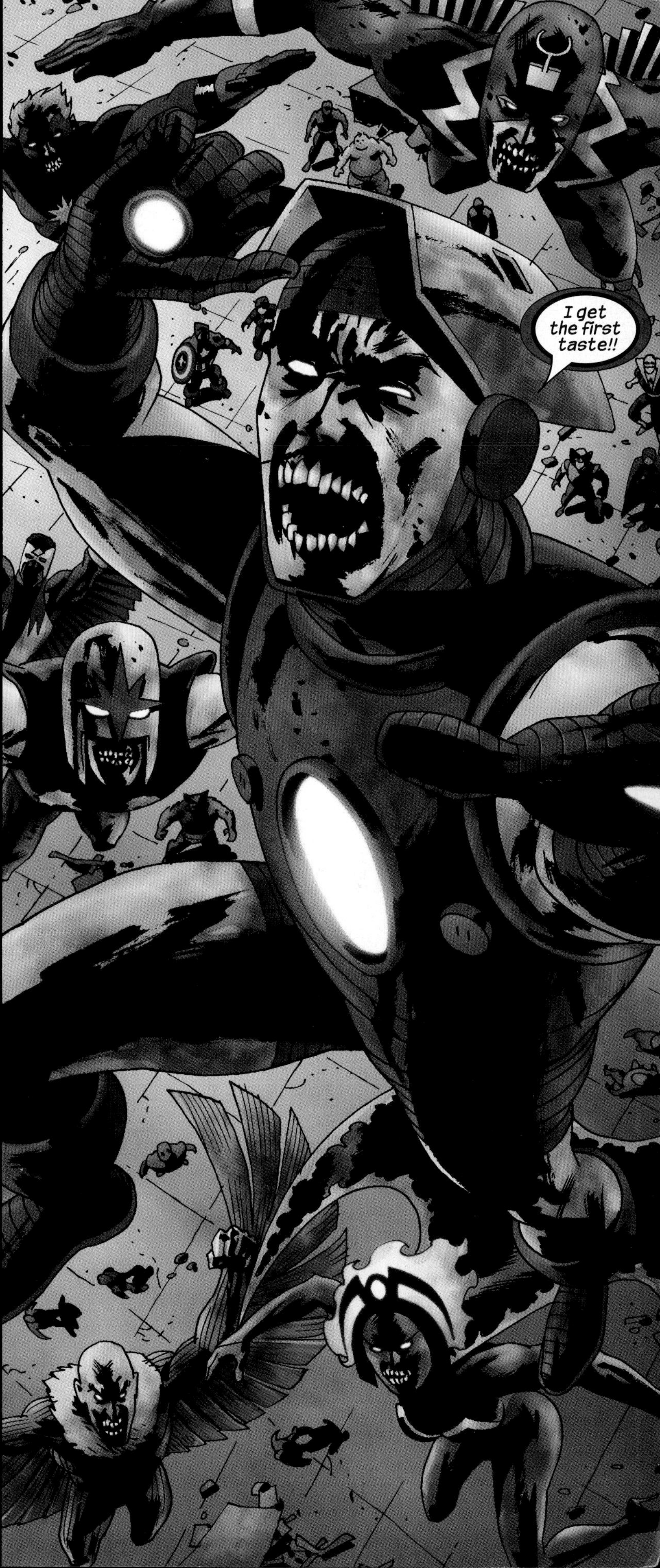
I get the first taste!!

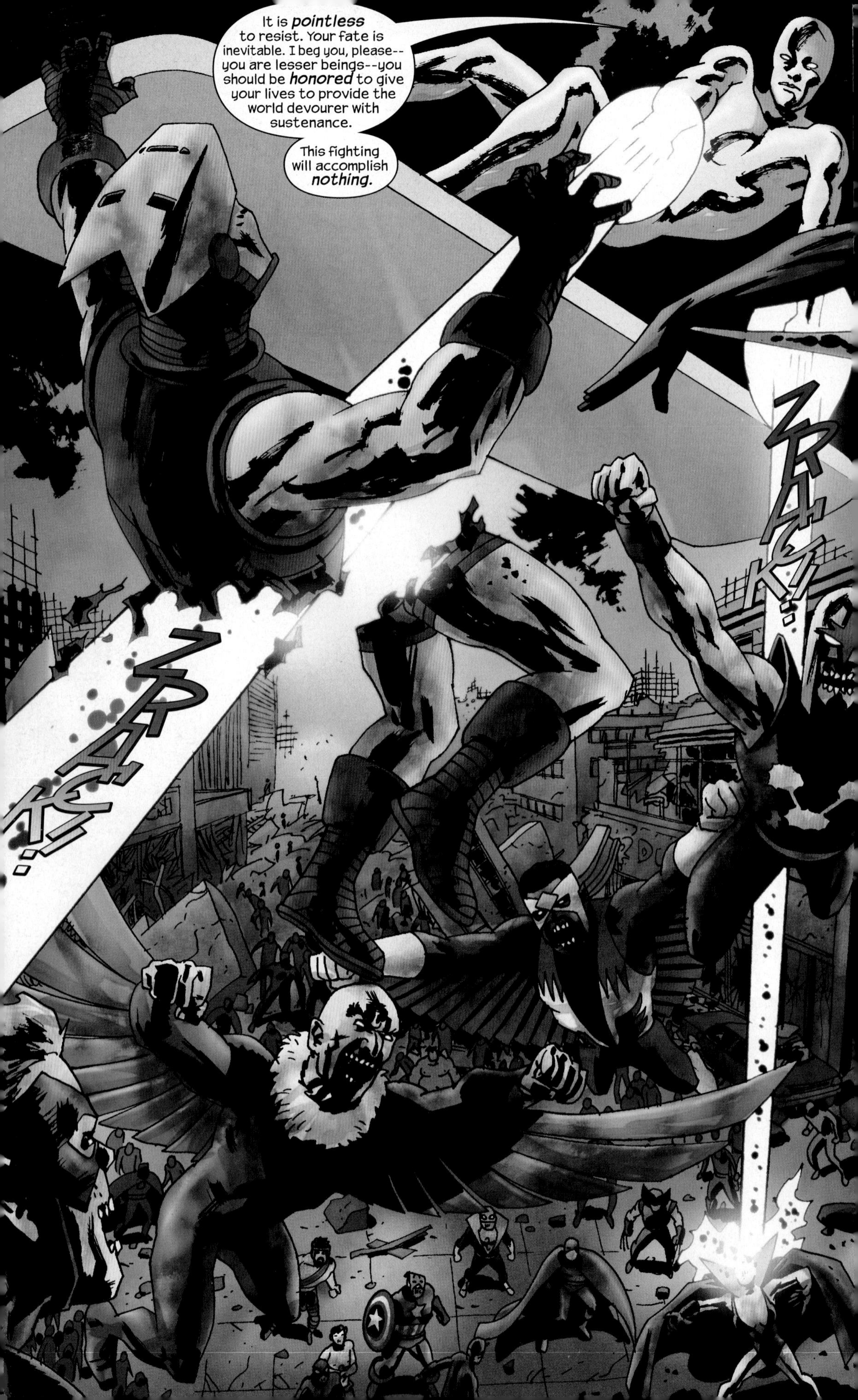

It is pointless to resist. Your fate is inevitable. I beg you, please-- you are lesser beings--you should be honored to give your lives to provide the world devourer with sustenance.
This fighting will accomplish nothing.
ZRAACK!!
ZRAACK!!

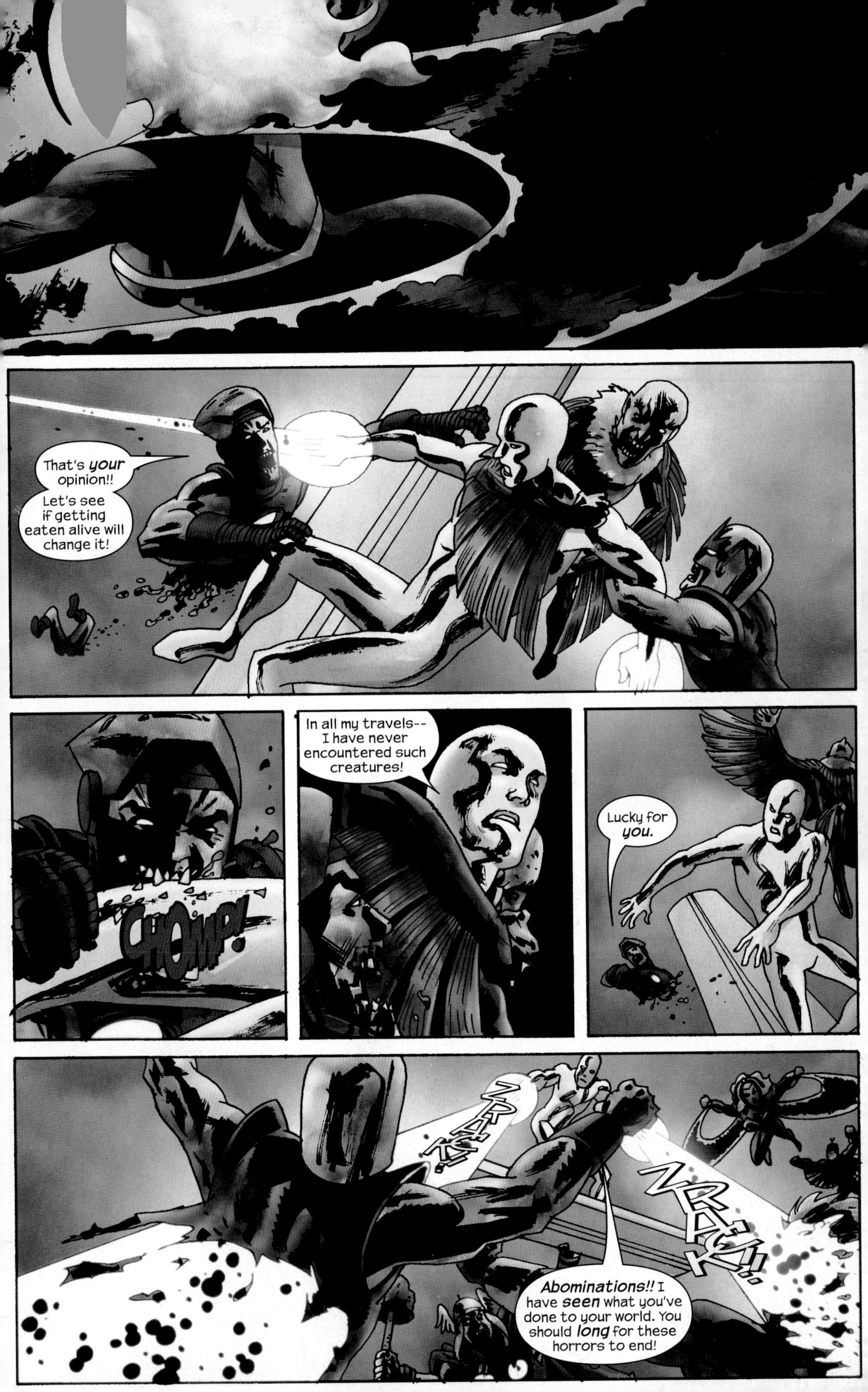
That's your opinion!!
Let's see if getting eaten alive will change it!
CHOMP!
In all my travels-- I have never encountered such creatures!
Lucky for you.
ZRAK!
ZRAK!!
Abominations!! I have seen what you've done to your world. You should long for these horrors to end!

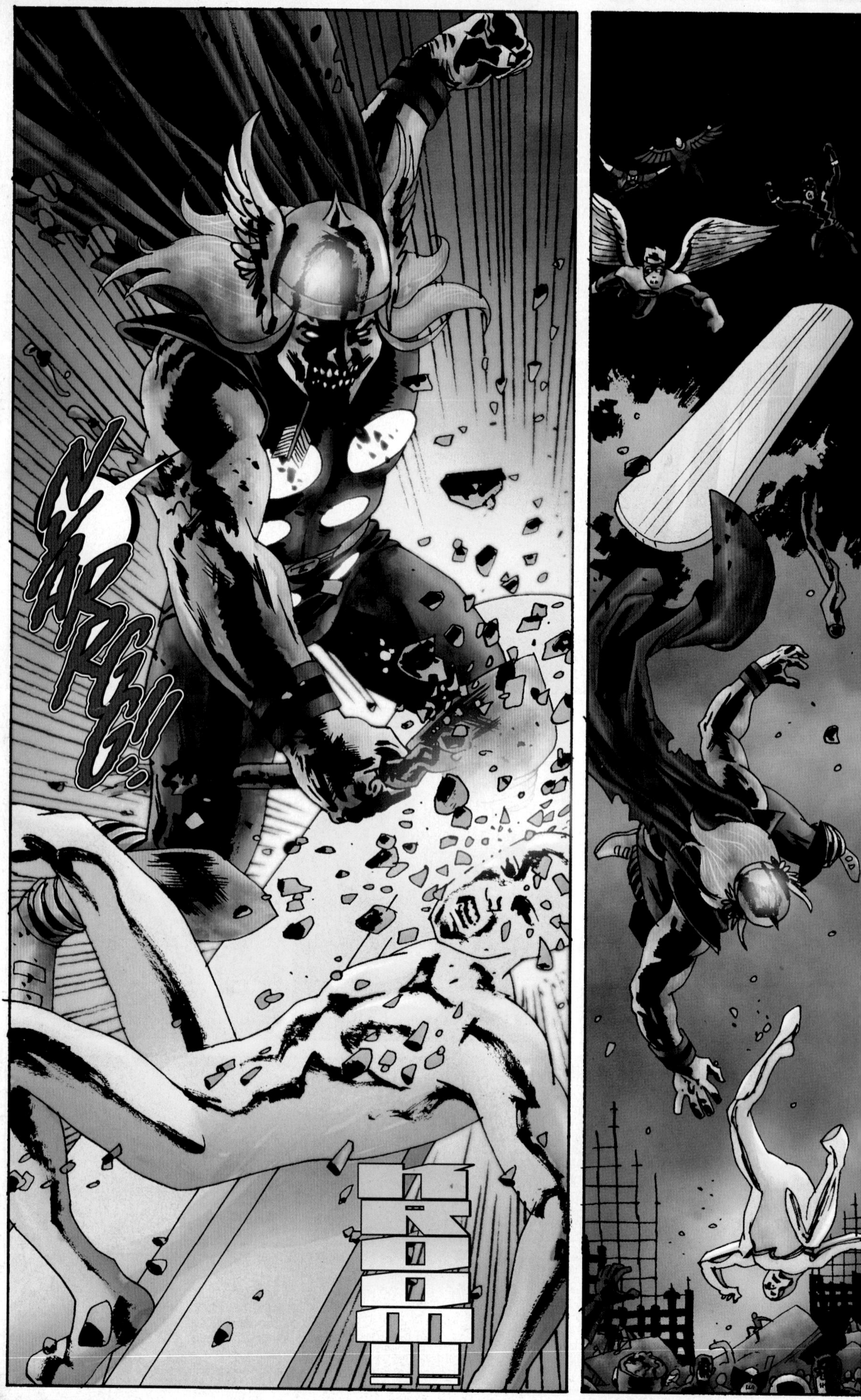
NYARRGG!!..
KROOM!!

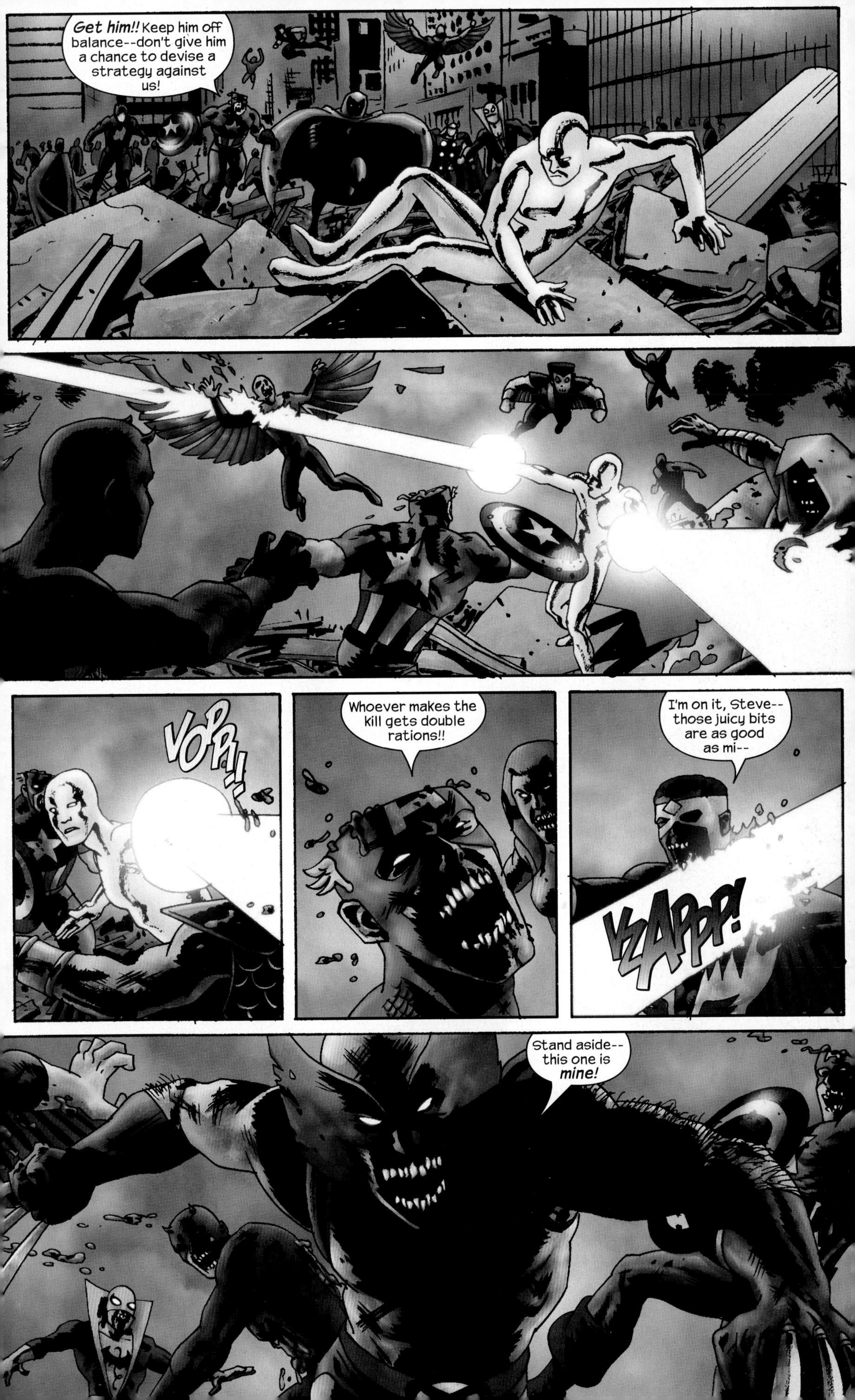
Get him!! Keep him off balance--don't give him a chance to devise a strategy against us!
VOPP!!
Whoever makes the kill gets double rations!!
I'm on it, Steve--those juicy bits are as good as mi--
VZAPP!
Stand aside--this one is mine!

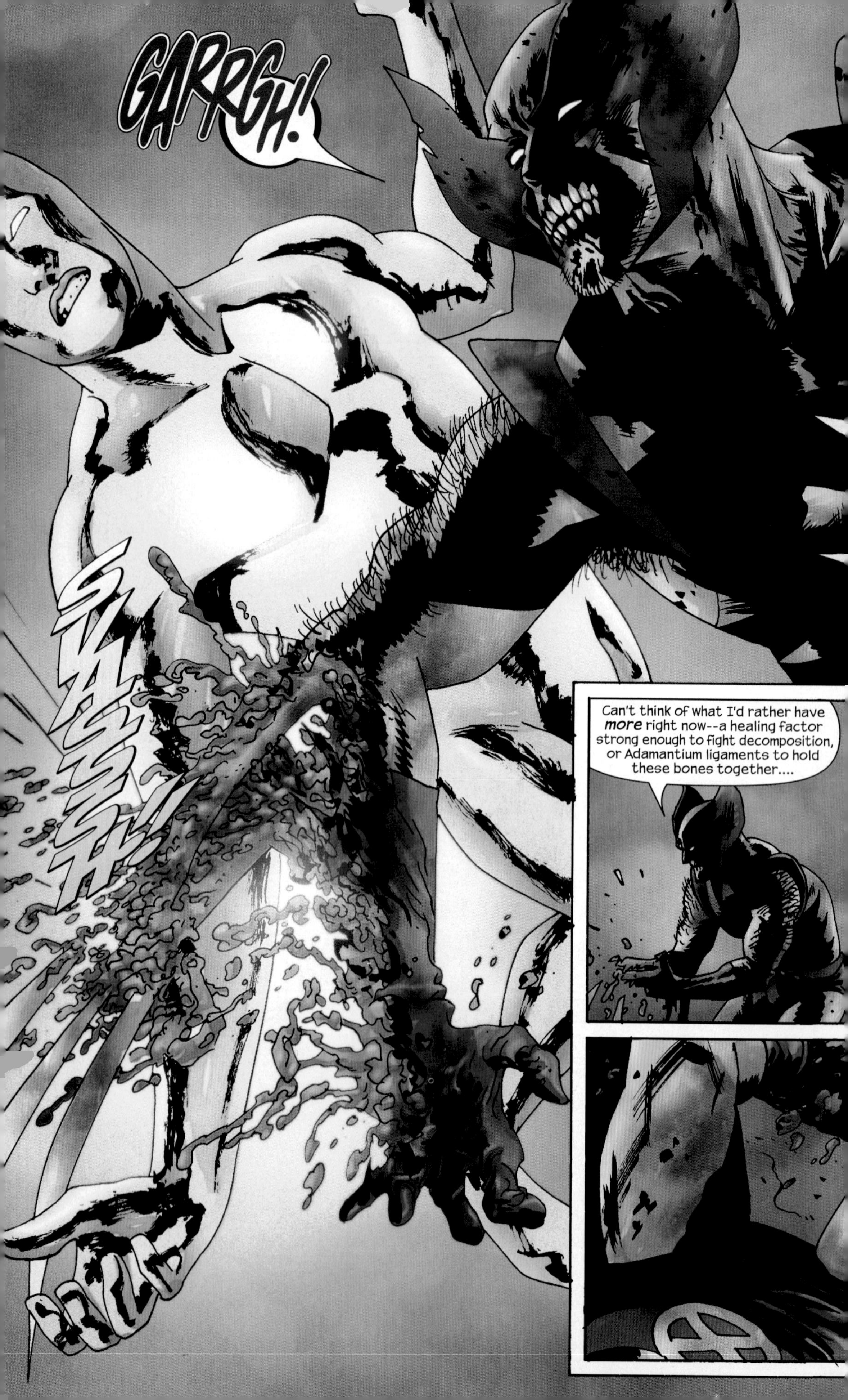
GARRGH!!
SHHUNNKK!!
Can't think of what I'd rather have *more* right now--a healing factor strong enough to fight decomposition, or Adamantium ligaments to hold these bones together....

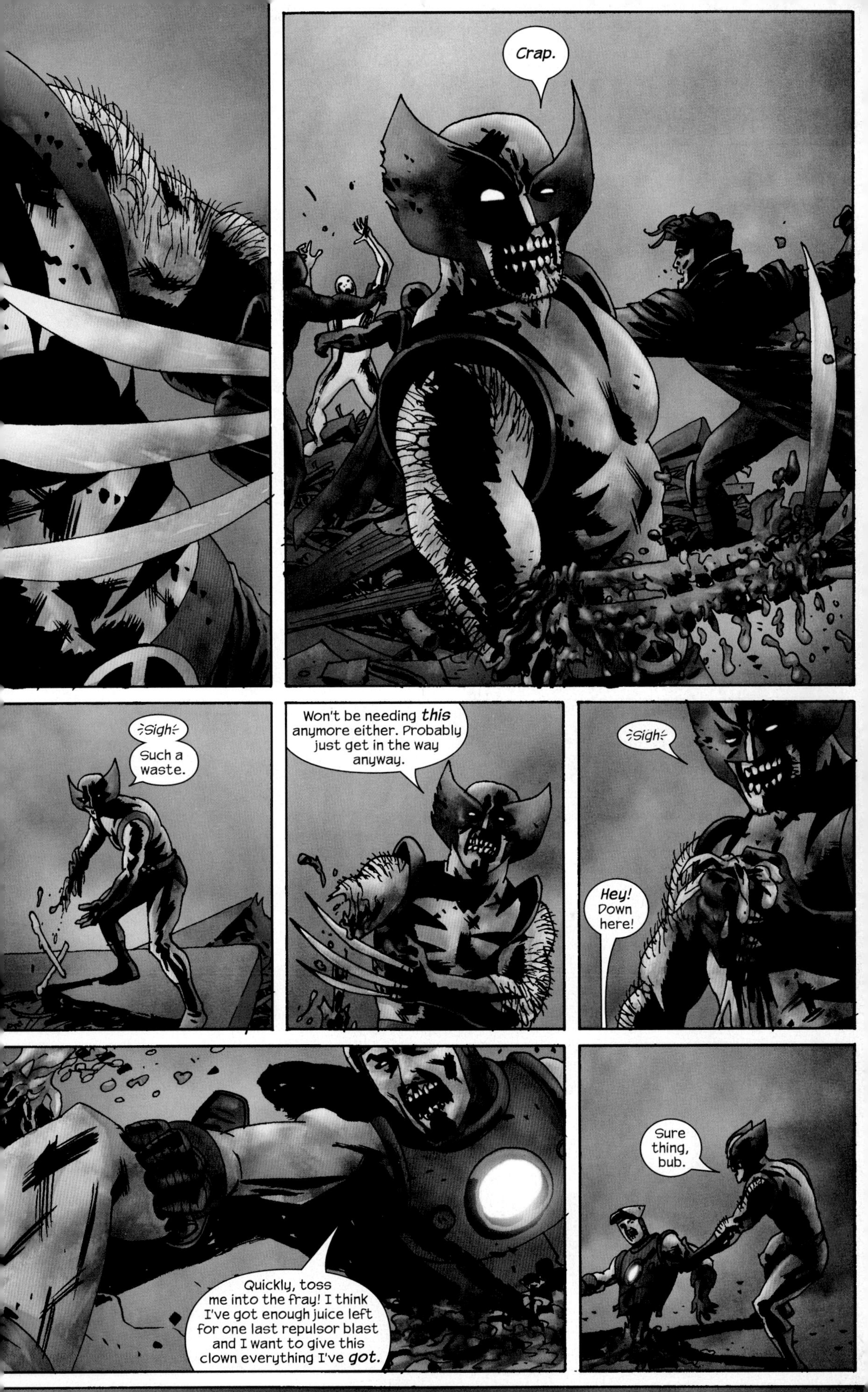
Crap.
Sigh
Such a waste.
Won't be needing this anymore either. Probably just get in the way anyway.
Sigh
Hey! Down here!
Quickly, toss me into the fray! I think I've got enough juice left for one last repulsor blast and I want to give this clown everything I've got.
Sure thing, bub.

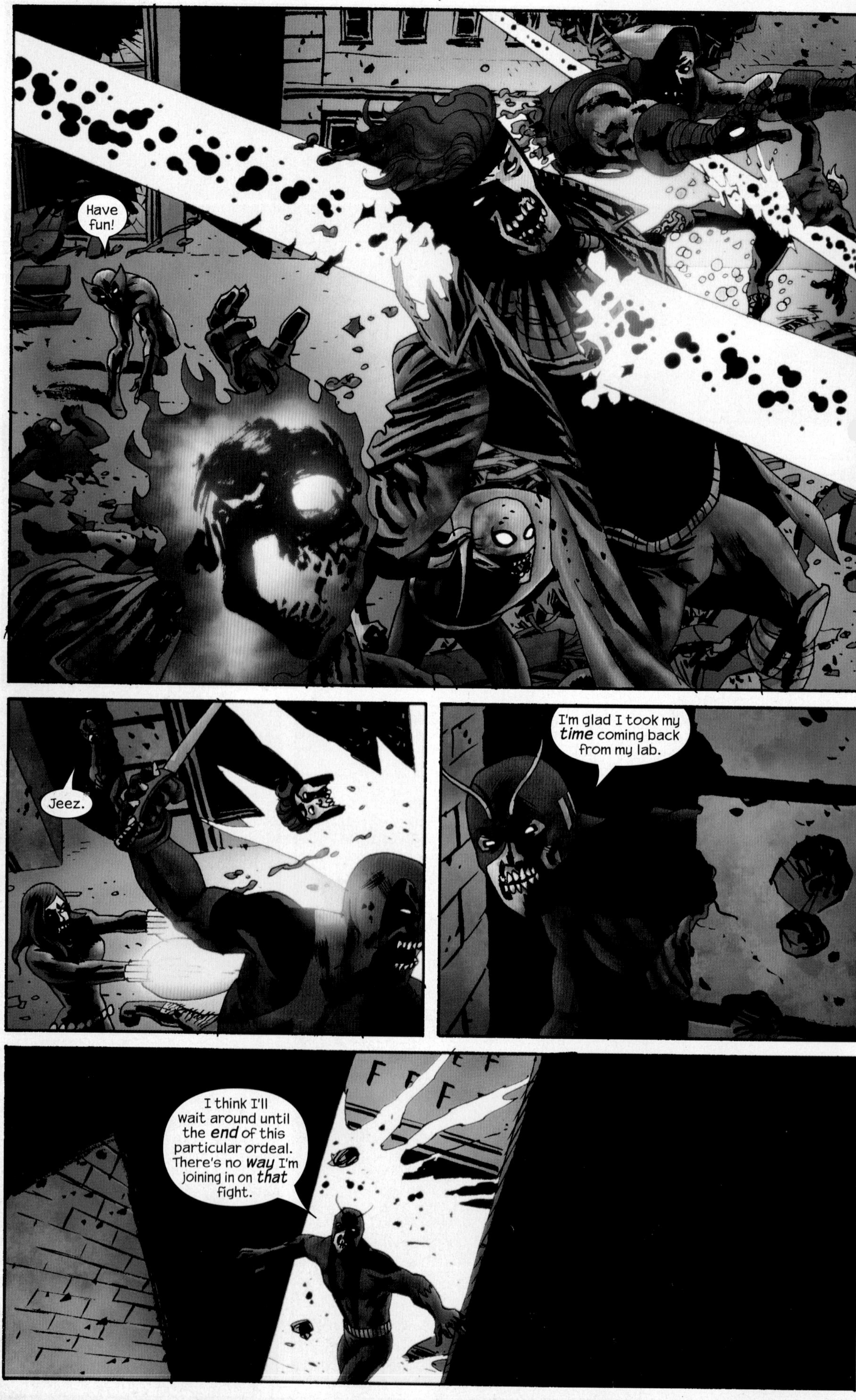
Have fun!
Jeez.
I'm glad I took my *time* coming back from my lab.
I think I'll wait around until the ***end*** of this particular ordeal. There's no ***way*** I'm joining in on ***that*** fight.

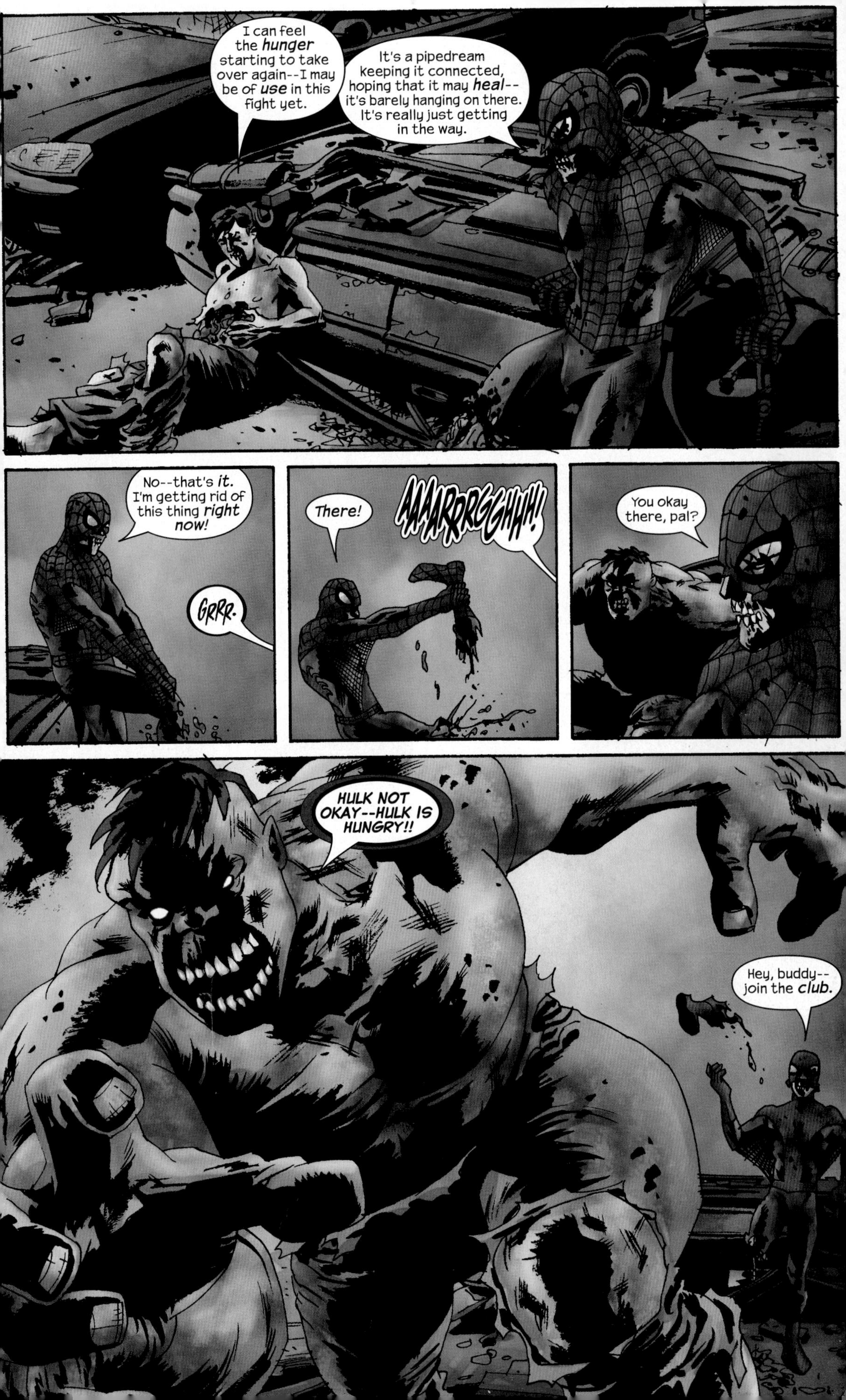
I can feel the hunger starting to take over again--I may be of use in this fight yet.
It's a pipedream keeping it connected, hoping that it may heal-- it's barely hanging on there. It's really just getting in the way.
No--that's it. I'm getting rid of this thing right now!
GRRR.
There!
AAAARRRGGHHH!
You okay there, pal?
HULK NOT OKAY--HULK IS HUNGRY!!
Hey, buddy-- join the club.

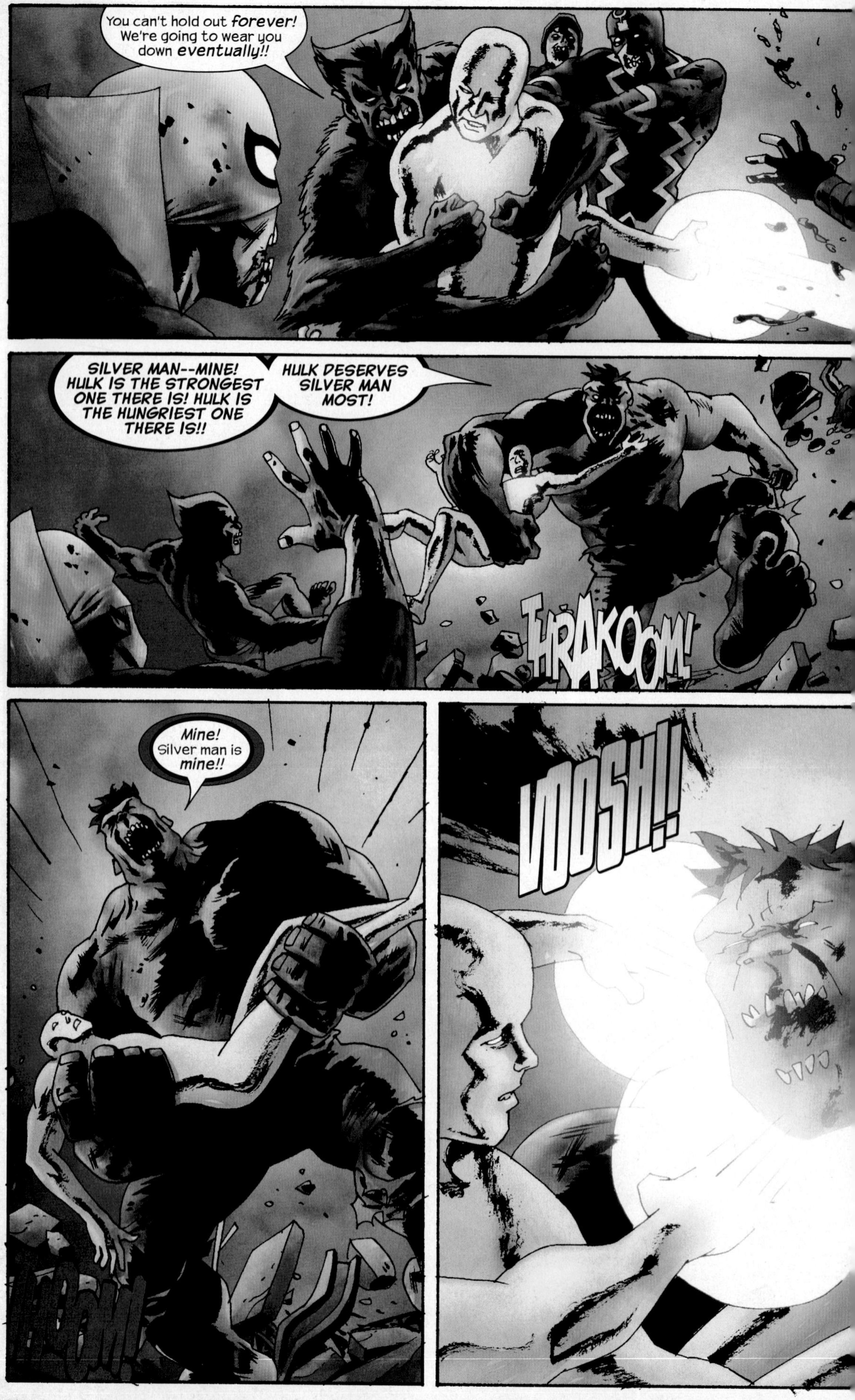
You can't hold out forever! We're going to wear you down eventually!!
SILVER MAN--MINE! HULK IS THE STRONGEST ONE THERE IS! HULK IS THE HUNGRIEST ONE THERE IS!!
HULK DESERVES SILVER MAN MOST!
THRAKOOM!
Mine! Silver man is mine!!
VOOSH!!

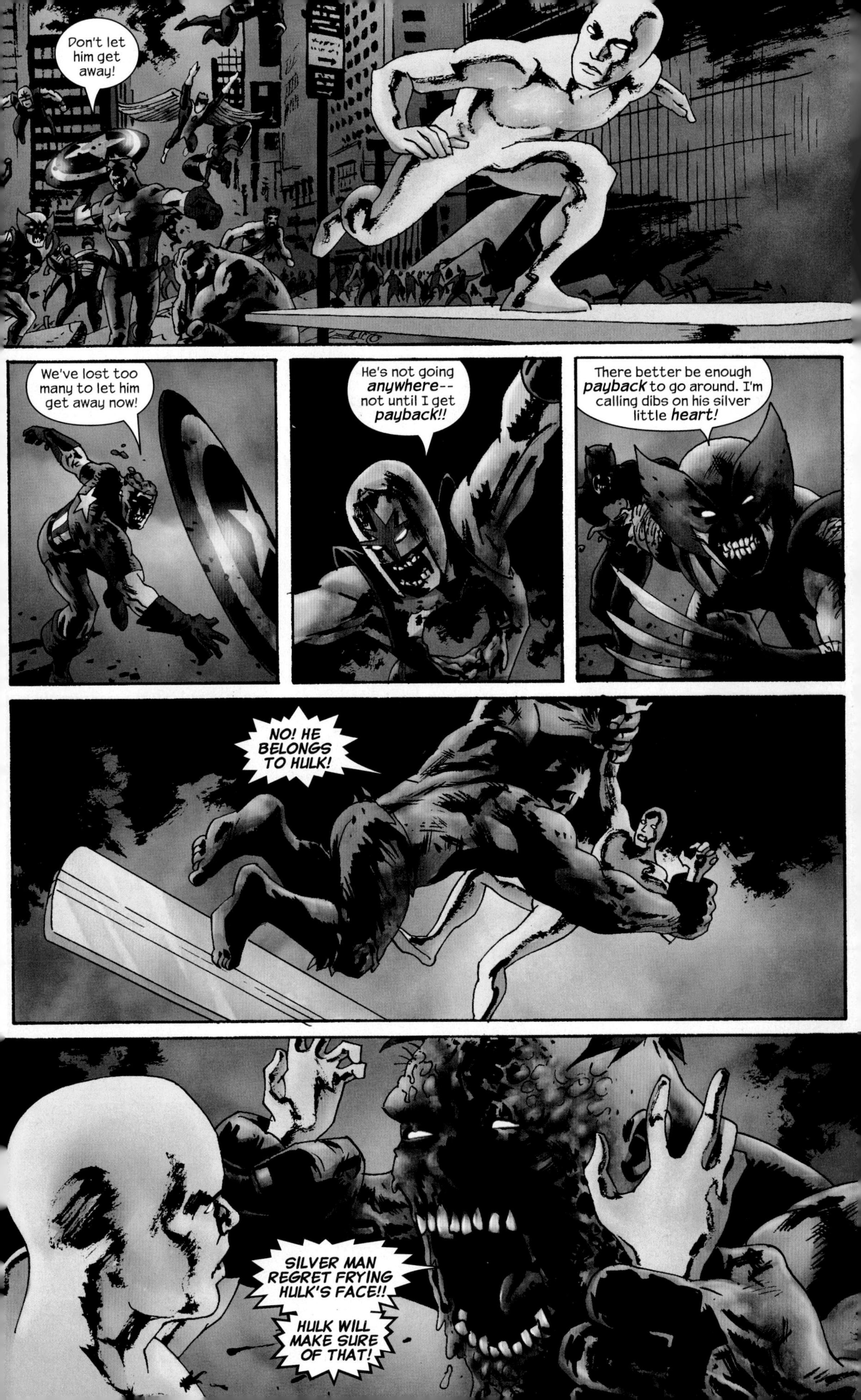
Don't let him get away!
We've lost too many to let him get away now!
He's not going *anywhere*-- not until I get *payback*!!
There better be enough *payback* to go around. I'm calling dibs on his silver little *heart!*
NO! HE BELONGS TO HULK!
SILVER MAN REGRET FRYING HULK'S FACE!!
HULK WILL MAKE SURE OF THAT!

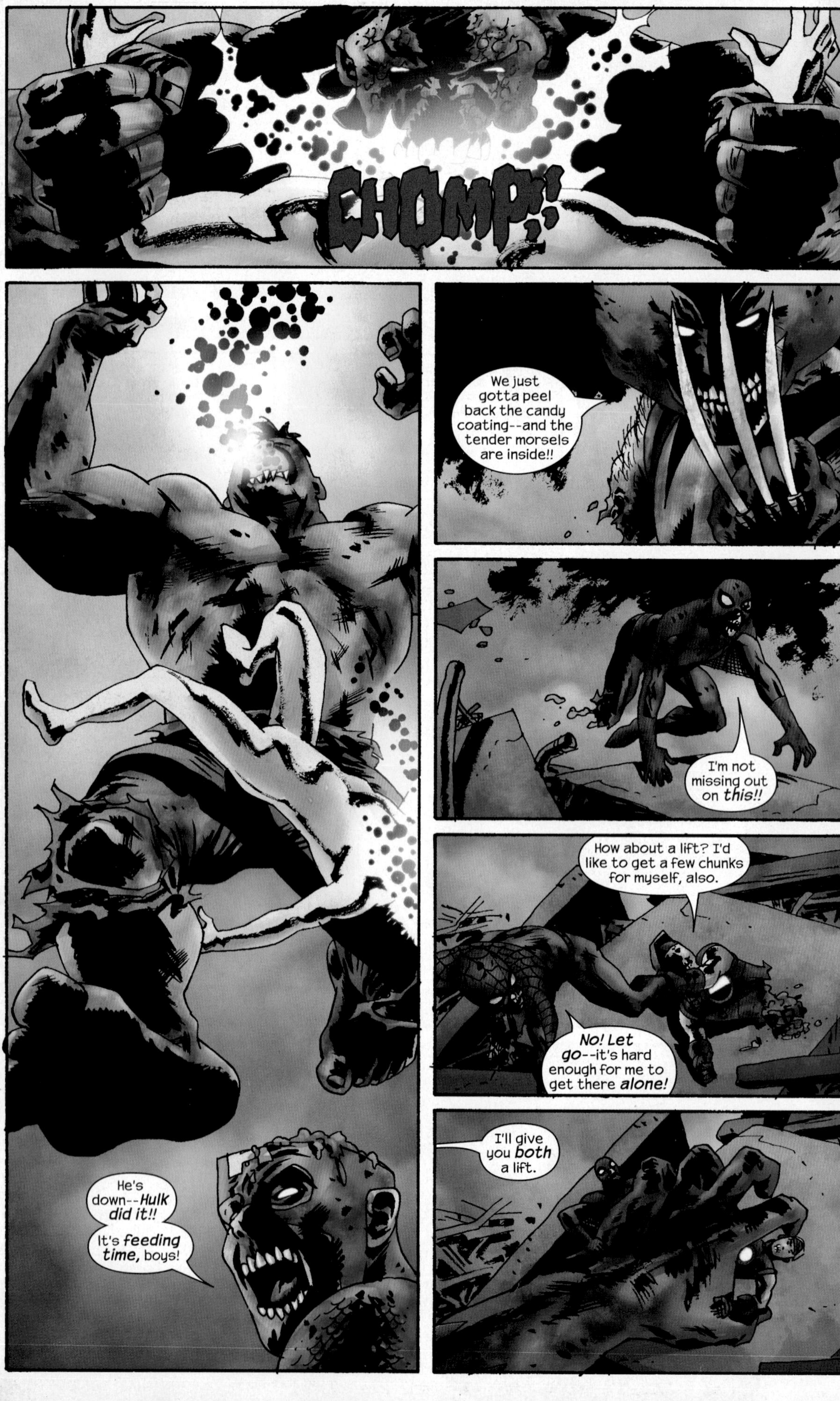
CHOMP!!
We just gotta peel back the candy coating--and the tender morsels are inside!!
He's down--Hulk did it!!
It's feeding time, boys!
I'm not missing out on this!!
How about a lift? I'd like to get a few chunks for myself, also.
No! Let go--it's hard enough for me to get there alone!
I'll give you both a lift.

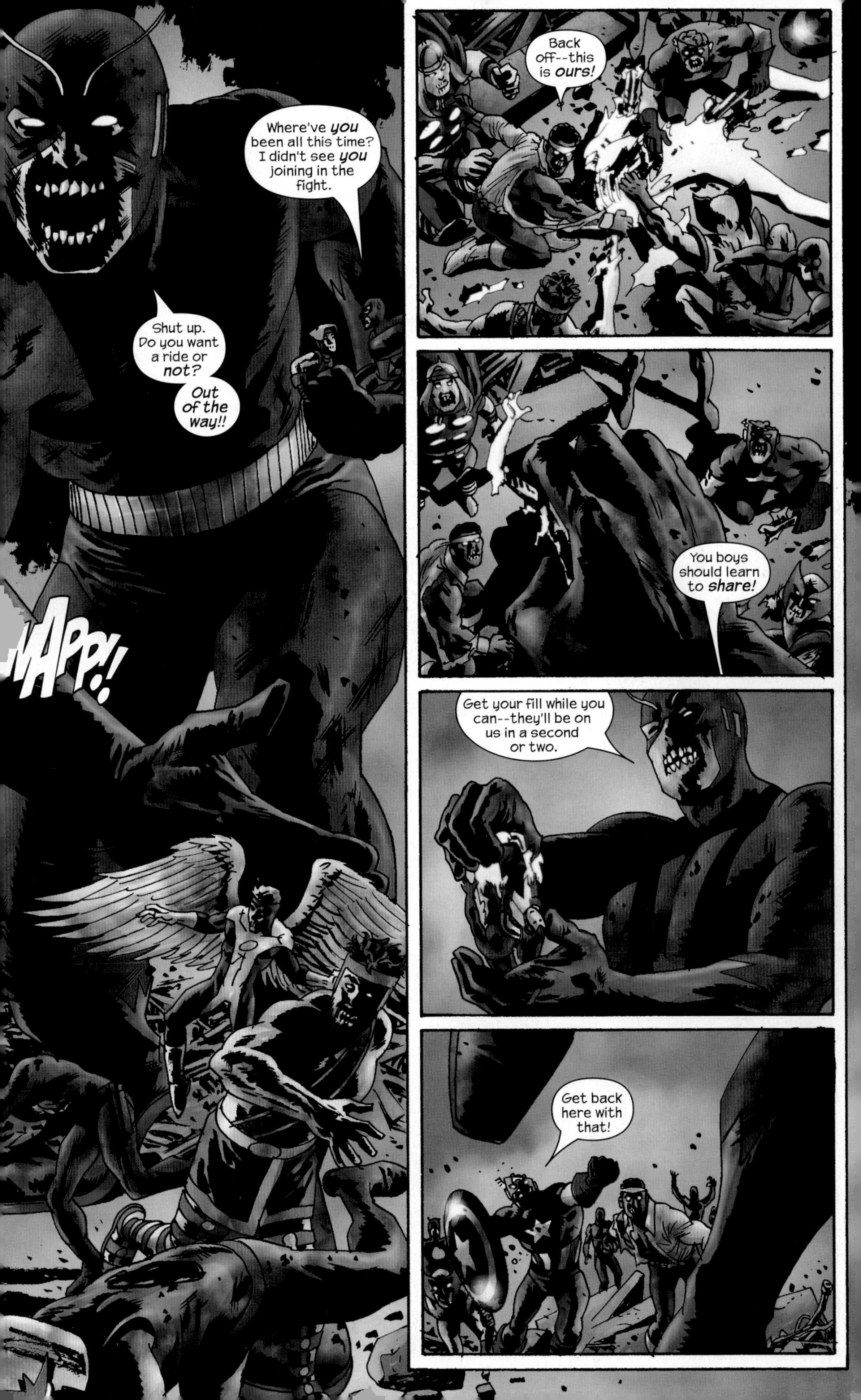
Where've *you* been all this time? I didn't see *you* joining in the fight.
Shut up. Do you want a ride or *not?*
Out of the way!!
MAPP!!
Back off--this is *ours!*
You boys should learn to *share!*
Get your fill while you can--they'll be on us in a second or two.
Get back here with that!

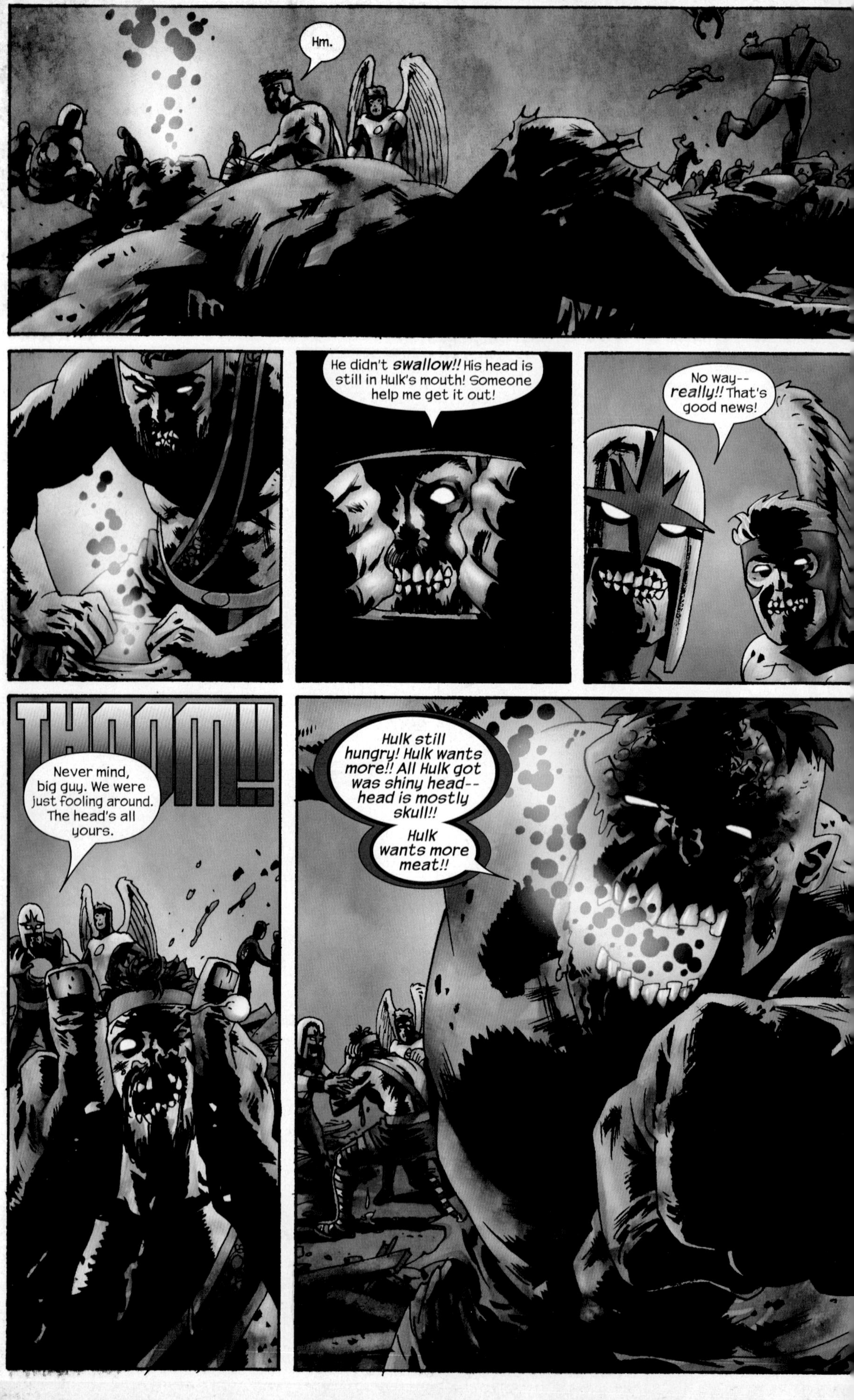
Hm.
He didn't *swallow!!* His head is still in Hulk's mouth! Someone help me get it out!
No way-- *really!!* That's good news!
THOOM!!
Never mind, big guy. We were just fooling around. The head's all yours.
Hulk still hungry! Hulk wants more!! All Hulk got was shiny head-- head is mostly skull!!
Hulk wants more meat!!

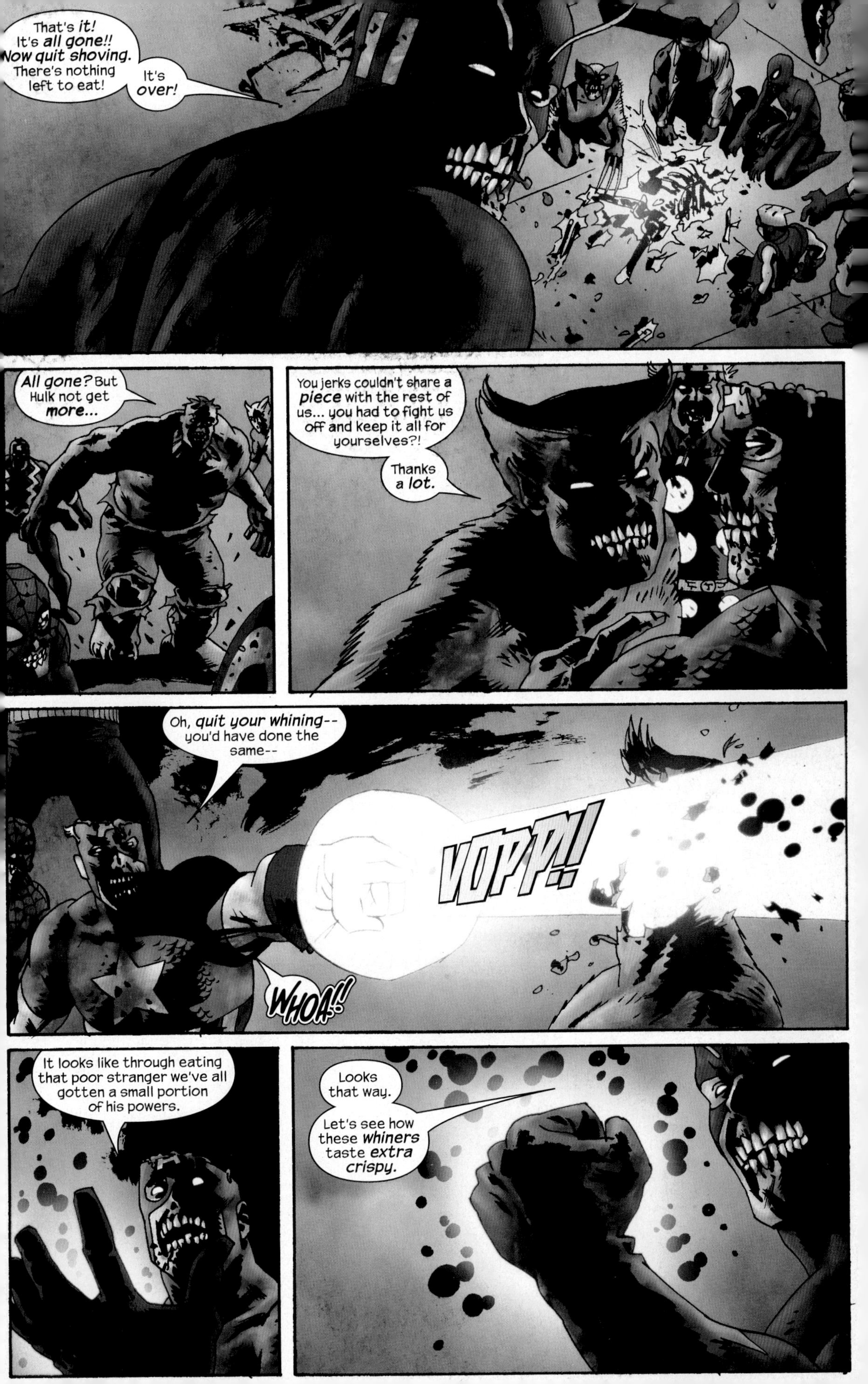
That's it! It's all gone!! Now quit shoving. There's nothing left to eat!
It's over!
All gone? But Hulk not get more...
You jerks couldn't share a piece with the rest of us... you had to fight us off and keep it all for yourselves?!
Thanks a lot.
Oh, quit your whining-- you'd have done the same--
VOPP!!
WHOA!!
It looks like through eating that poor stranger we've all gotten a small portion of his powers.
Looks that way.
Let's see how these whiners taste extra crispy.

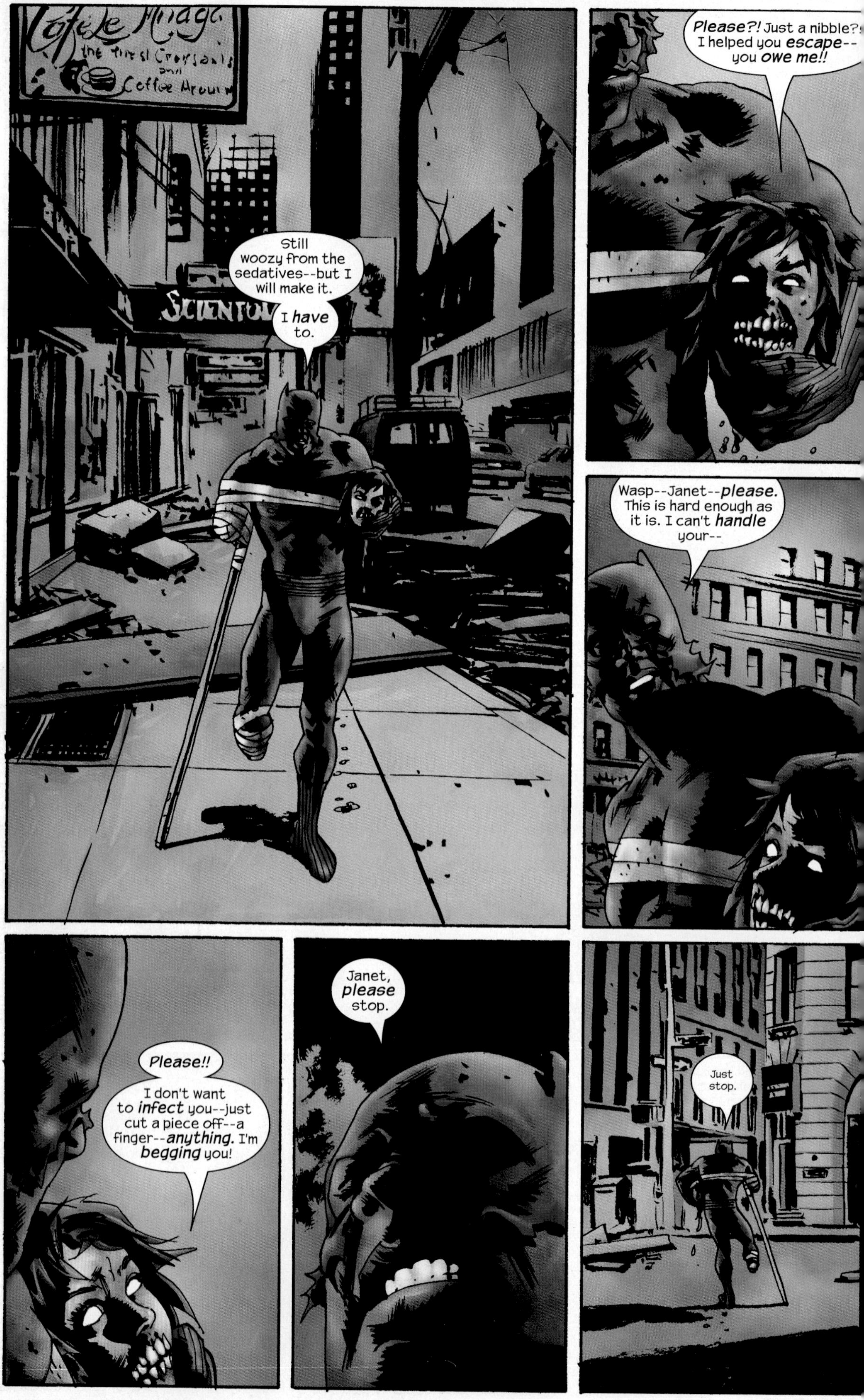

Still woozy from the sedatives--but I will make it.
I have to.
Please?! Just a nibble?! I helped you escape--you owe me!!
Wasp--Janet--please. This is hard enough as it is. I can't handle your--
Please!!
I don't want to infect you--just cut a piece off--a finger--anything. I'm begging you!
Janet, please stop.
Just stop.

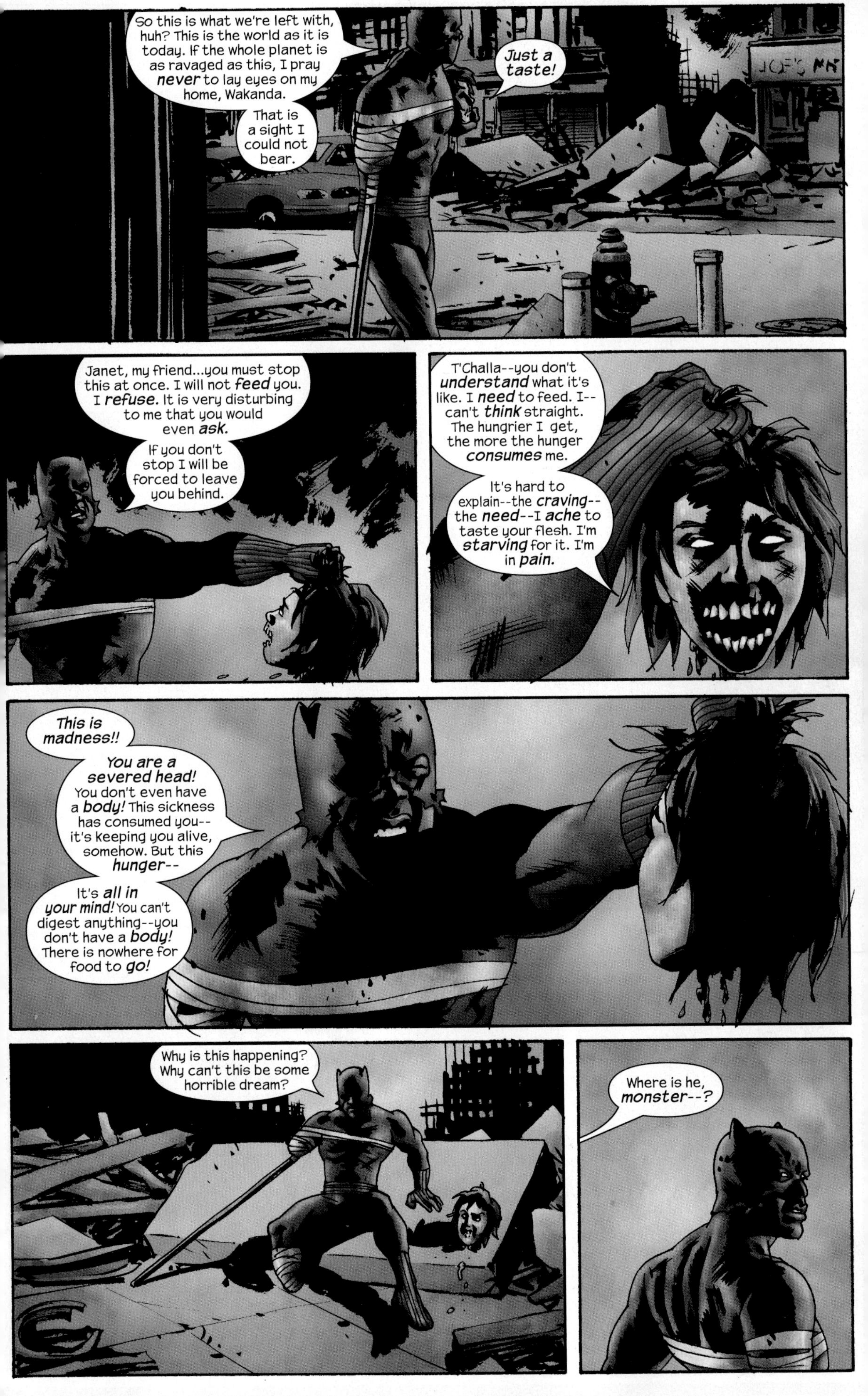
So this is what we're left with, huh? This is the world as it is today. If the whole planet is as ravaged as this, I pray never to lay eyes on my home, Wakanda.
That is a sight I could not bear.
Just a taste!
Janet, my friend...you must stop this at once. I will not feed you. I refuse. It is very disturbing to me that you would even ask.
If you don't stop I will be forced to leave you behind.
T'Challa--you don't understand what it's like. I need to feed. I--can't think straight. The hungrier I get, the more the hunger consumes me.
It's hard to explain--the craving--the need--I ache to taste your flesh. I'm starving for it. I'm in pain.
This is madness!!
You are a severed head! You don't even have a body! This sickness has consumed you--it's keeping you alive, somehow. But this hunger--
It's all in your mind! You can't digest anything--you don't have a body! There is nowhere for food to go!
Why is this happening? Why can't this be some horrible dream?
Where is he, monster--?

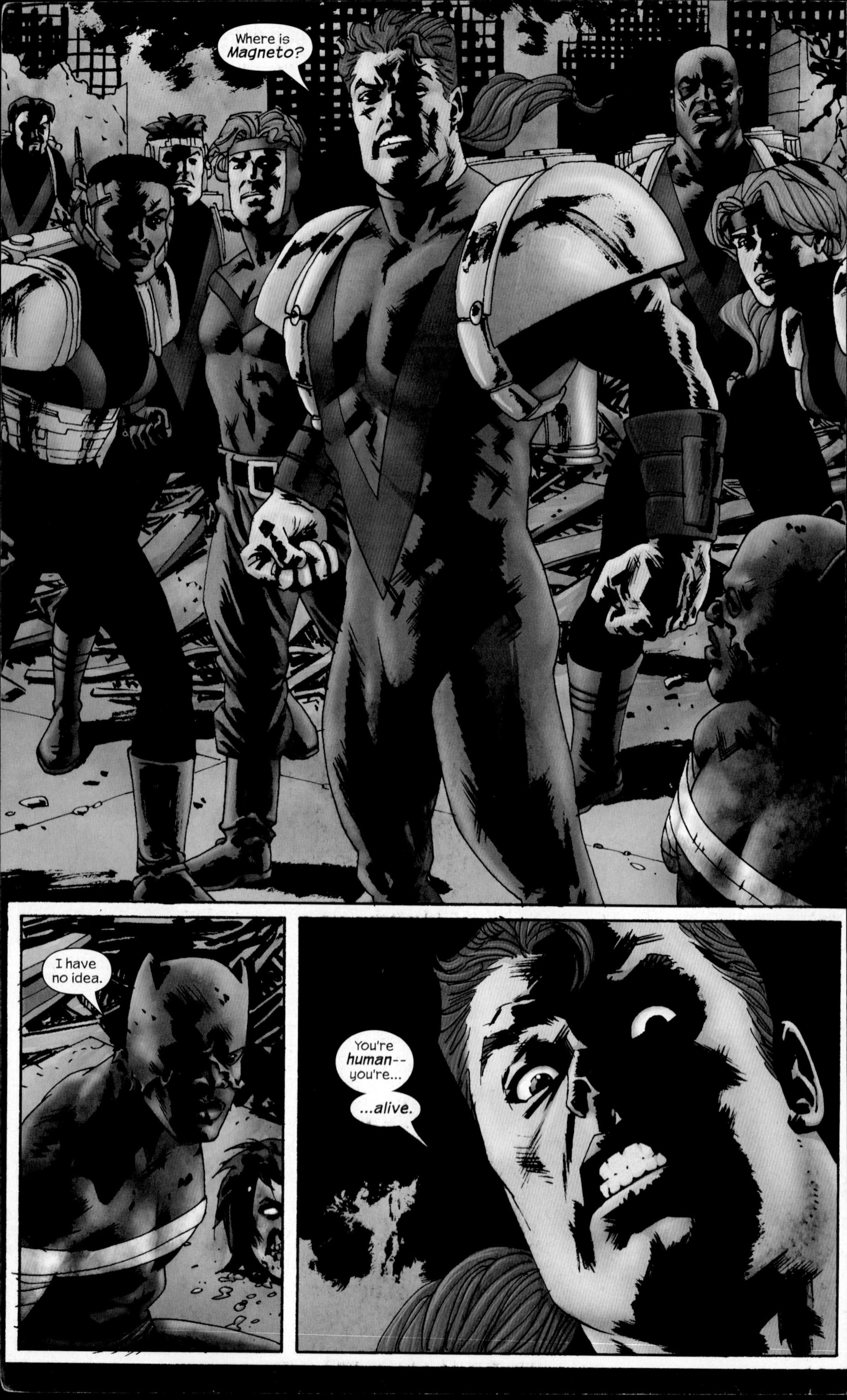
Where is *Magneto?*
I have no idea.
You're *human*-- you're...
...*alive.*

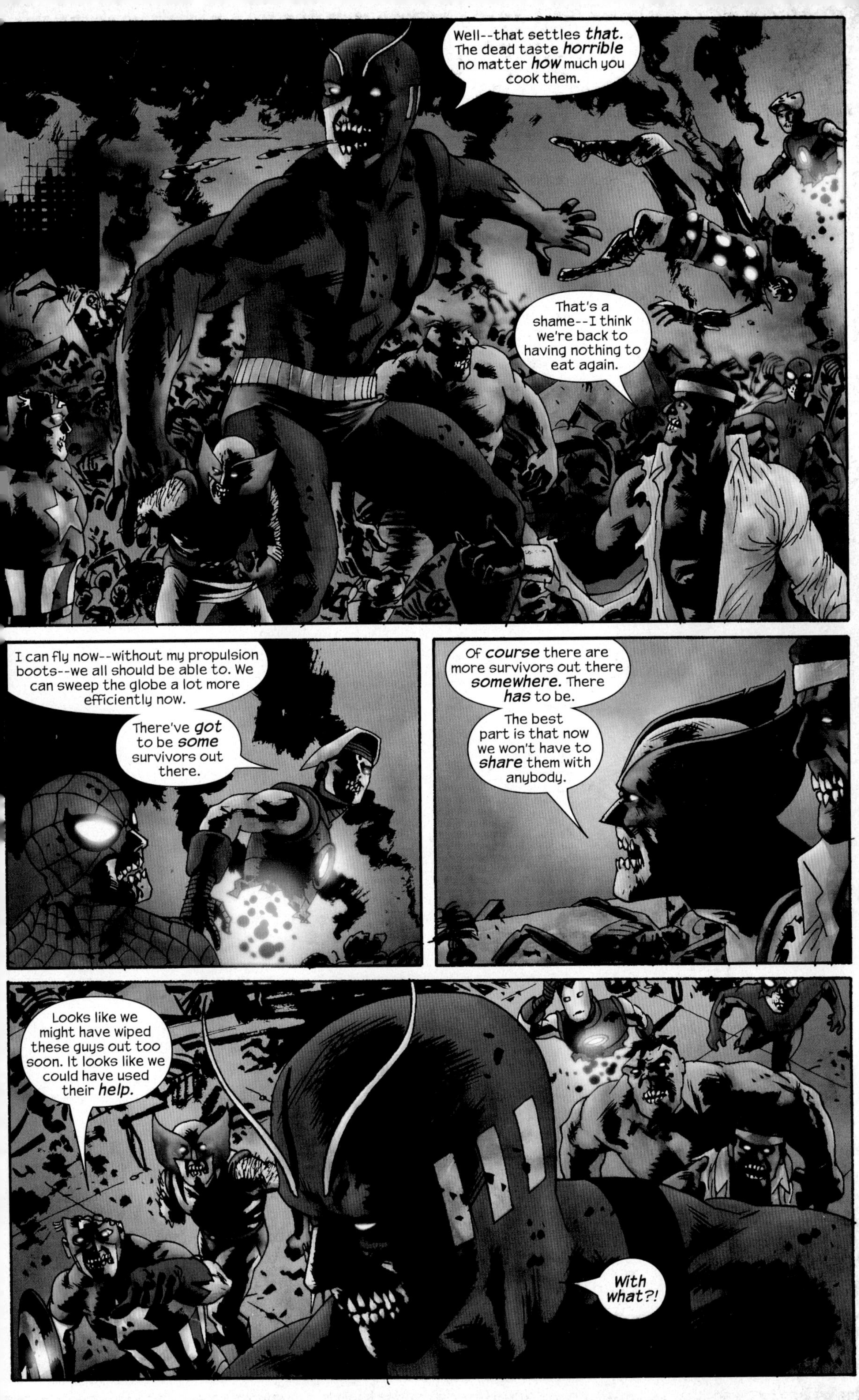
Well--that settles *that*. The dead taste *horrible* no matter *how* much you cook them.
That's a shame--I think we're back to having nothing to eat again.
I can fly now--without my propulsion boots--we all should be able to. We can sweep the globe a lot more efficiently now.
There've *got* to be *some* survivors out there.
Of *course* there are more survivors out there *somewhere*. There *has* to be.
The best part is that now we won't have to *share* them with anybody.
Looks like we might have wiped these guys out too soon. It looks like we could have used their *help*.
With what?!

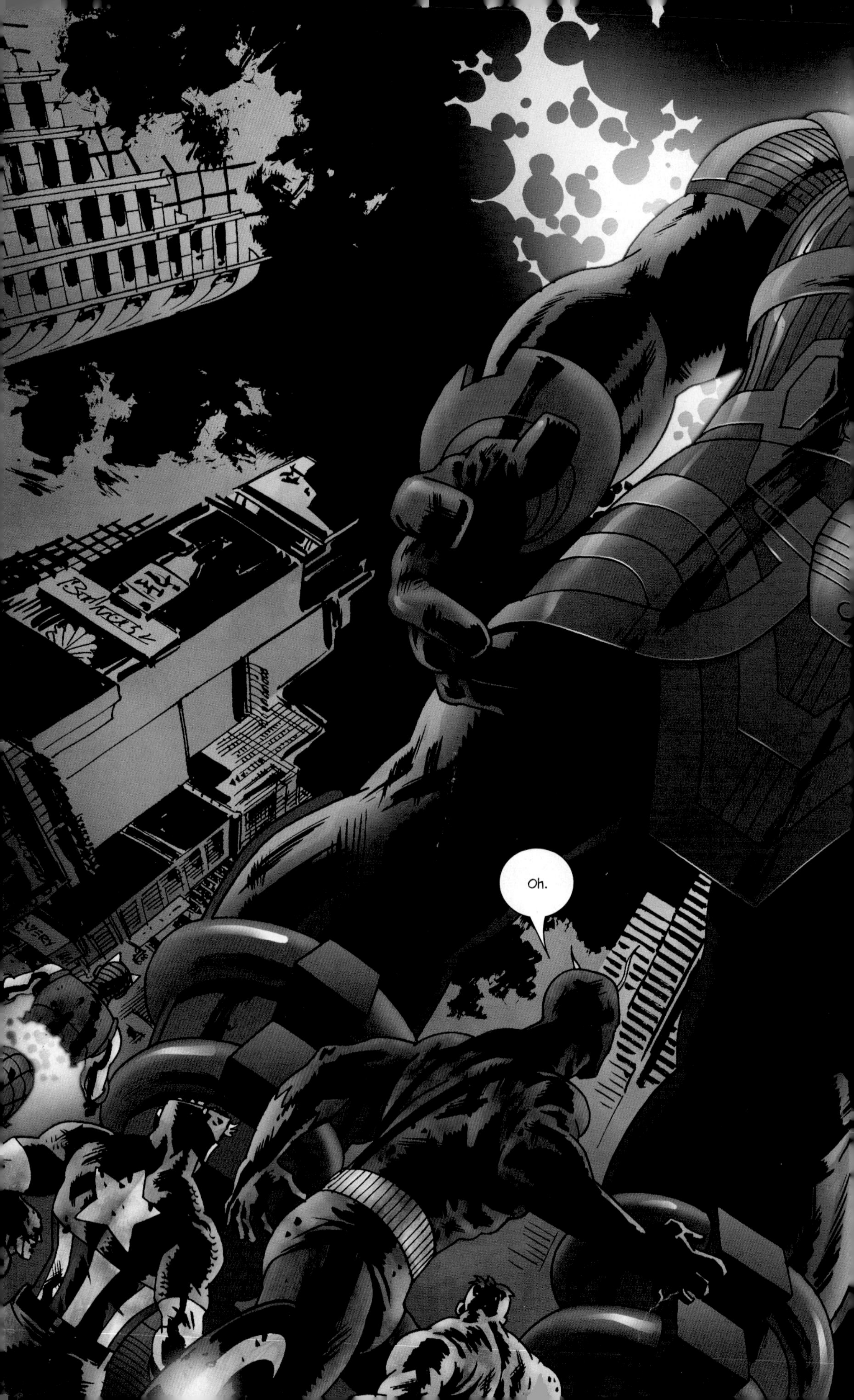
Oh.

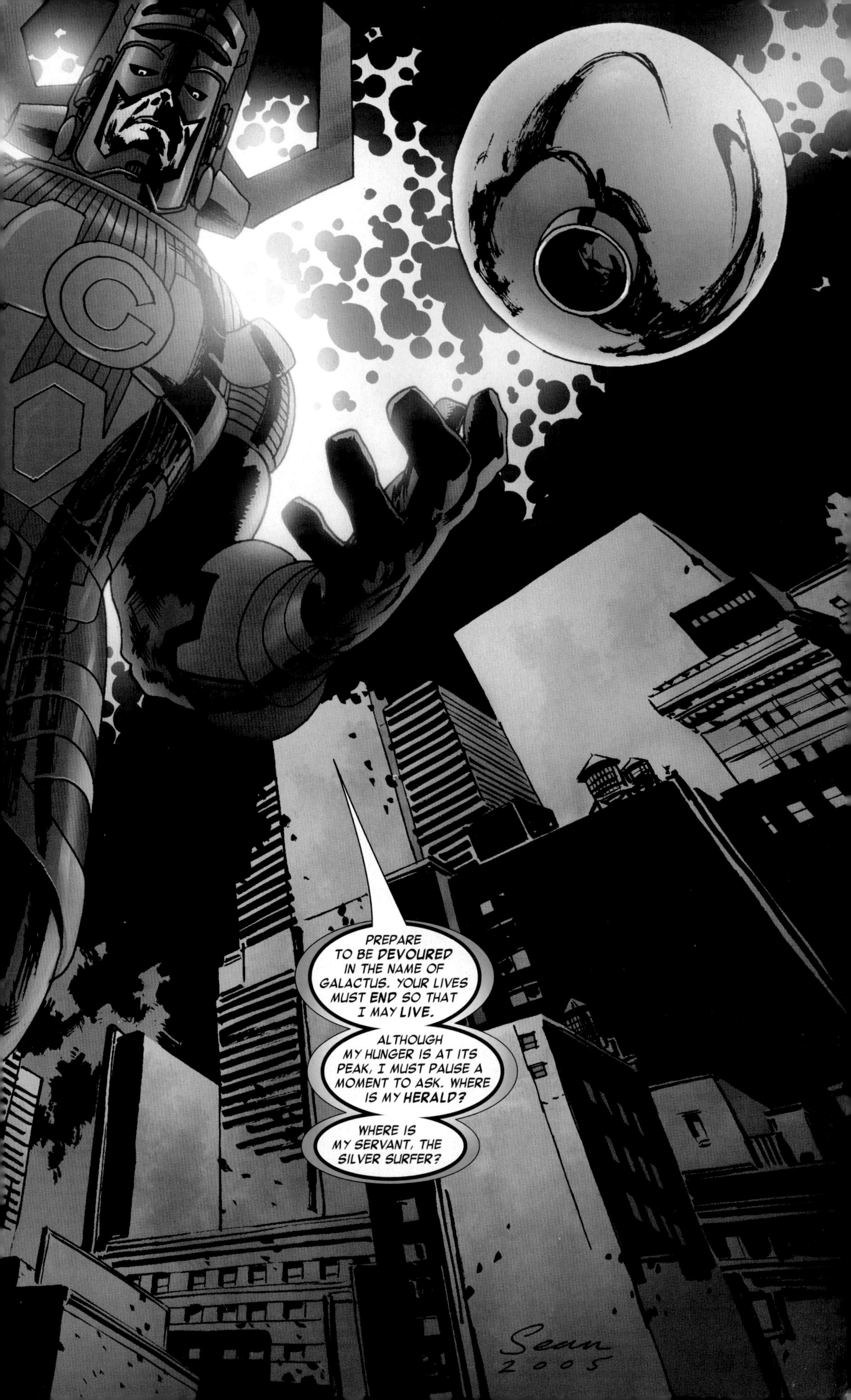

PREPARE TO BE DEVOURED IN THE NAME OF GALACTUS. YOUR LIVES MUST END SO THAT I MAY LIVE.
ALTHOUGH MY HUNGER IS AT ITS PEAK, I MUST PAUSE A MOMENT TO ASK. WHERE IS MY HERALD?
WHERE IS MY SERVANT, THE SILVER SURFER?
Sean 2005

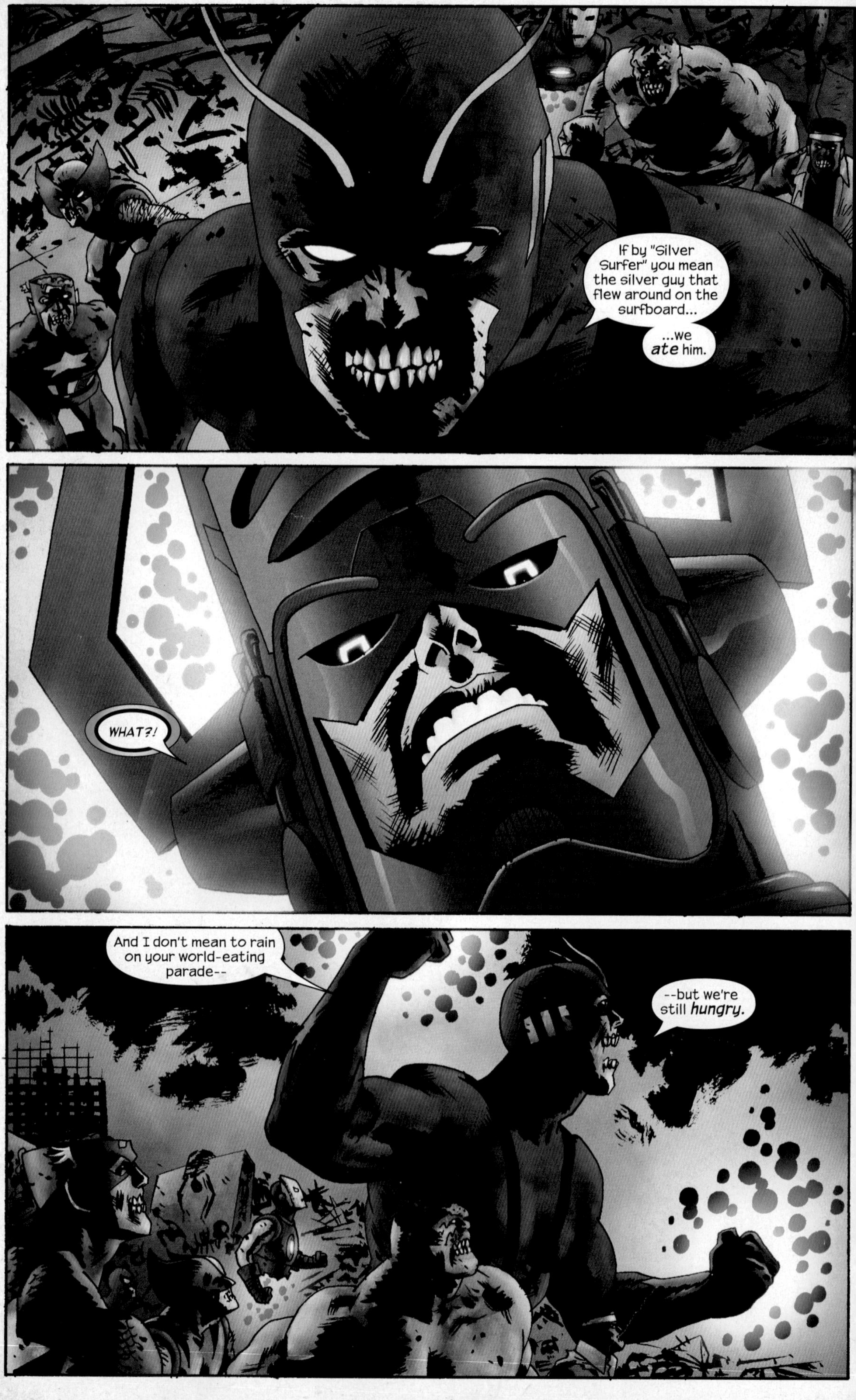
If by "Silver Surfer" you mean the silver guy that flew around on the surfboard...
...we ate him.
WHAT?!
And I don't mean to rain on your world-eating parade--
--but we're still hungry.

MARVEL ZOMBIES

PART 4 OF 5

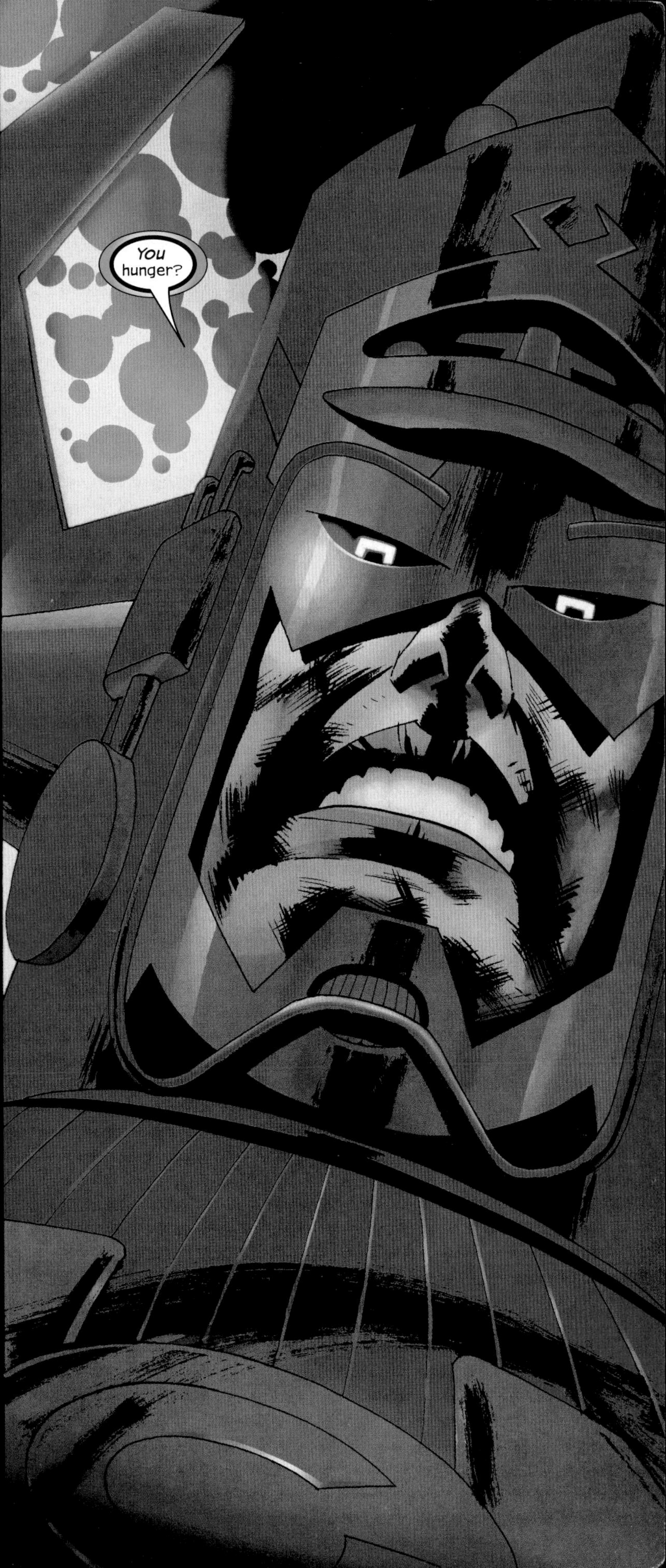
You hunger?

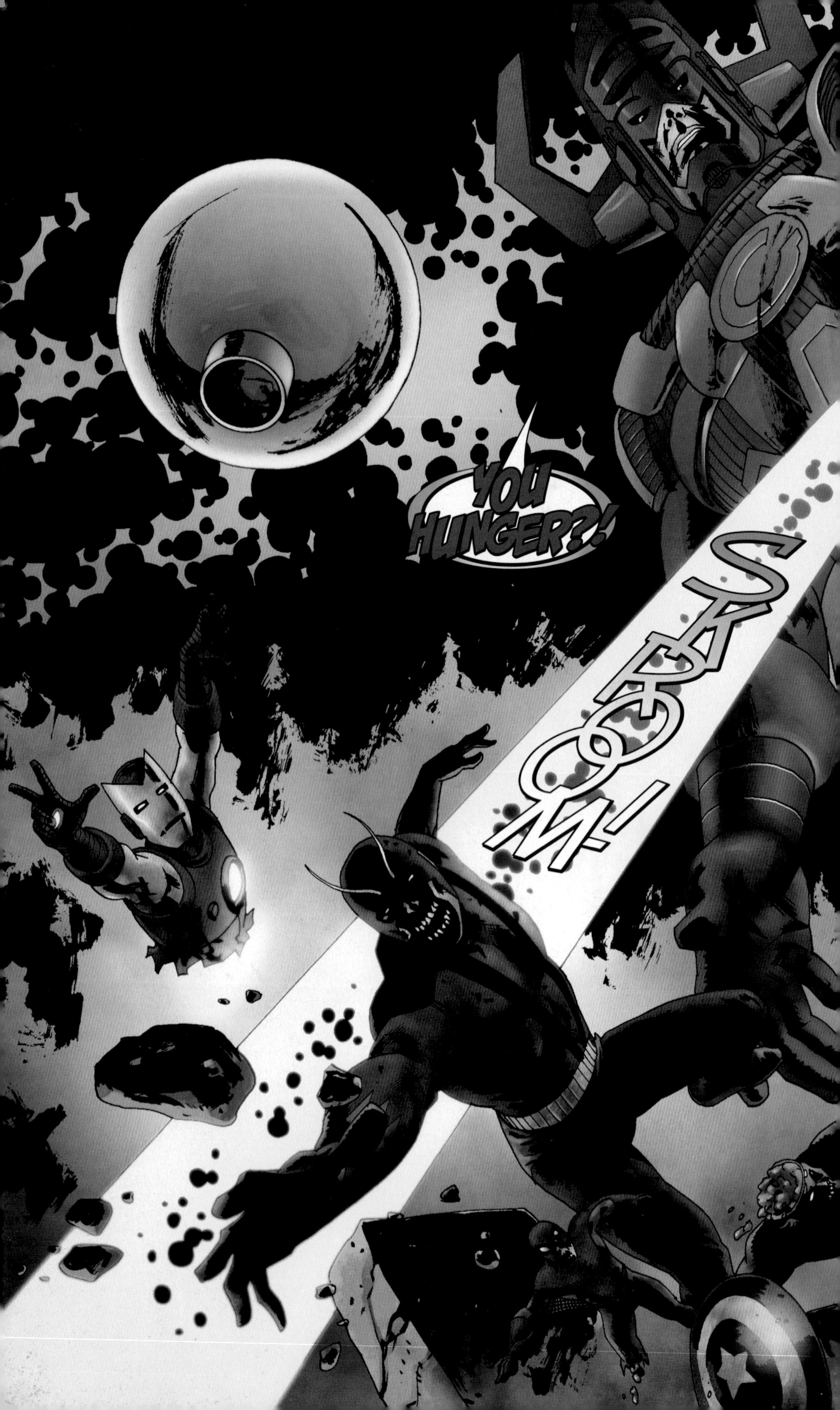
YOU HUNGER?!
SKROOM!

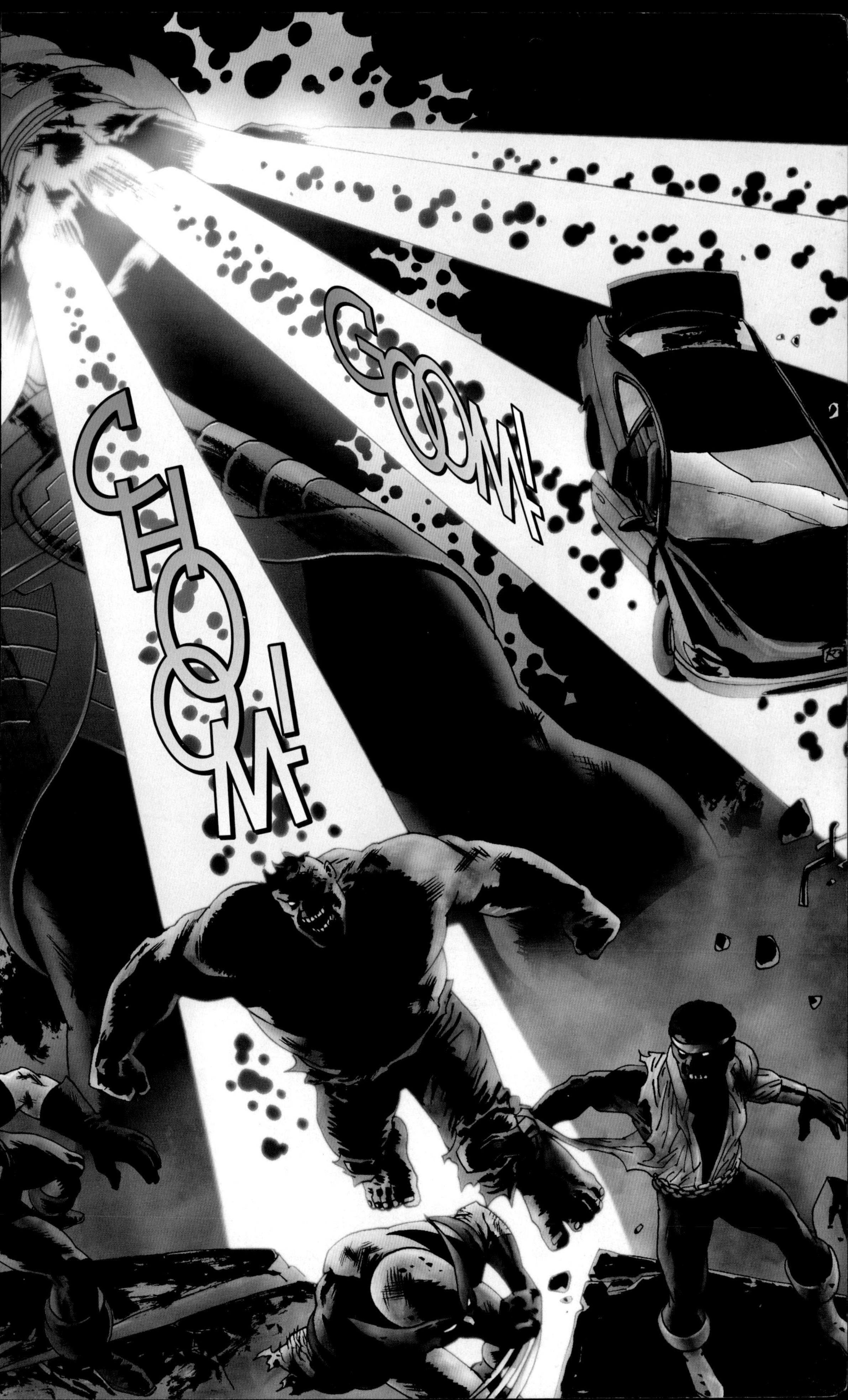
GOOM!
CHOOM!

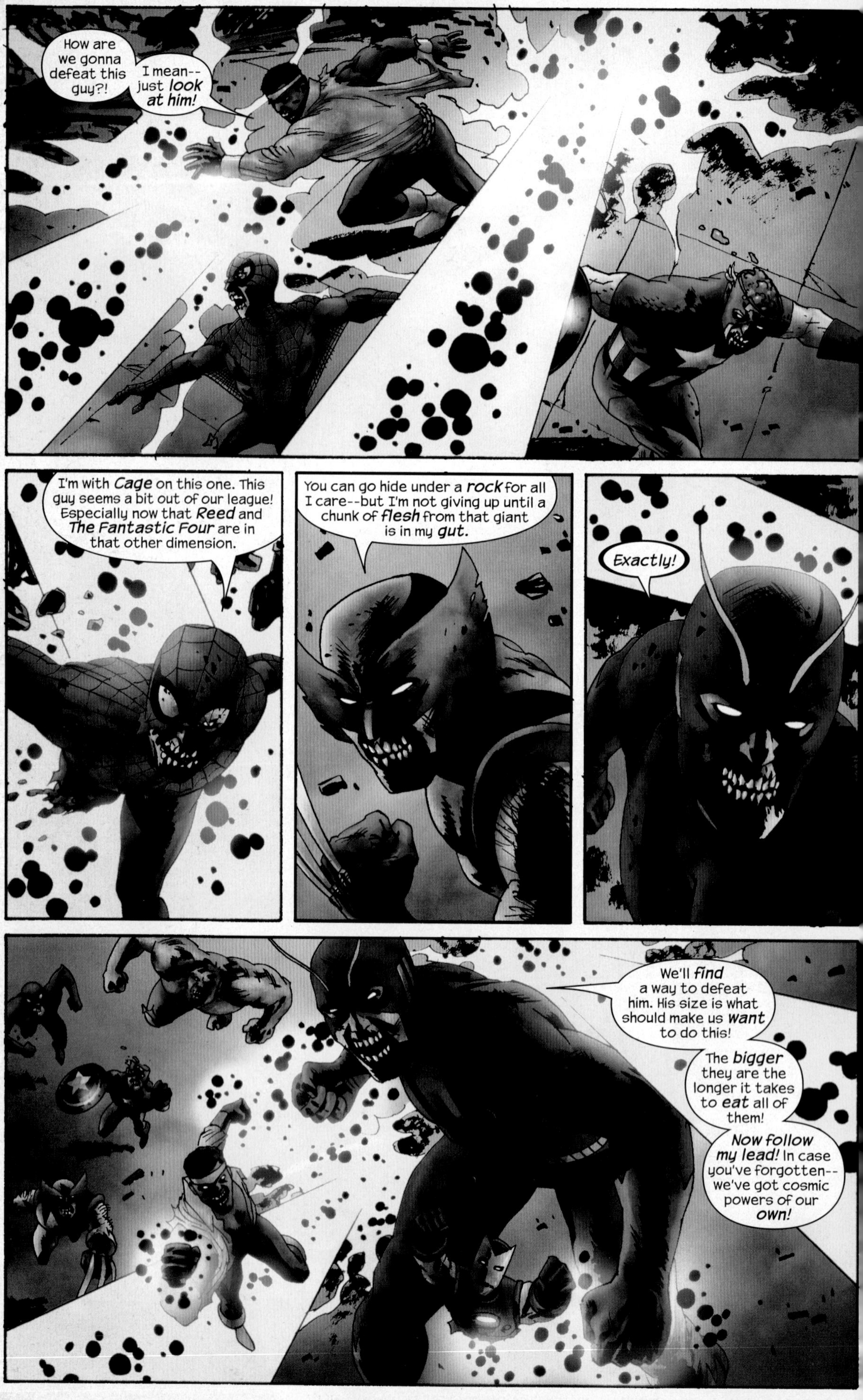
How are we gonna defeat this guy?!
I mean-- just look at him!
I'm with Cage on this one. This guy seems a bit out of our league! Especially now that Reed and The Fantastic Four are in that other dimension.
You can go hide under a rock for all I care--but I'm not giving up until a chunk of flesh from that giant is in my gut.
Exactly!
We'll find a way to defeat him. His size is what should make us want to do this!
The bigger they are the longer it takes to eat all of them!
Now follow my lead! In case you've forgotten-- we've got cosmic powers of our own!

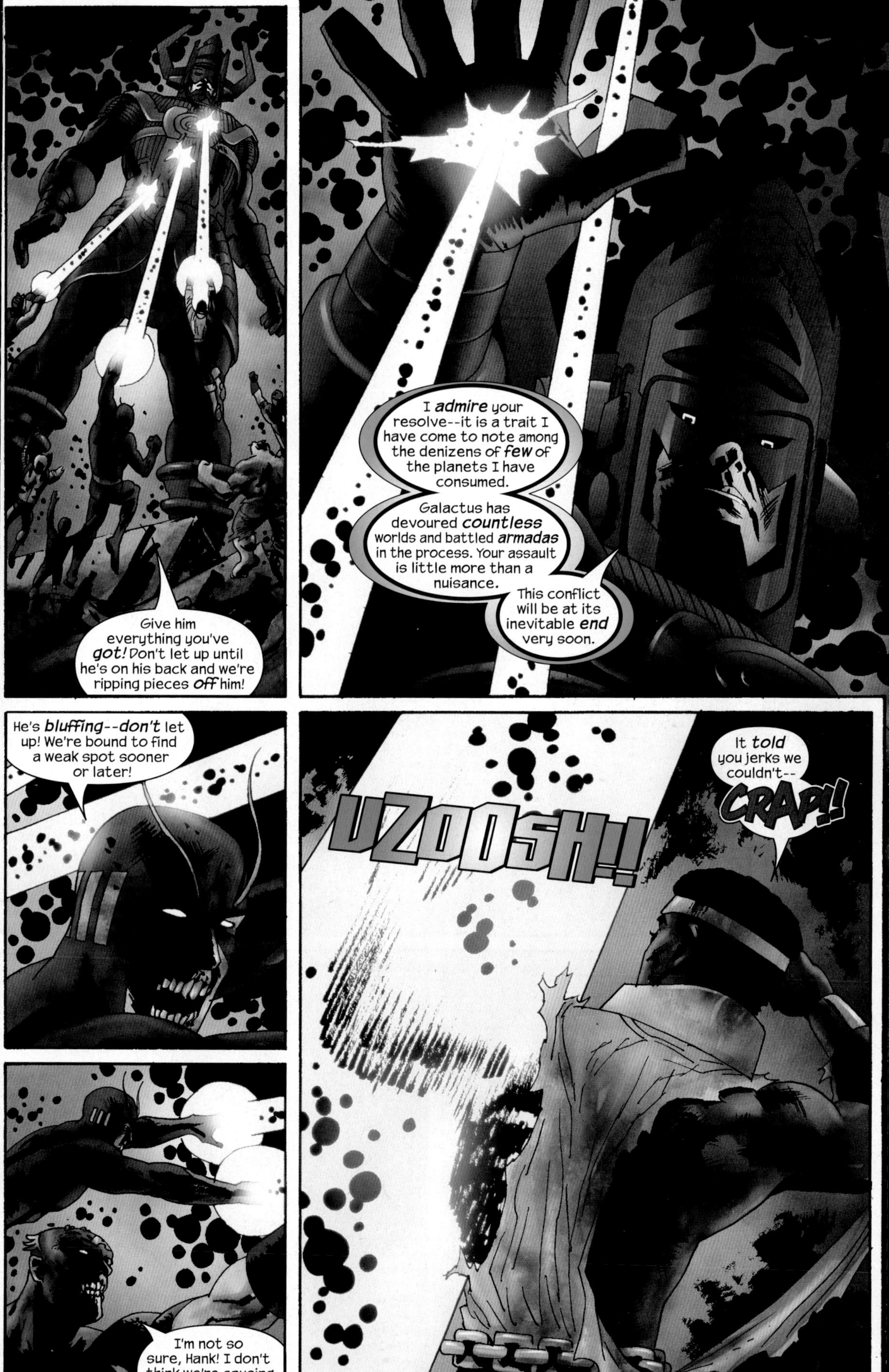
Give him everything you've got! Don't let up until he's on his back and we're ripping pieces off him!
I admire your resolve--it is a trait I have come to note among the denizens of few of the planets I have consumed.
Galactus has devoured countless worlds and battled armadas in the process. Your assault is little more than a nuisance.
This conflict will be at its inevitable end very soon.
He's bluffing--don't let up! We're bound to find a weak spot sooner or later!
I'm not so sure, Hank! I don't think we're causing him a lick of pain!
VZOOSH!!
It told you jerks we couldn't--
CRAP!!

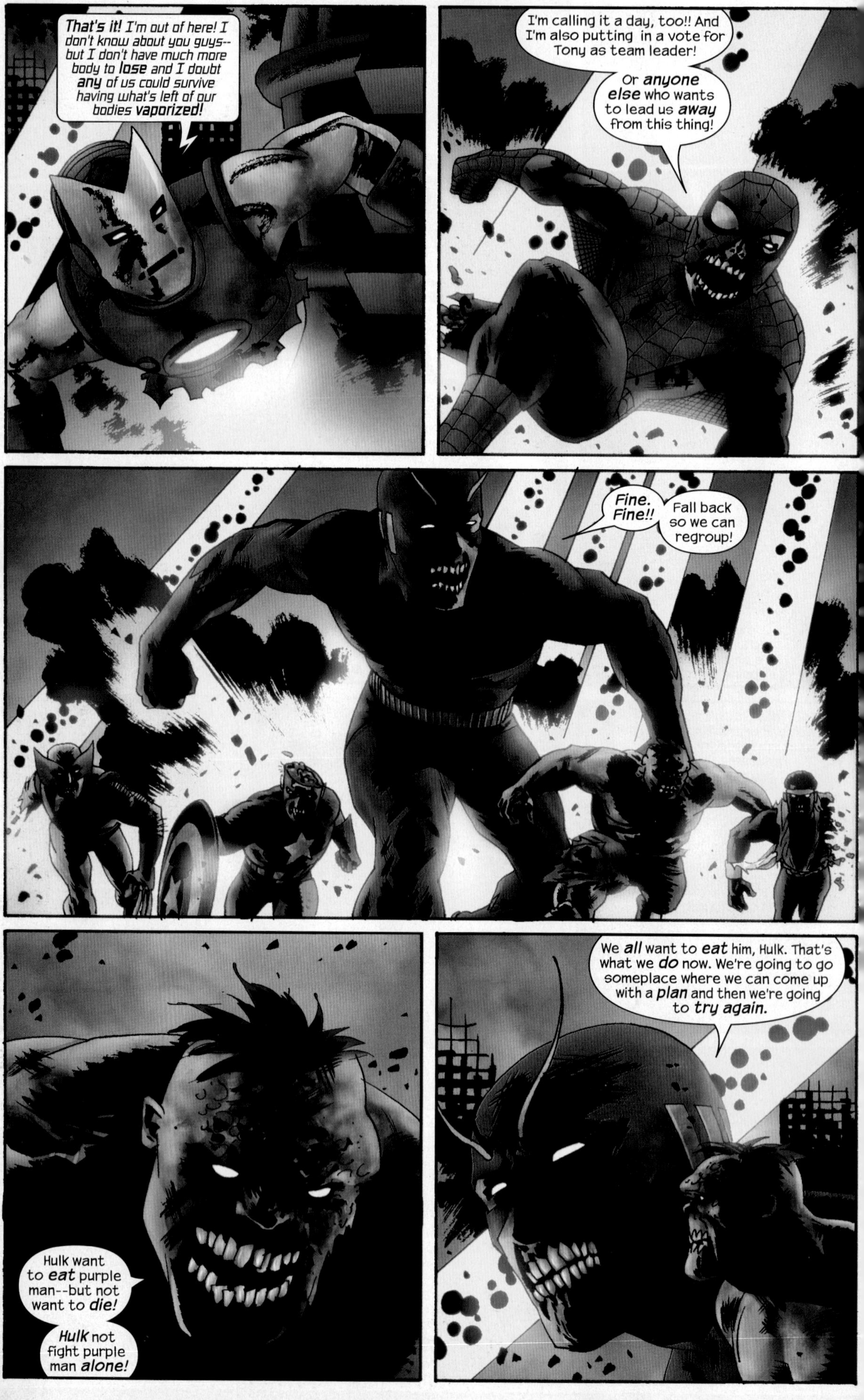
That's it! I'm out of here! I don't know about you guys--but I don't have much more body to lose and I doubt any of us could survive having what's left of our bodies vaporized!
I'm calling it a day, too!! And I'm also putting in a vote for Tony as team leader!
Or anyone else who wants to lead us away from this thing!
Fine. Fine!!
Fall back so we can regroup!
Hulk want to eat purple man--but not want to die!
Hulk not fight purple man alone!
We all want to eat him, Hulk. That's what we do now. We're going to go someplace where we can come up with a plan and then we're going to try again.

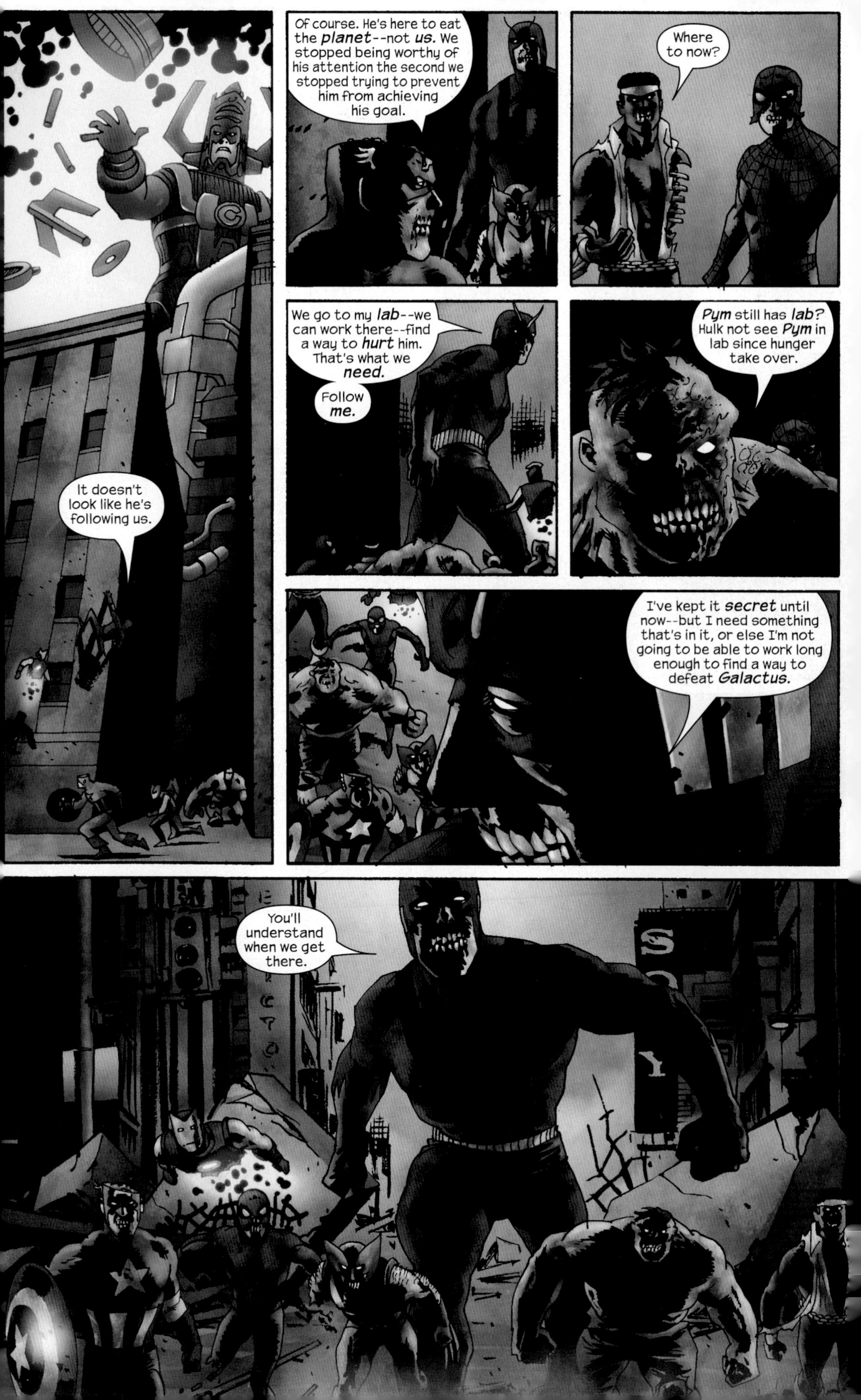
It doesn't look like he's following us.
Of course. He's here to eat the planet--not us. We stopped being worthy of his attention the second we stopped trying to prevent him from achieving his goal.
Where to now?
We go to my lab--we can work there--find a way to hurt him. That's what we need.
Follow me.
Pym still has lab? Hulk not see Pym in lab since hunger take over.
I've kept it secret until now--but I need something that's in it, or else I'm not going to be able to work long enough to find a way to defeat Galactus.
You'll understand when we get there.

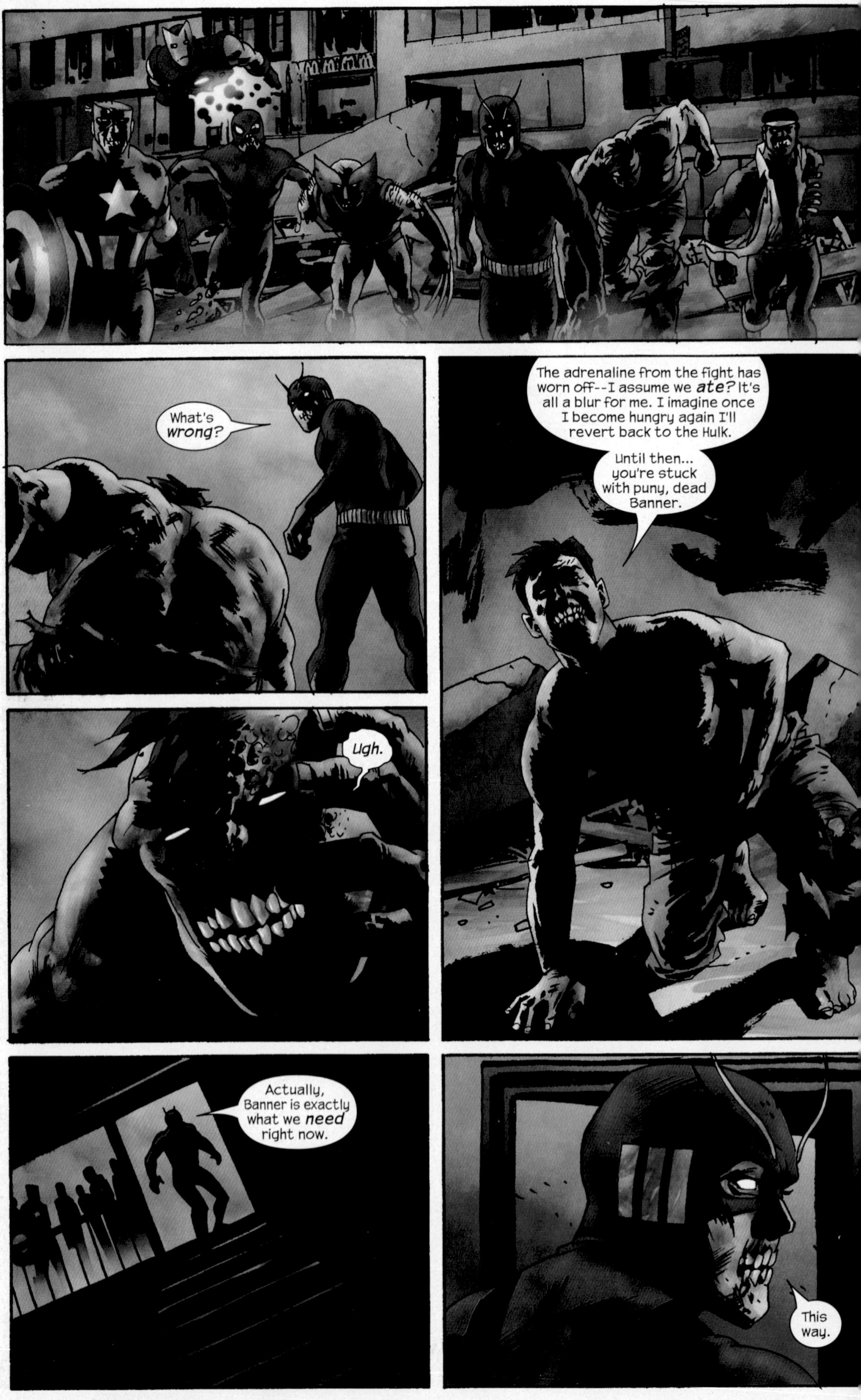
What's *wrong?*
The adrenaline from the fight has worn off--I assume we *ate?* It's all a blur for me. I imagine once I become hungry again I'll revert back to the Hulk.
Until then... you're stuck with puny, dead Banner.
Ugh.
Actually, Banner is exactly what we *need* right now.
This way.

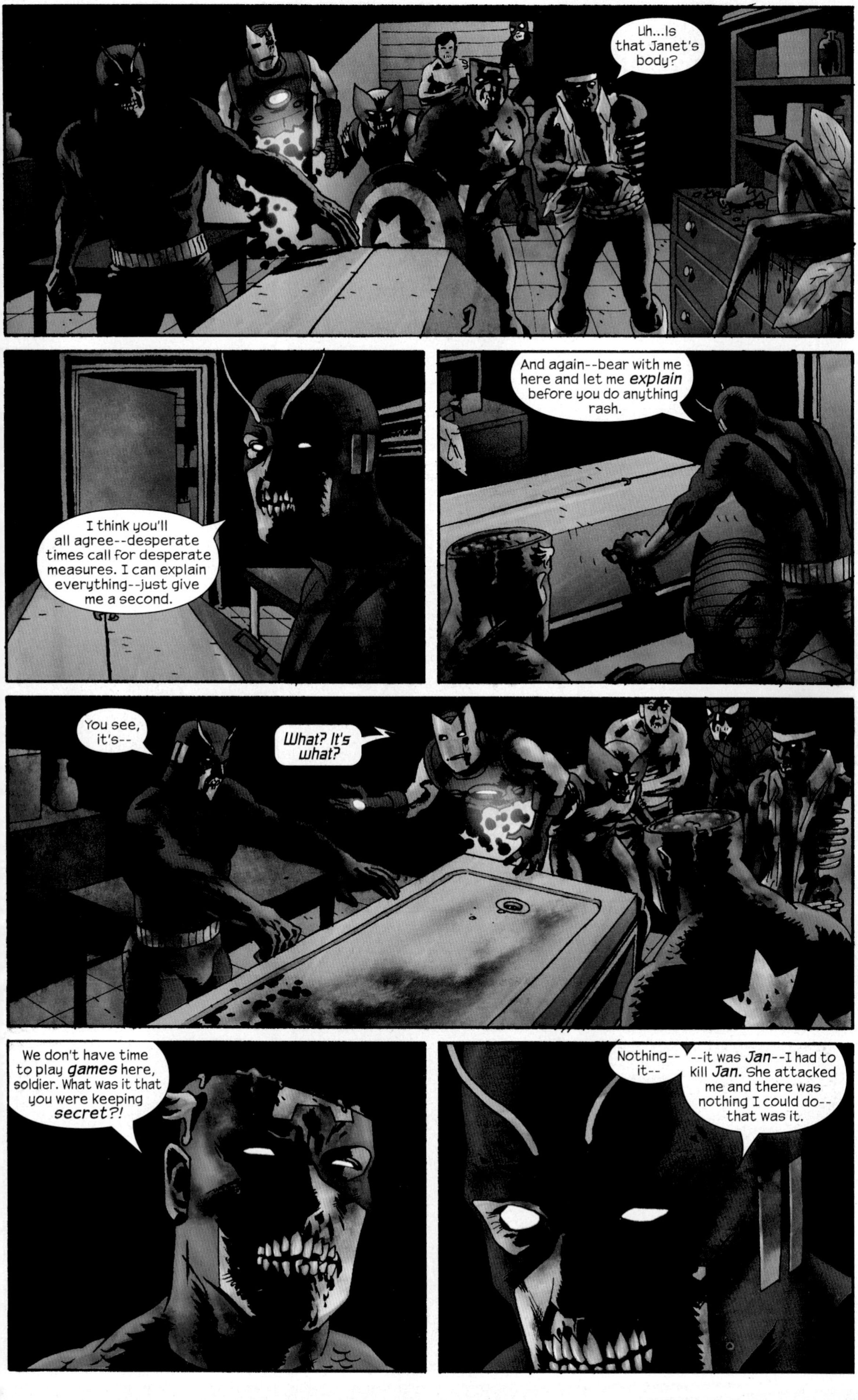
Uh...Is that Janet's body?
I think you'll all agree--desperate times call for desperate measures. I can explain everything--just give me a second.
And again--bear with me here and let me *explain* before you do anything rash.
You see, it's--
What? It's what?
We don't have time to play *games* here, soldier. What was it that you were keeping *secret?!*
Nothing-- it--
--it was *Jan*--I had to kill *Jan.* She attacked me and there was nothing I could do--that was it.

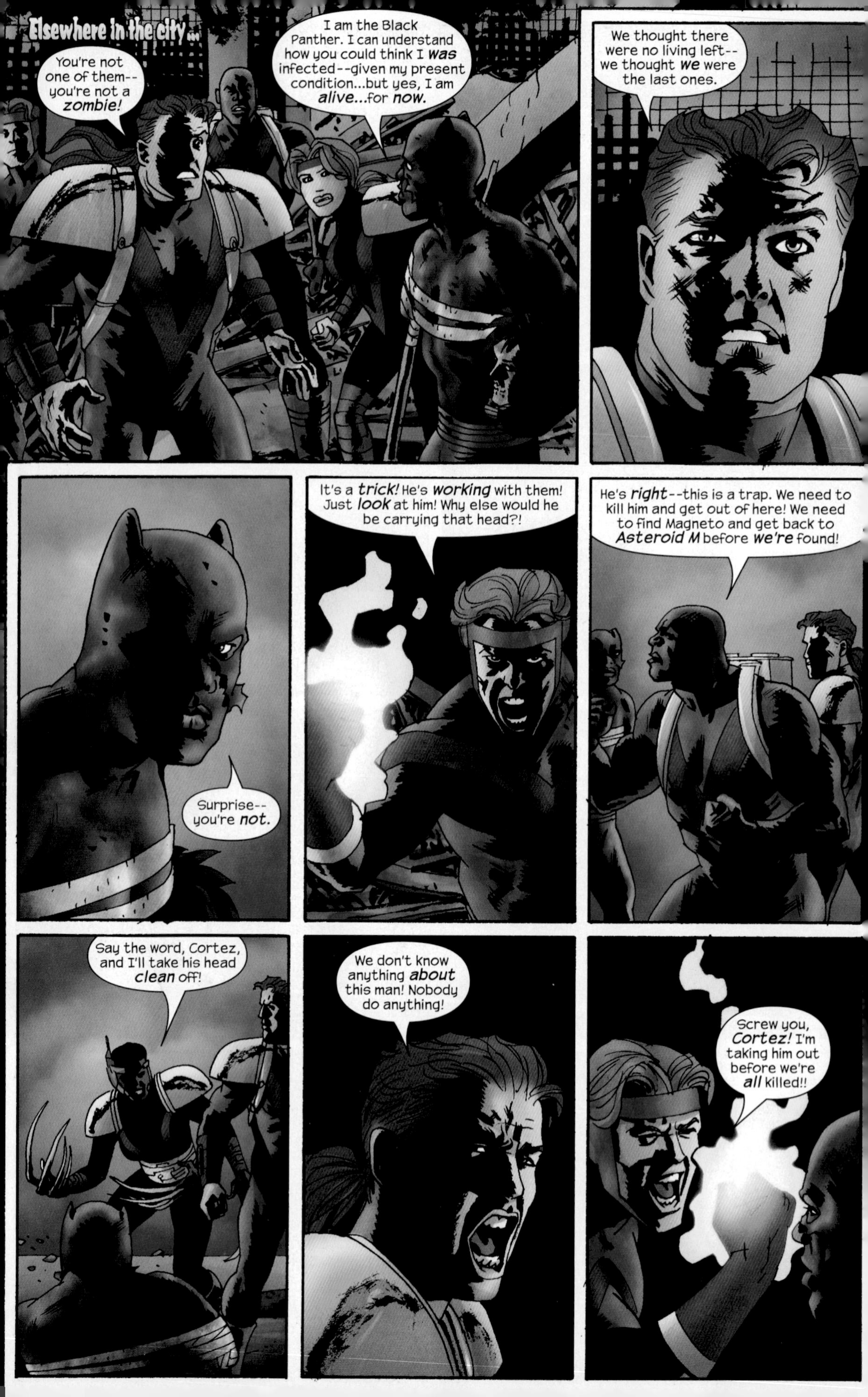
Elsewhere in the city...
You're not one of them--you're not a zombie!
I am the Black Panther. I can understand how you could think I was infected--given my present condition...but yes, I am alive...for now.
We thought there were no living left--we thought we were the last ones.
Surprise--you're not.
It's a trick! He's working with them! Just look at him! Why else would he be carrying that head?!
He's right--this is a trap. We need to kill him and get out of here! We need to find Magneto and get back to Asteroid M before we're found!
Say the word, Cortez, and I'll take his head clean off!
We don't know anything about this man! Nobody do anything!
Screw you, Cortez! I'm taking him out before we're all killed!!

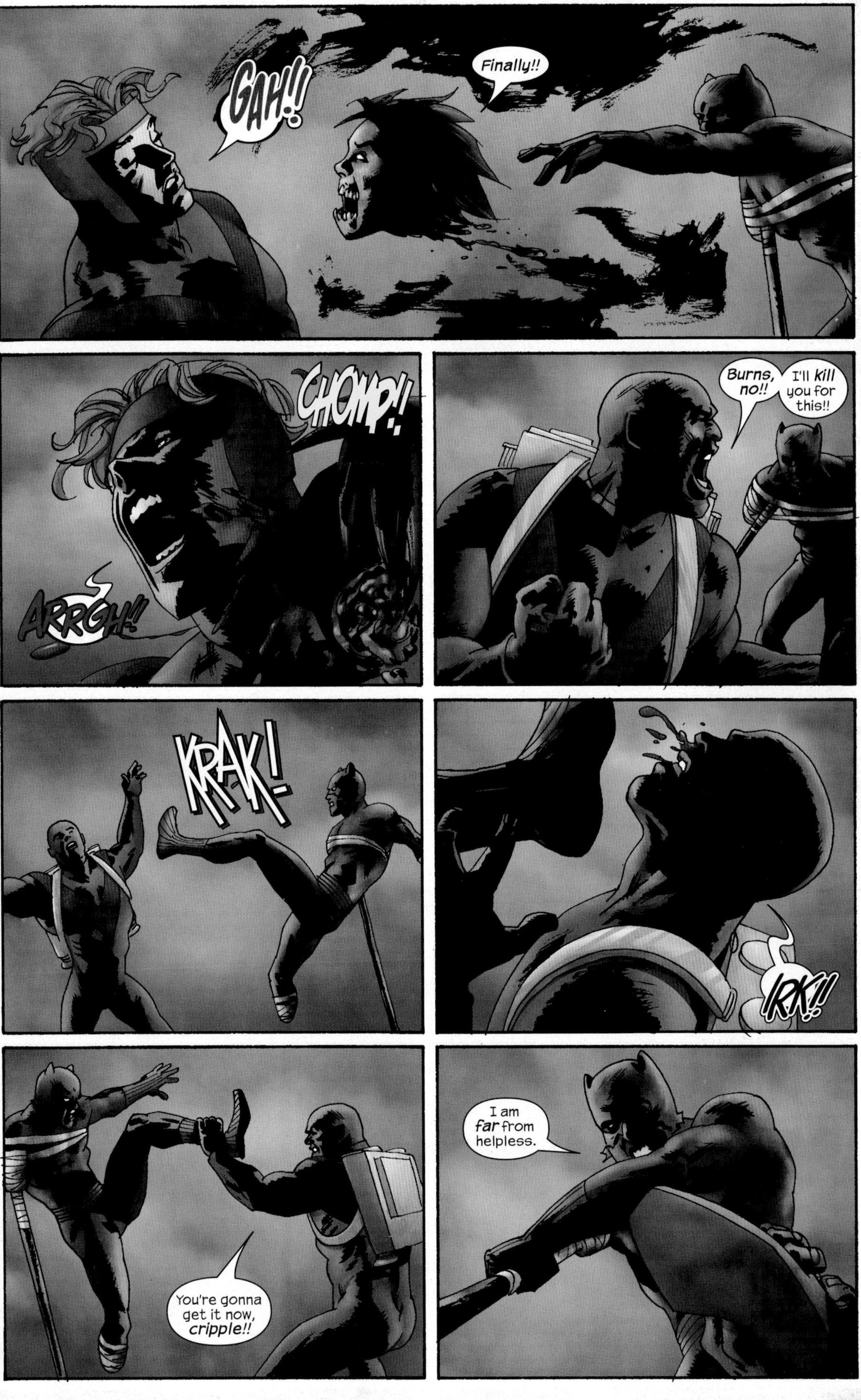
GAH!!
Finally!!
CHOMP!!
ARRGH!!
Burns, no!!
I'll kill you for this!!
KRAK!
IRK!!
You're gonna get it now, cripple!!
I am far from helpless.

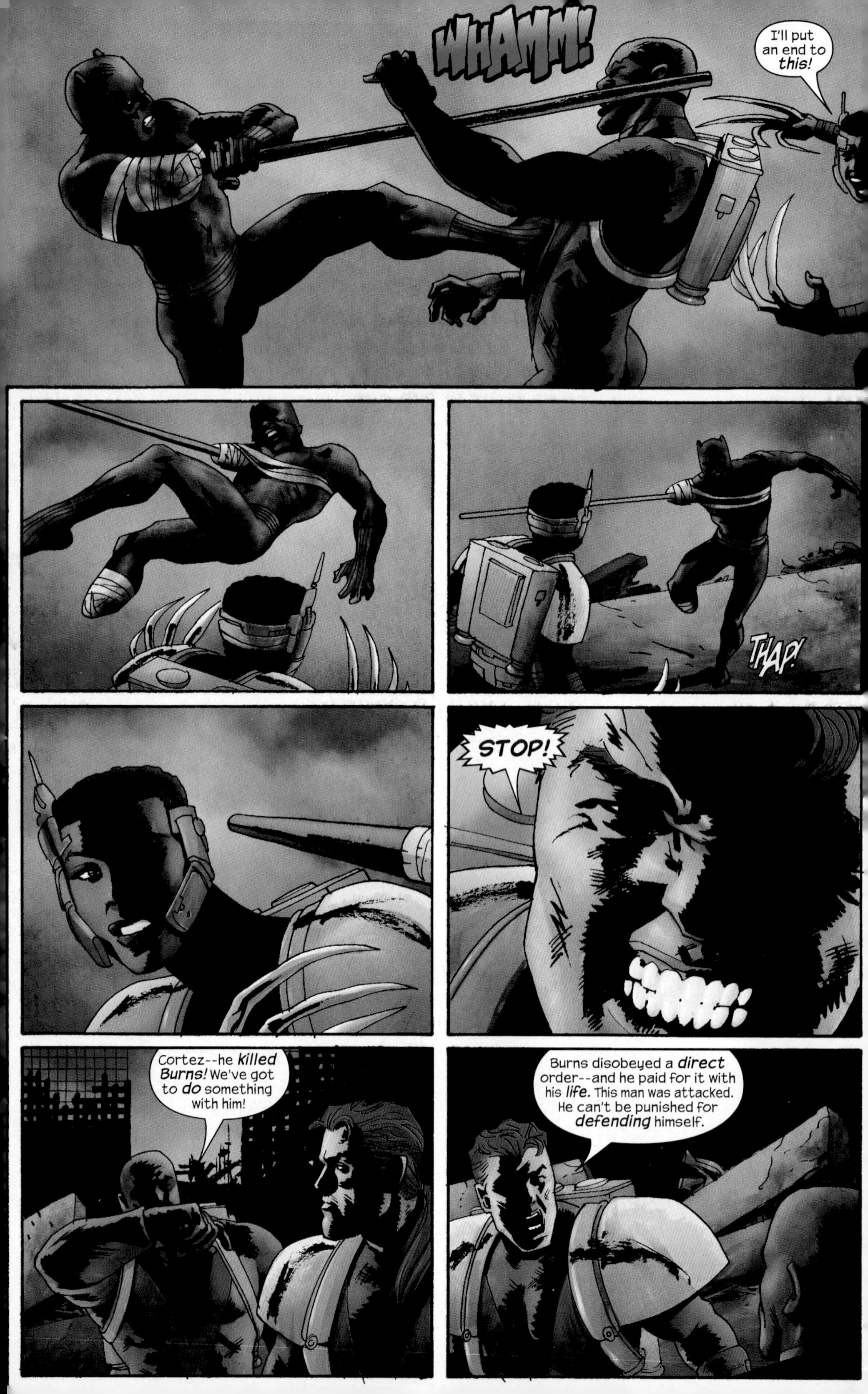
WHAMM!
I'll put an end to *this!*
THAP!
STOP!
Cortez--he *killed Burns!* We've got to *do* something with him!
Burns disobeyed a *direct* order--and he paid for it with his *life.* This man was attacked. He can't be punished for *defending* himself.

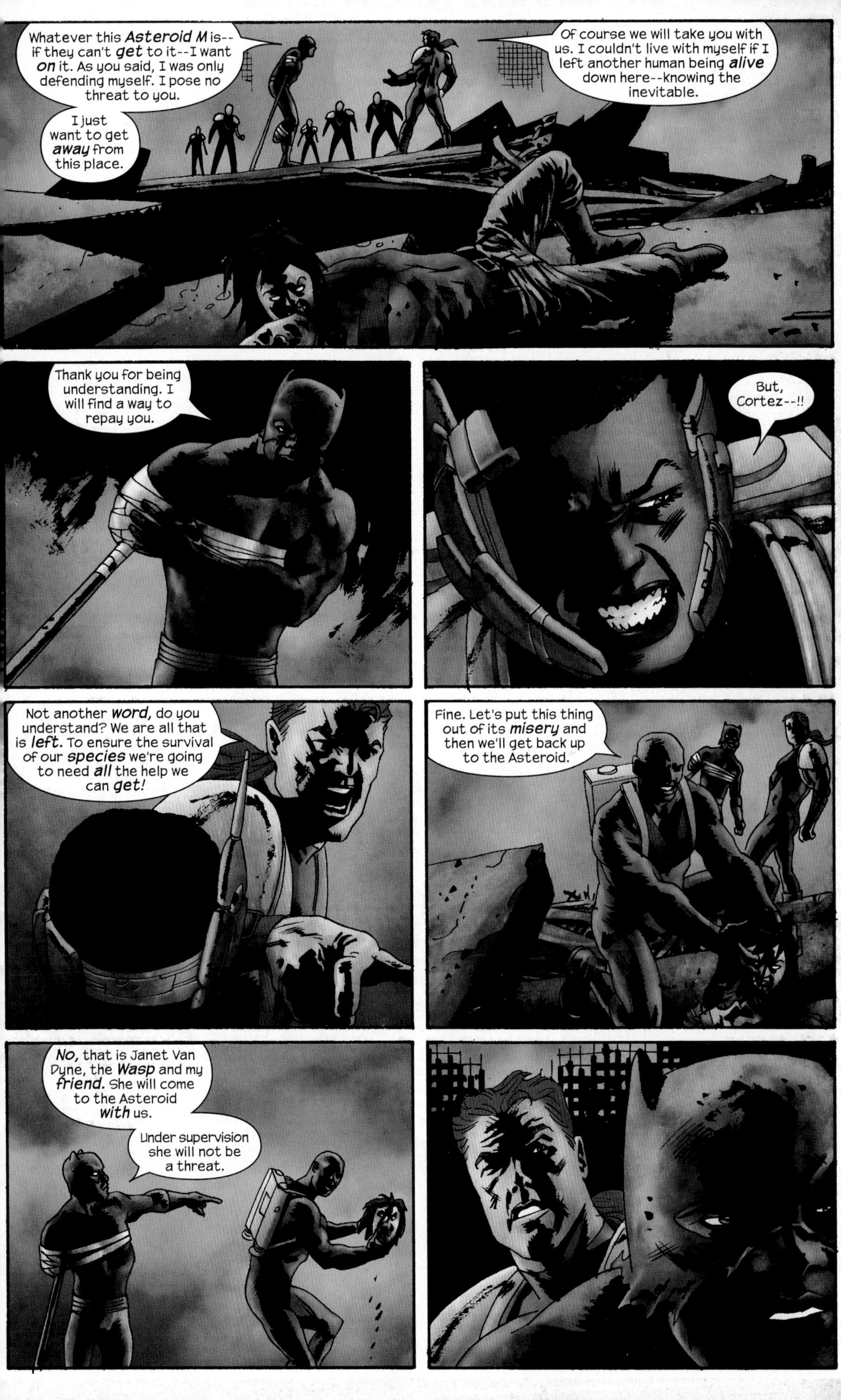

Whatever this Asteroid M is--if they can't get to it--I want on it. As you said, I was only defending myself. I pose no threat to you.
I just want to get away from this place.
Of course we will take you with us. I couldn't live with myself if I left another human being alive down here--knowing the inevitable.
Thank you for being understanding. I will find a way to repay you.
But, Cortez--!!
Not another word, do you understand? We are all that is left. To ensure the survival of our species we're going to need all the help we can get!
Fine. Let's put this thing out of its misery and then we'll get back up to the Asteroid.
No, that is Janet Van Dyne, the Wasp and my friend. She will come to the Asteroid with us.
Under supervision she will not be a threat.

We've been here for *days*— do you think they're going to figure something out before that giant eats the planet?

Let's just let the big brains think and do their thing. Do you have a *seven*?

Go fish.

Stark, Banner, and Pym are working together on this. They're some of the brightest minds on the planet. They're not going to let us get eaten.

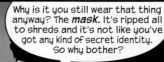

Why is it you still wear that thing anyway? The *mask*. It's ripped all to shreds and it's not like you've got any kind of secret identity. So why bother?

The hunger—the way it is—I *know* I would do it again *right now* if I had the chance. That's just the way things *are* now.

But after doing it—after eating my *wife* and *aunt*, the only two people *left* in this world that really *loved* me...after knowing what I've *become*...I couldn't ever look myself in the mirror— and I don't want to *chance* it.

Right—forget I *asked*, you *sissy*. You got any *jacks*?

Just wanted to let you kids know—he's *back*.

He's *back*?

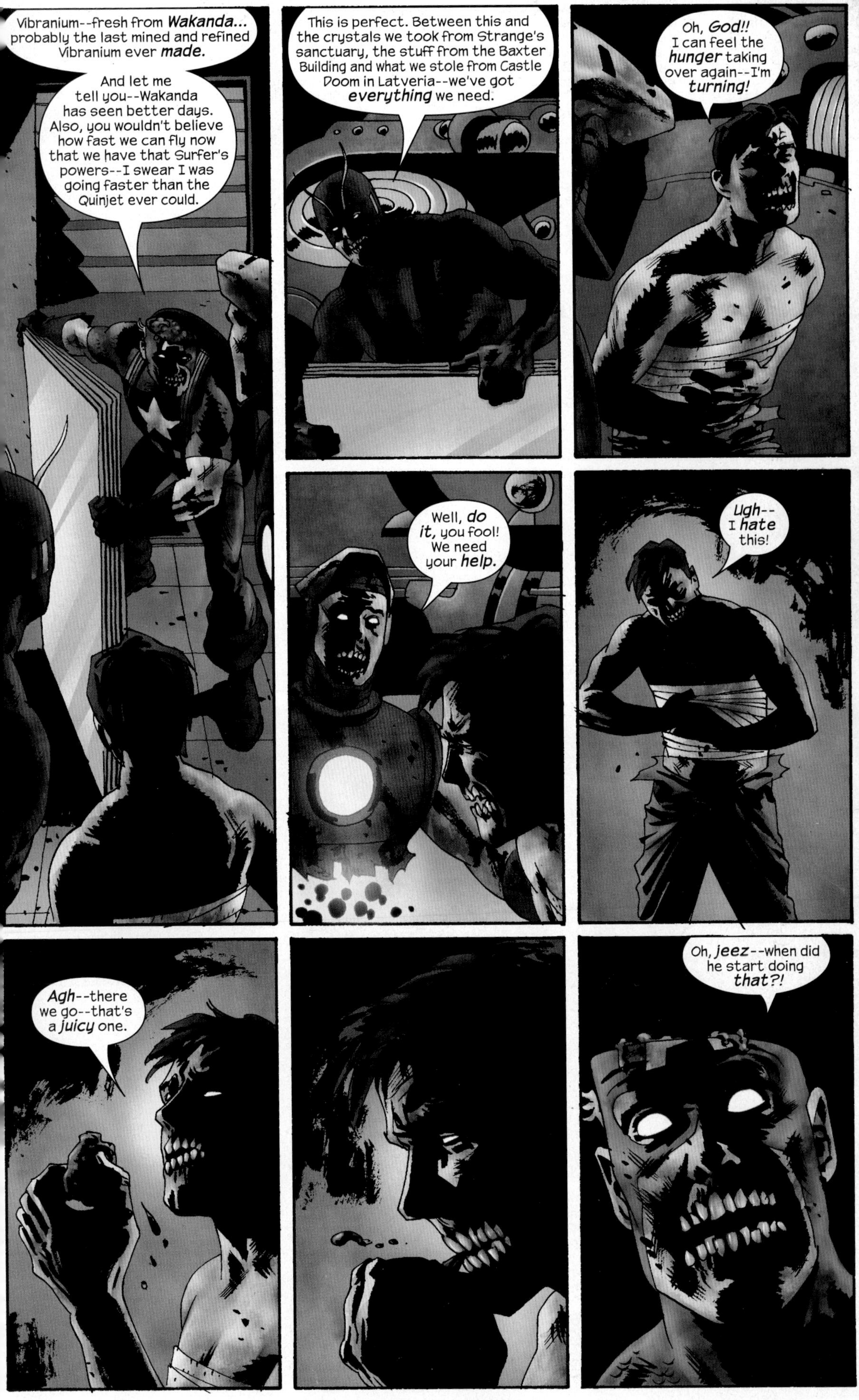
Vibranium--fresh from Wakanda... probably the last mined and refined Vibranium ever made.
And let me tell you--Wakanda has seen better days. Also, you wouldn't believe how fast we can fly now that we have that Surfer's powers--I swear I was going faster than the Quinjet ever could.
This is perfect. Between this and the crystals we took from Strange's sanctuary, the stuff from the Baxter Building and what we stole from Castle Doom in Latveria--we've got everything we need.
Oh, God!! I can feel the hunger taking over again--I'm turning!
Well, do it, you fool! We need your help.
Ugh--I hate this!
Agh--there we go--that's a juicy one.
Oh, jeez--when did he start doing that?!

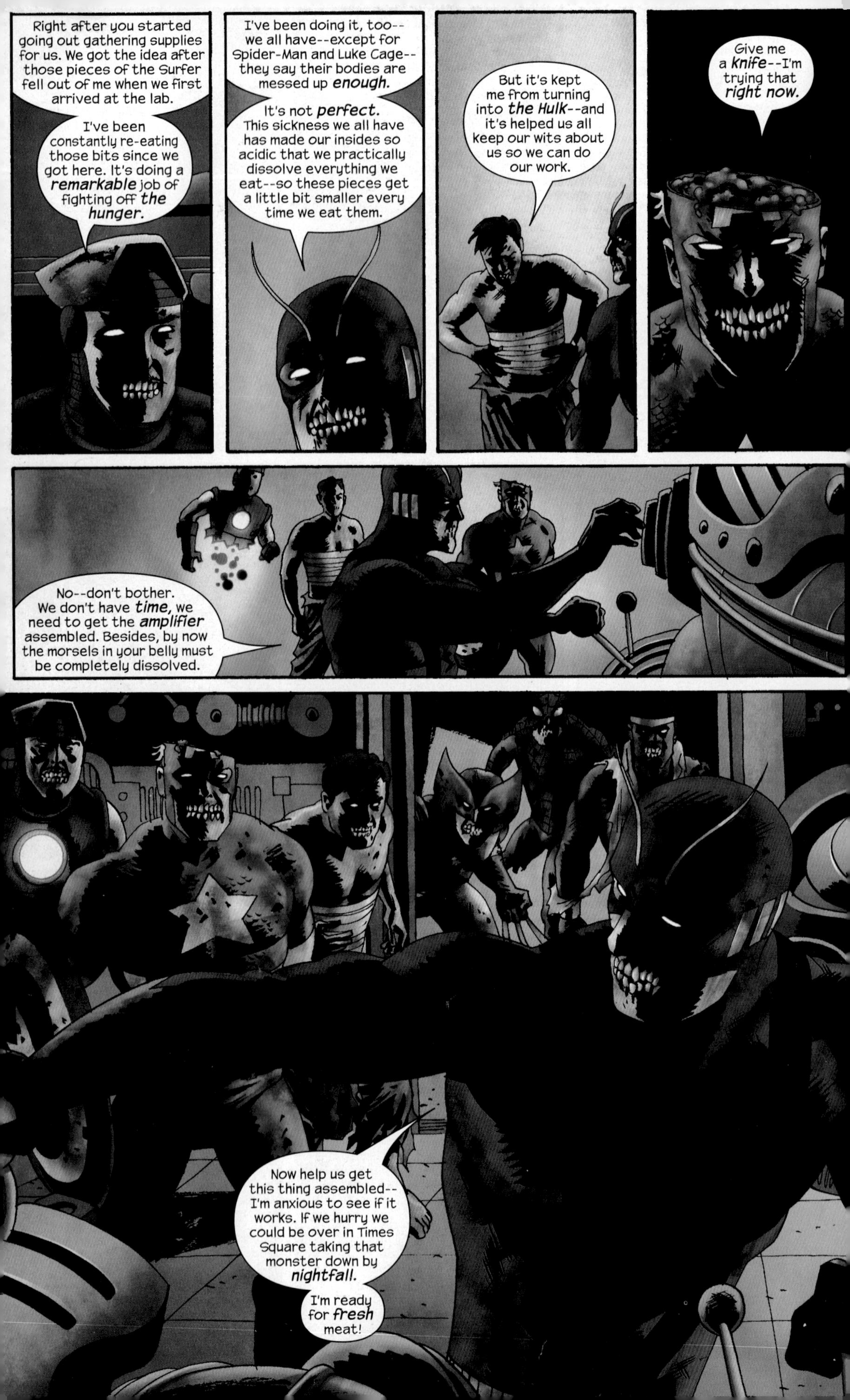
Right after you started going out gathering supplies for us. We got the idea after those pieces of the Surfer fell out of me when we first arrived at the lab.
I've been constantly re-eating those bits since we got here. It's doing a remarkable job of fighting off the hunger.
I've been doing it, too--we all have--except for Spider-Man and Luke Cage--they say their bodies are messed up enough.
It's not perfect. This sickness we all have has made our insides so acidic that we practically dissolve everything we eat--so these pieces get a little bit smaller every time we eat them.
But it's kept me from turning into the Hulk--and it's helped us all keep our wits about us so we can do our work.
Give me a knife--I'm trying that right now.
No--don't bother. We don't have time, we need to get the amplifier assembled. Besides, by now the morsels in your belly must be completely dissolved.
Now help us get this thing assembled--I'm anxious to see if it works. If we hurry we could be over in Times Square taking that monster down by nightfall.
I'm ready for fresh meat!

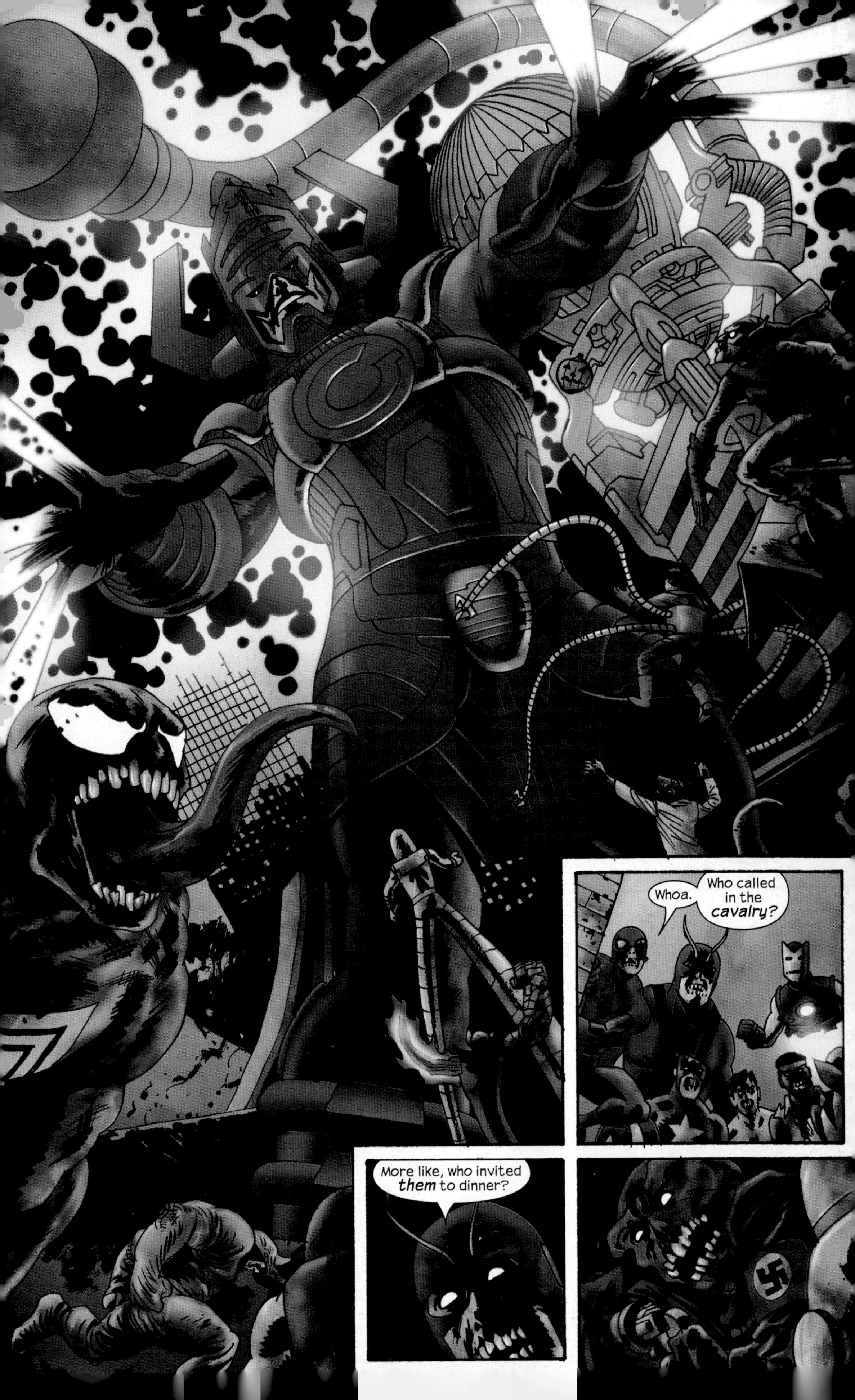
Whoa.
Who called in the *cavalry*?
More like, who invited *them* to dinner?

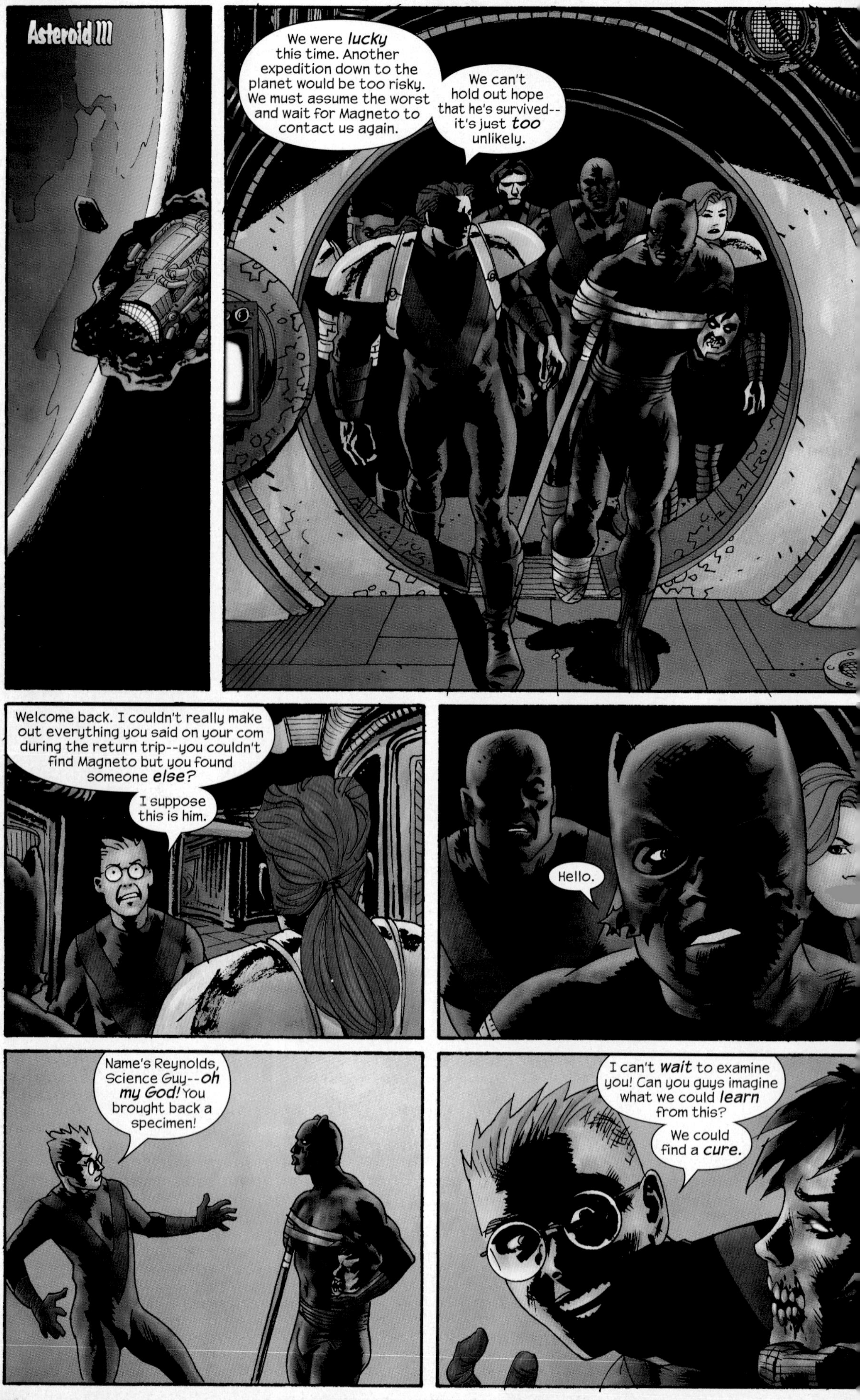

Asteroid M
We were *lucky* this time. Another expedition down to the planet would be too risky. We must assume the worst and wait for Magneto to contact us again.
We can't hold out hope that he's survived-- it's just *too* unlikely.
Welcome back. I couldn't really make out everything you said on your com during the return trip--you couldn't find Magneto but you found someone *else*?
I suppose this is him.
Hello.
Name's Reynolds, Science Guy--*oh my God!* You brought back a specimen!
I can't *wait* to examine you! Can you guys imagine what we could *learn* from this?
We could find a *cure.*

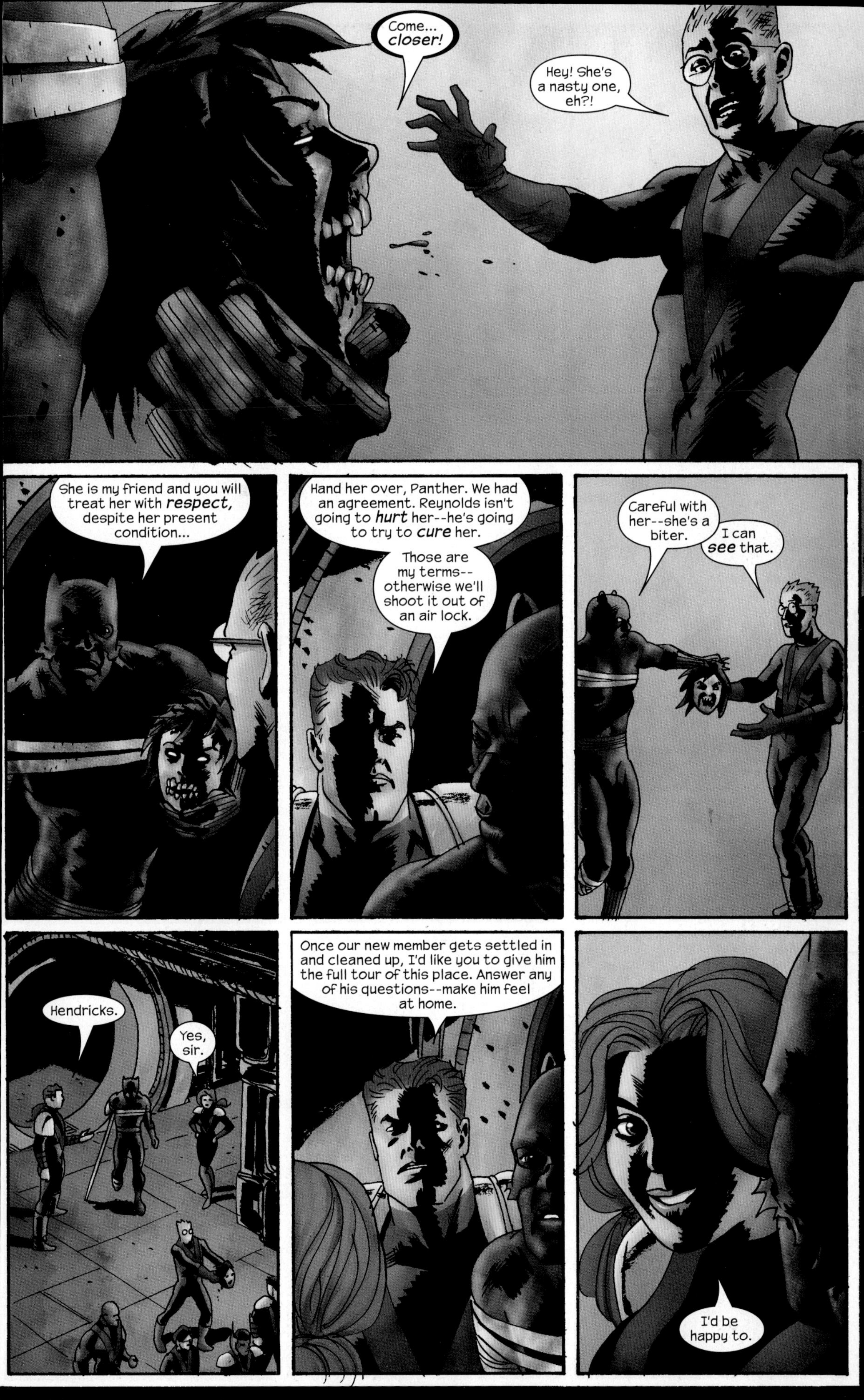

Come... closer!
Hey! She's a nasty one, eh?!
She is my friend and you will treat her with respect, despite her present condition...
Hand her over, Panther. We had an agreement. Reynolds isn't going to hurt her--he's going to try to cure her.
Those are my terms--otherwise we'll shoot it out of an air lock.
Careful with her--she's a biter.
I can see that.
Hendricks.
Yes, sir.
Once our new member gets settled in and cleaned up, I'd like you to give him the full tour of this place. Answer any of his questions--make him feel at home.
I'd be happy to.

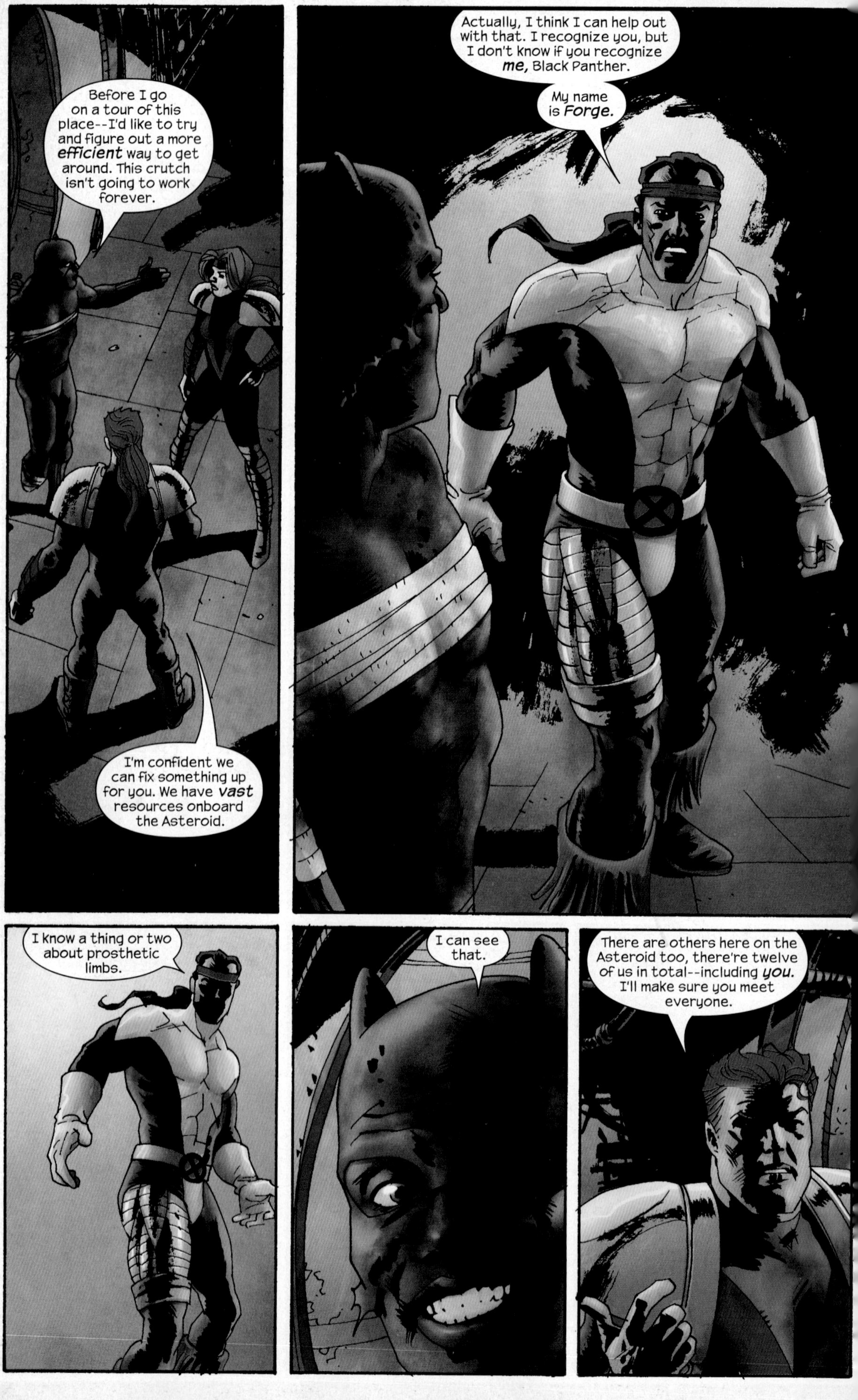
Before I go on a tour of this place--I'd like to try and figure out a more efficient way to get around. This crutch isn't going to work forever.
I'm confident we can fix something up for you. We have vast resources onboard the Asteroid.
Actually, I think I can help out with that. I recognize you, but I don't know if you recognize me, Black Panther.
My name is Forge.
I know a thing or two about prosthetic limbs.
I can see that.
There are others here on the Asteroid too, there're twelve of us in total--including you. I'll make sure you meet everyone.

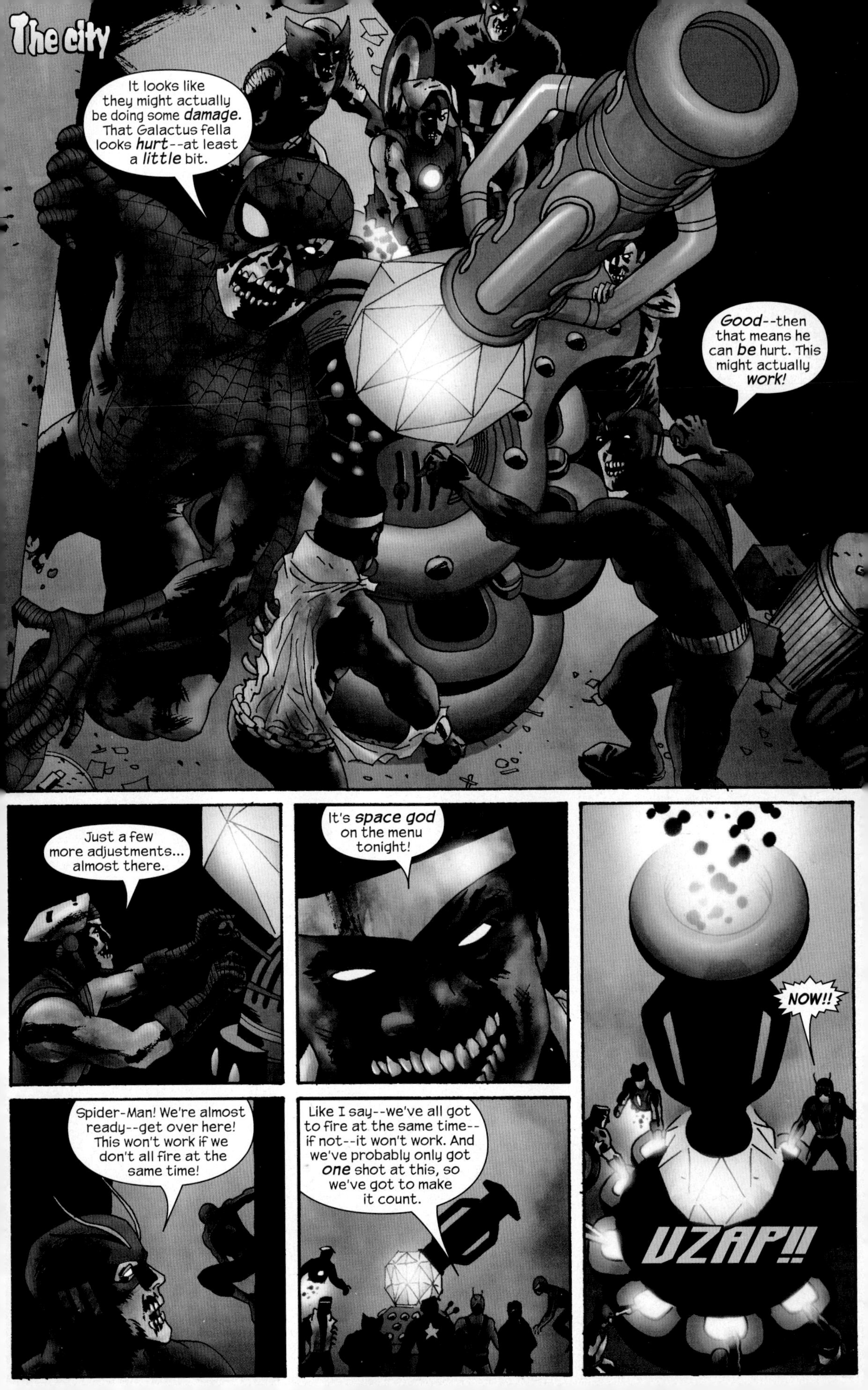
The city
It looks like they might actually be doing some *damage*. That Galactus fella looks *hurt*--at least a *little* bit.
Good--then that means he can *be* hurt. This might actually *work!*
Just a few more adjustments... almost there.
It's *space god* on the menu tonight!
Spider-Man! We're almost ready--get over here! This won't work if we don't all fire at the same time!
Like I say--we've all got to fire at the same time--if not--it won't work. And we've probably only got *one* shot at this, so we've got to make it count.
NOW!!
VZAP!!

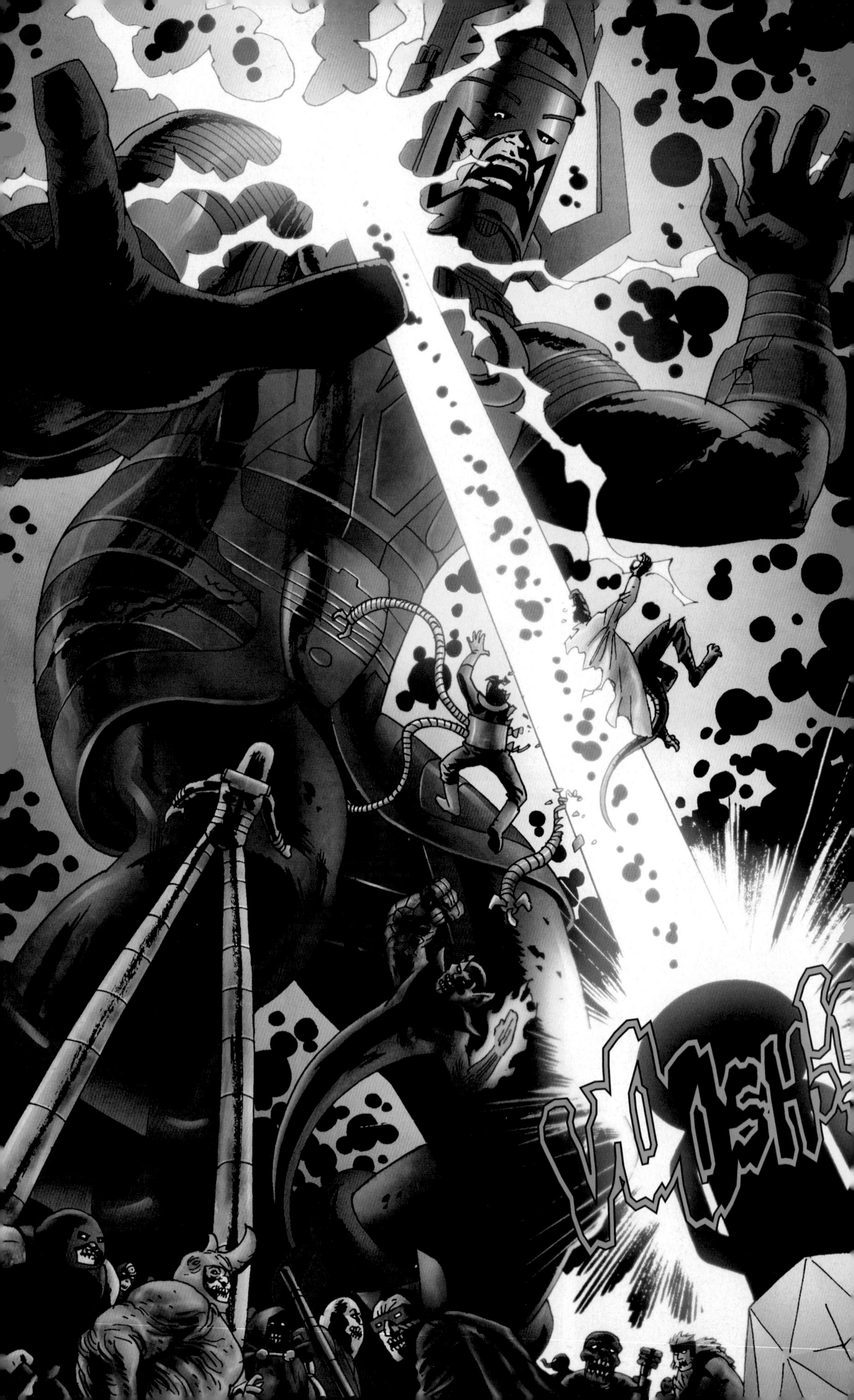
VOOSH

MARVEL ZOMBIES

CONCLUSION

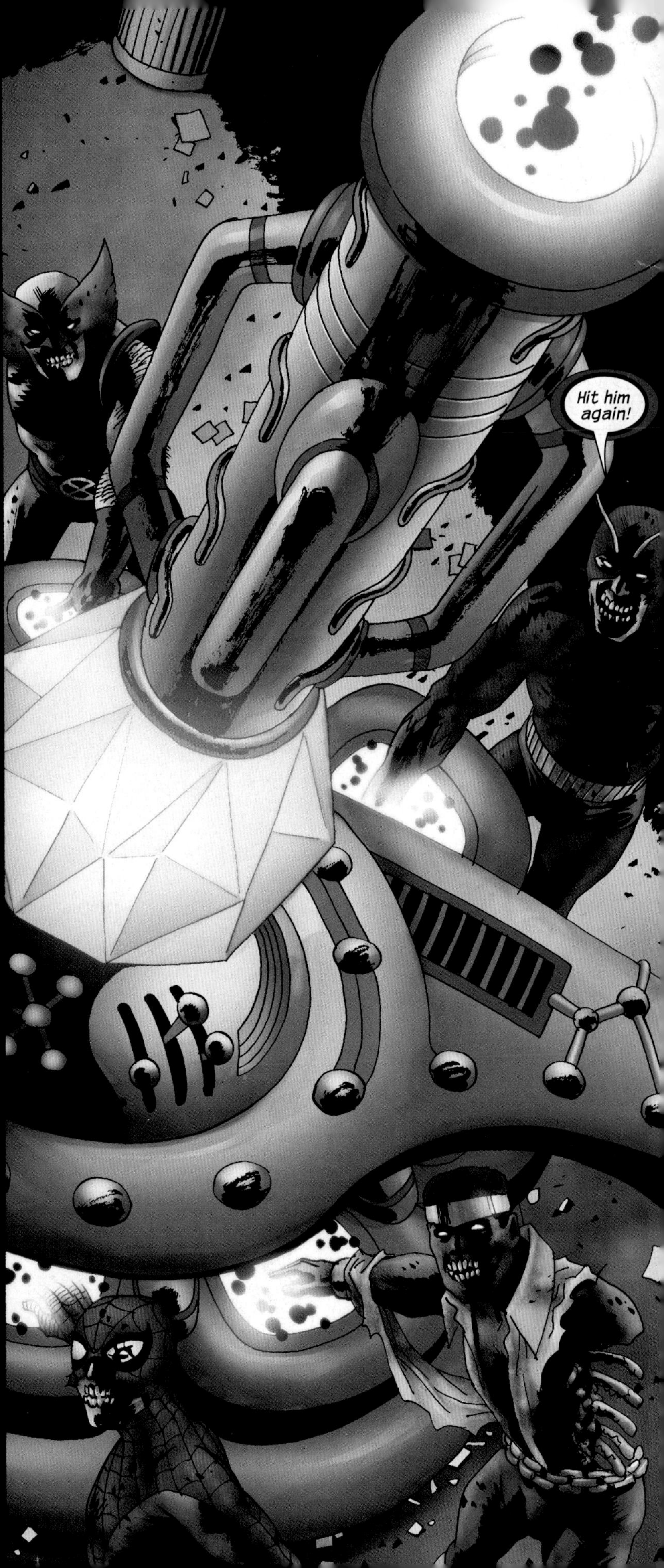

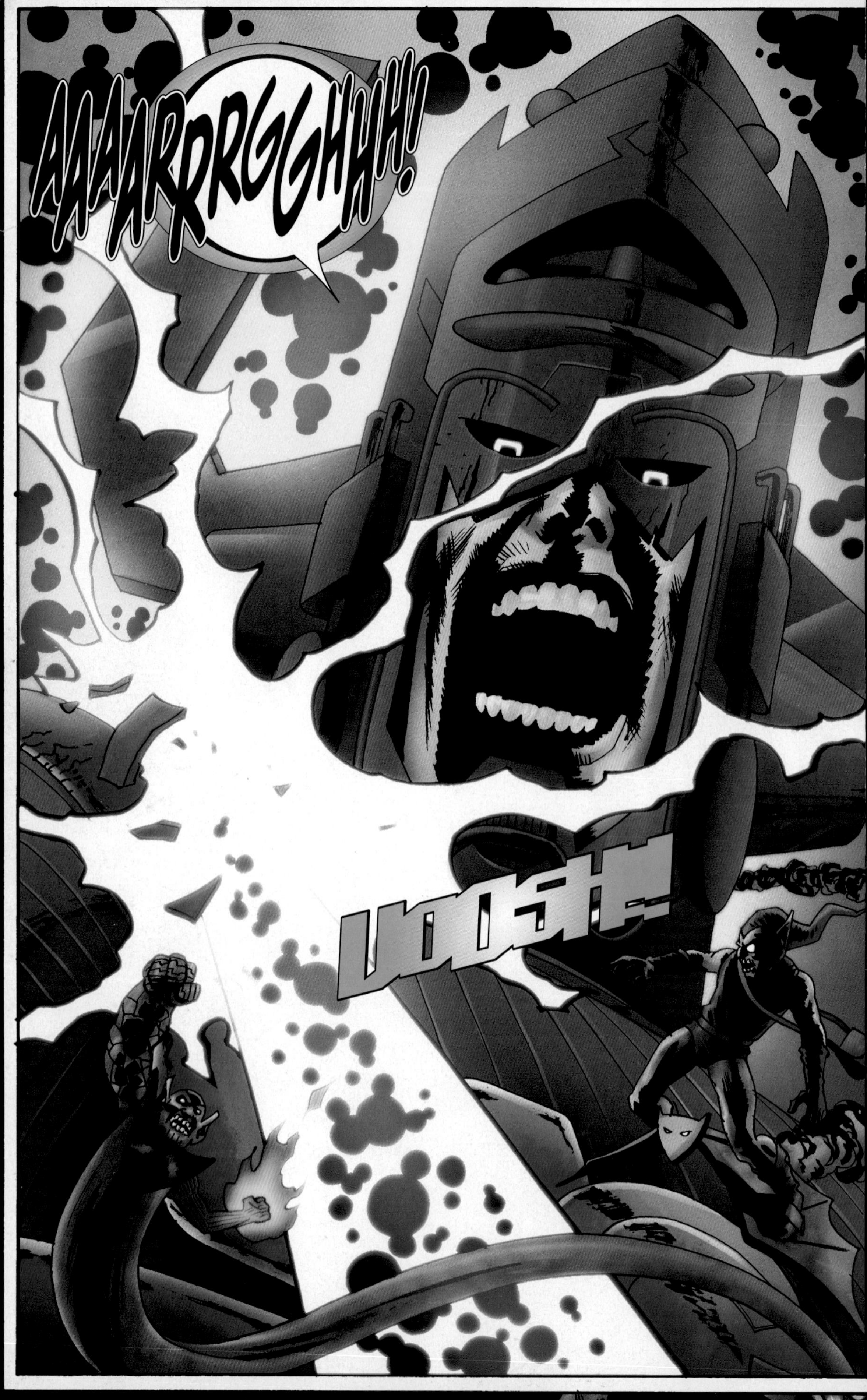
AAAARRRGHHH!
WOOSH!

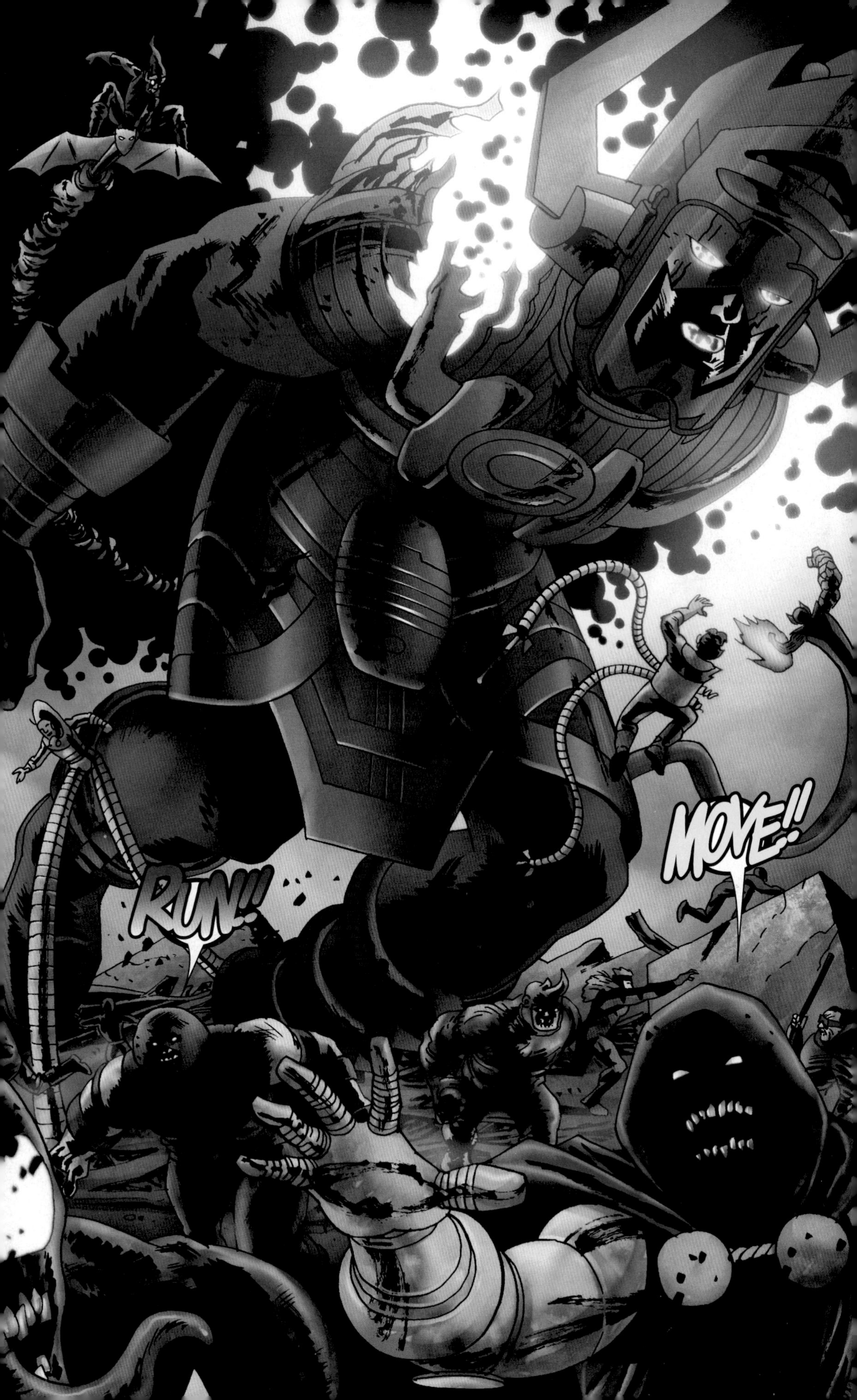
MOVE!!
RUN!!

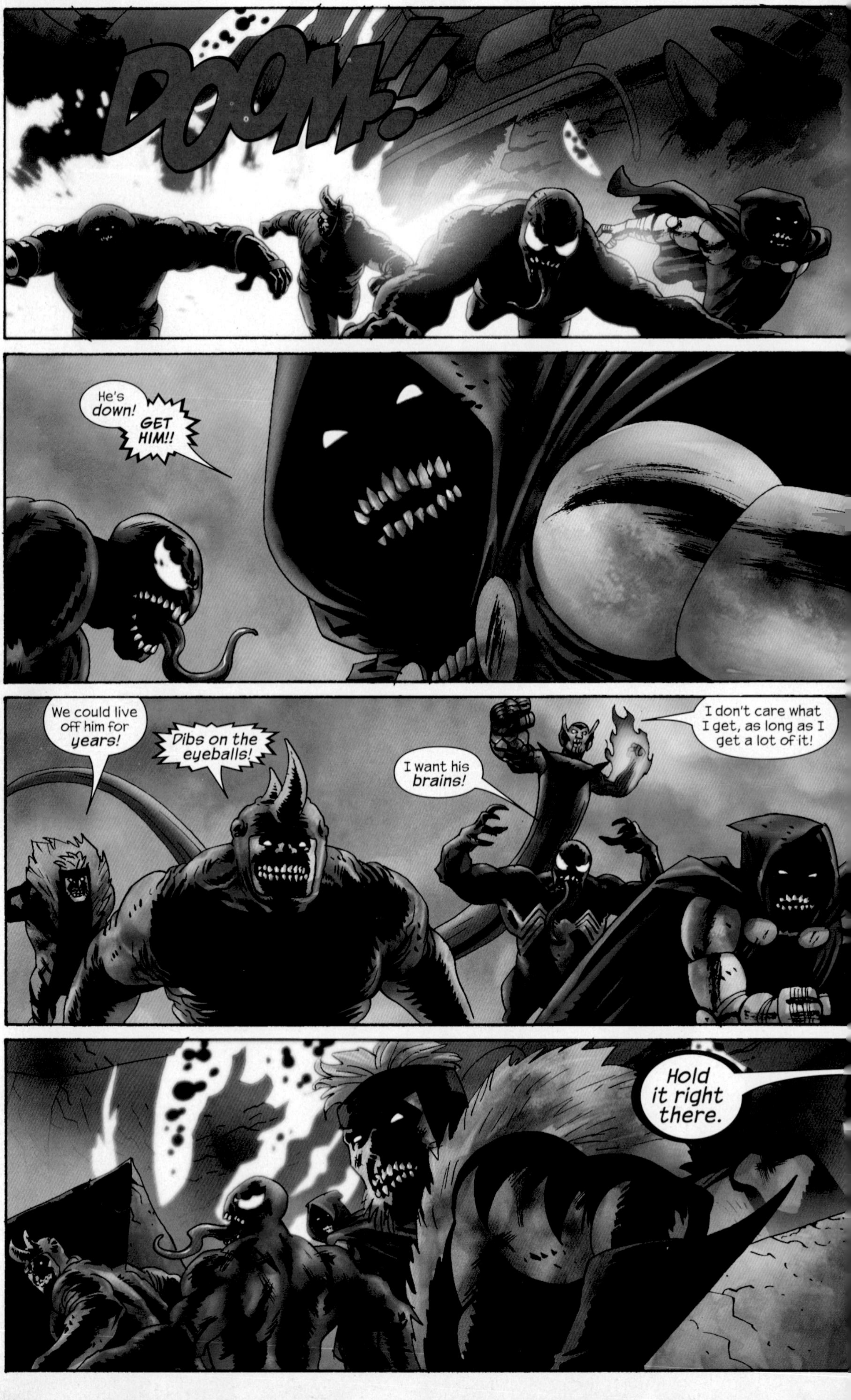
DOOM!!
He's down!
GET HIM!!
We could live off him for years!
Dibs on the eyeballs!
I want his brains!
I don't care what I get, as long as I get a lot of it!
Hold it right there.

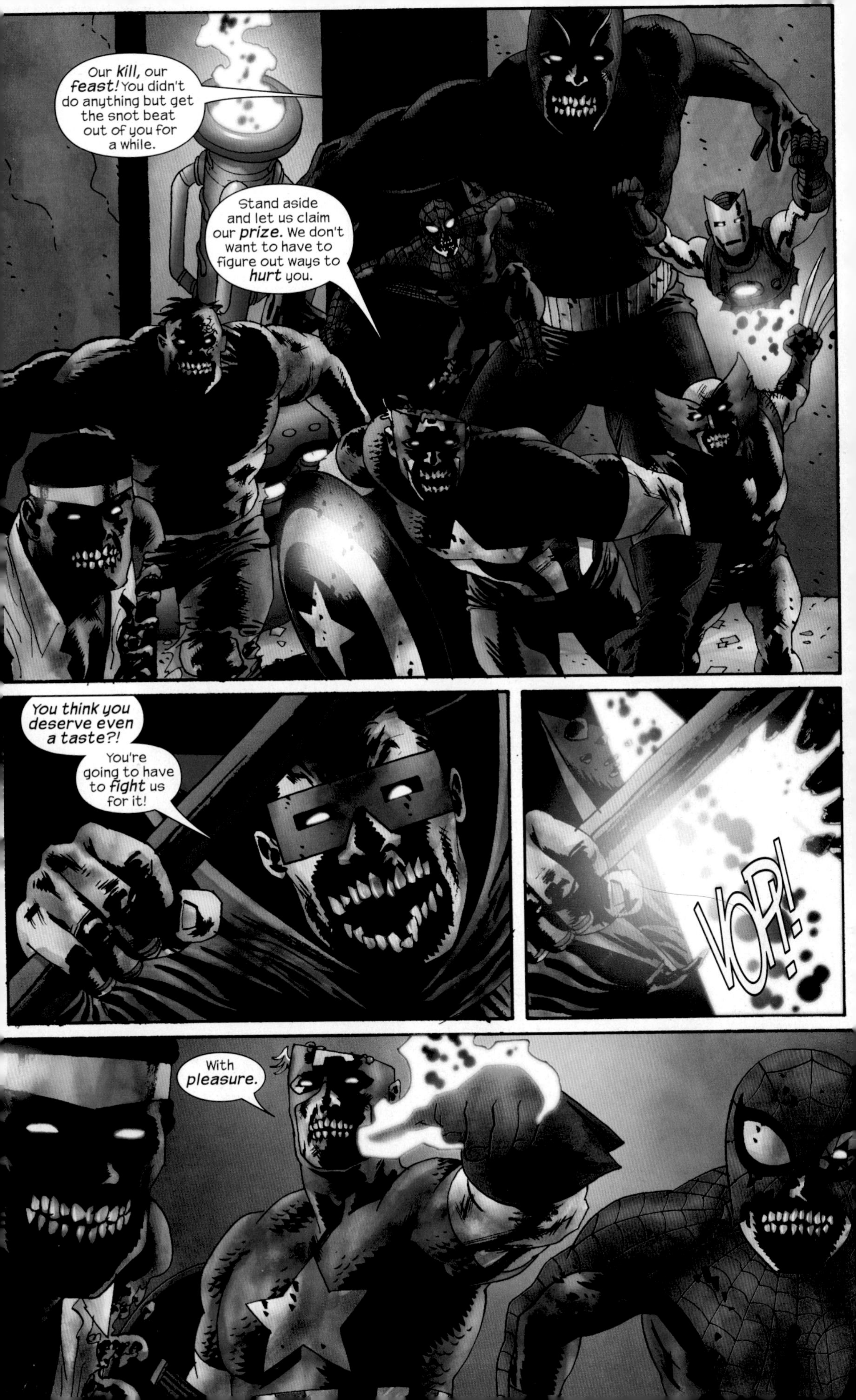
Our kill, our feast! You didn't do anything but get the snot beat out of you for a while.
Stand aside and let us claim our prize. We don't want to have to figure out ways to hurt you.
You think you deserve even a taste?!
You're going to have to fight us for it!
VOP!
With pleasure.

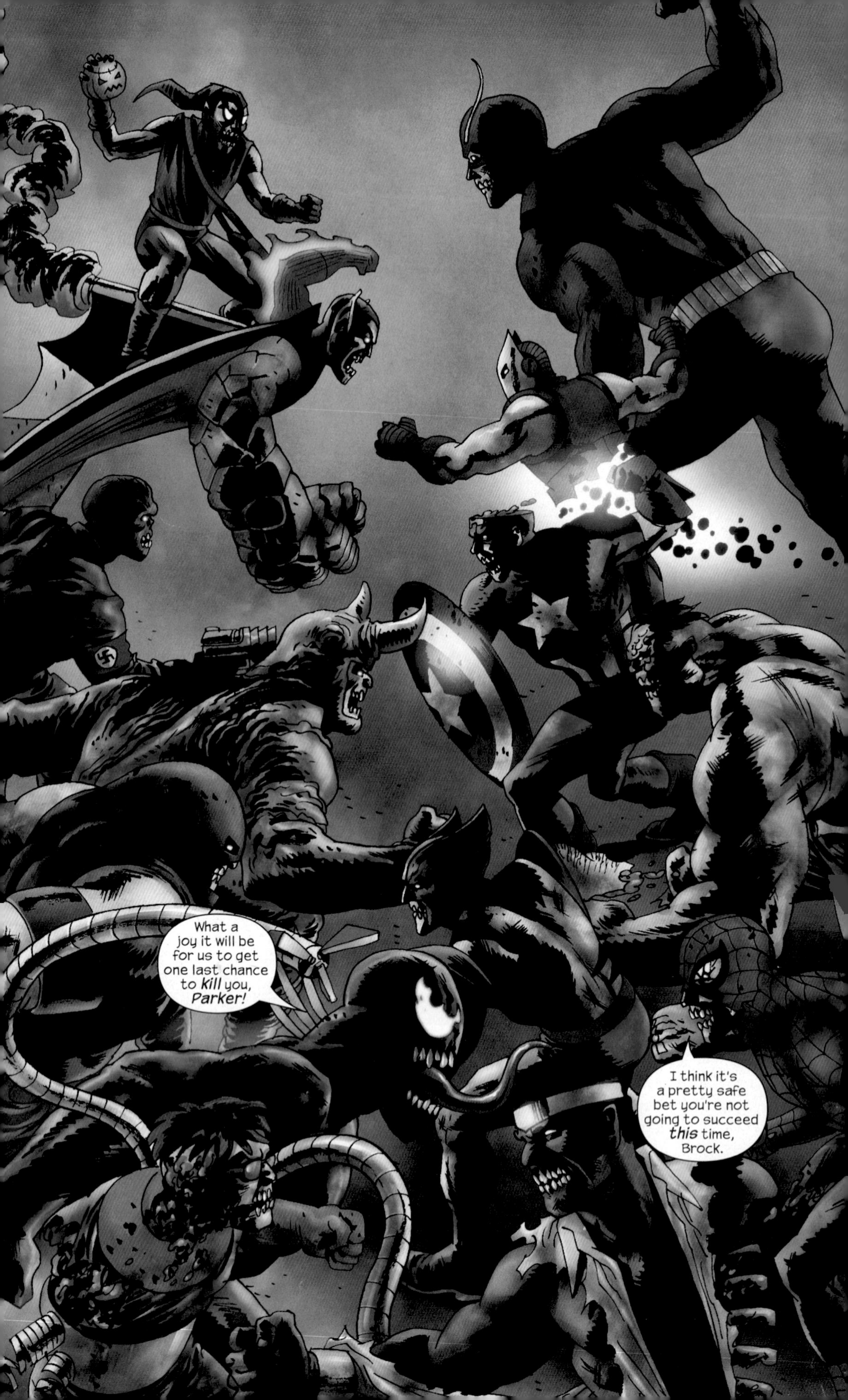
What a joy it will be for us to get one last chance to *kill* you, *Parker!*
I think it's a pretty safe bet you're not going to succeed *this* time, Brock.

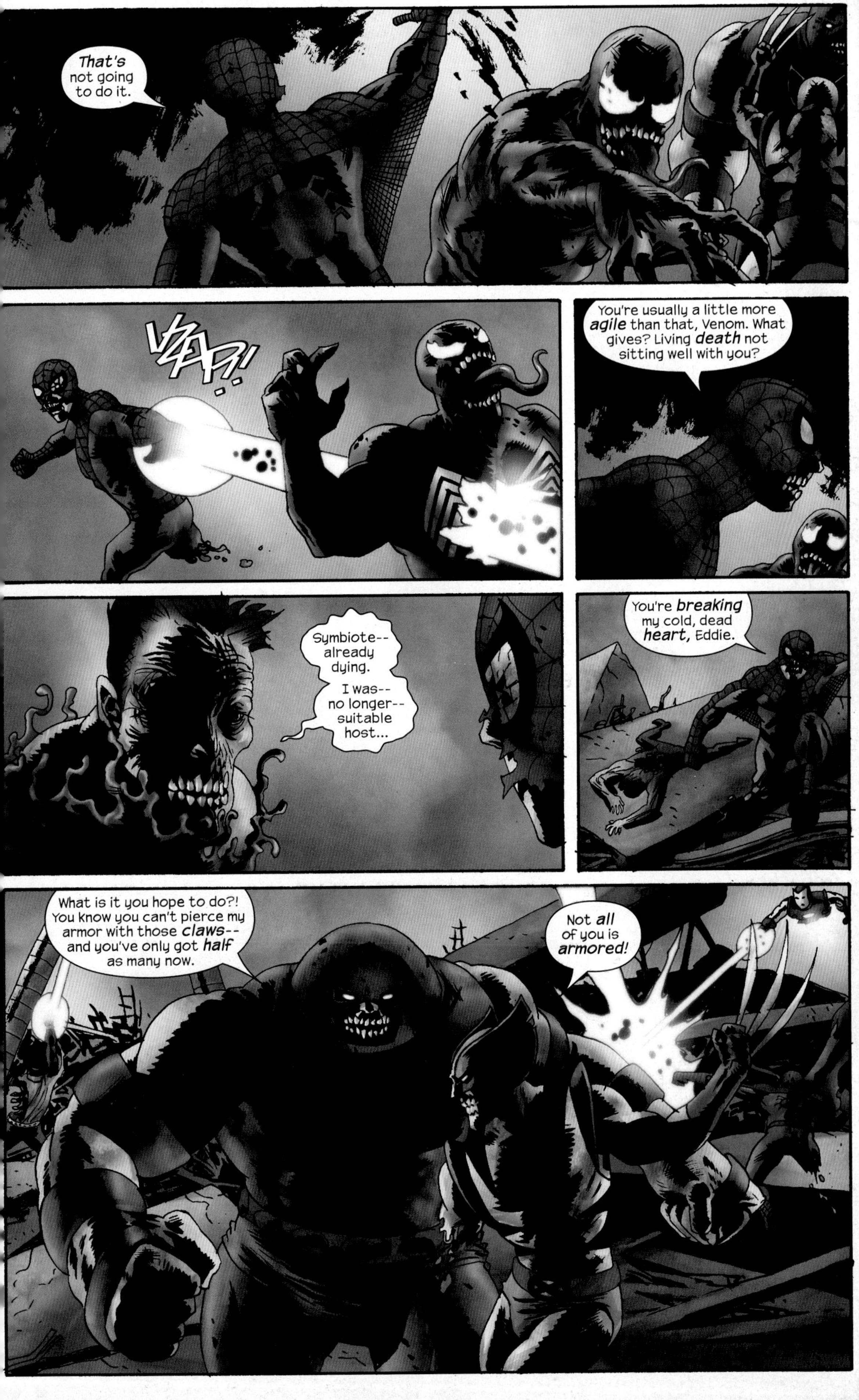
That's not going to do it.
VZZAP!!
You're usually a little more agile than that, Venom. What gives? Living death not sitting well with you?
Symbiote-- already dying.
I was-- no longer-- suitable host...
You're breaking my cold, dead heart, Eddie.
What is it you hope to do?! You know you can't pierce my armor with those claws-- and you've only got half as many now.
Not all of you is armored!

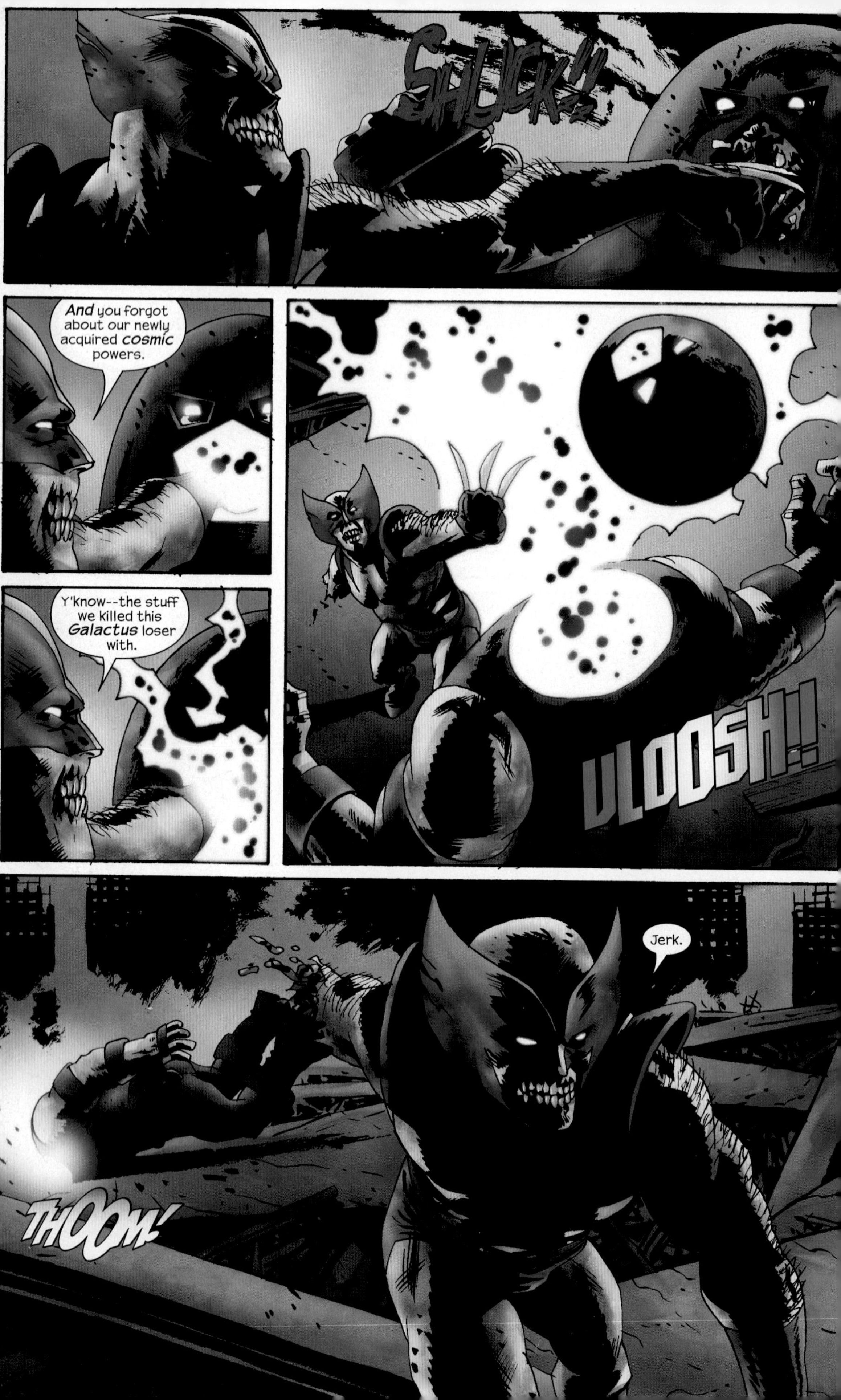
SHUCK!!
And you forgot about our newly acquired cosmic powers.
Y'know--the stuff we killed this Galactus loser with.
VLOOSH!!
Jerk.
THOOM!

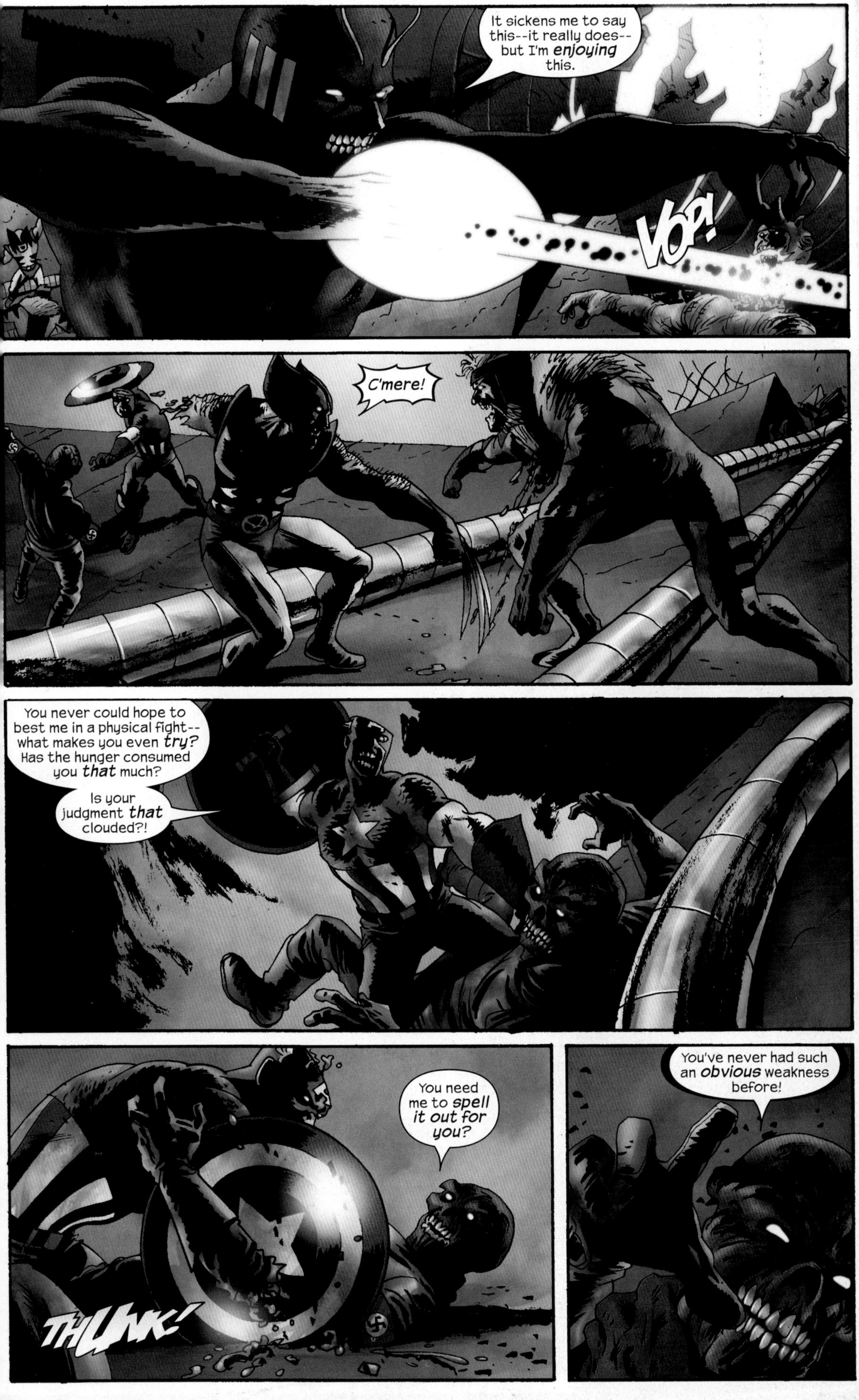
It sickens me to say this--it really does--but I'm *enjoying* this.
VOP!
C'mere!
You never could hope to best me in a physical fight--what makes you even *try?* Has the hunger consumed you *that* much?
Is your judgment *that* clouded?!
THUNK!
You need me to *spell it out for you?*
You've never had such an *obvious* weakness before!

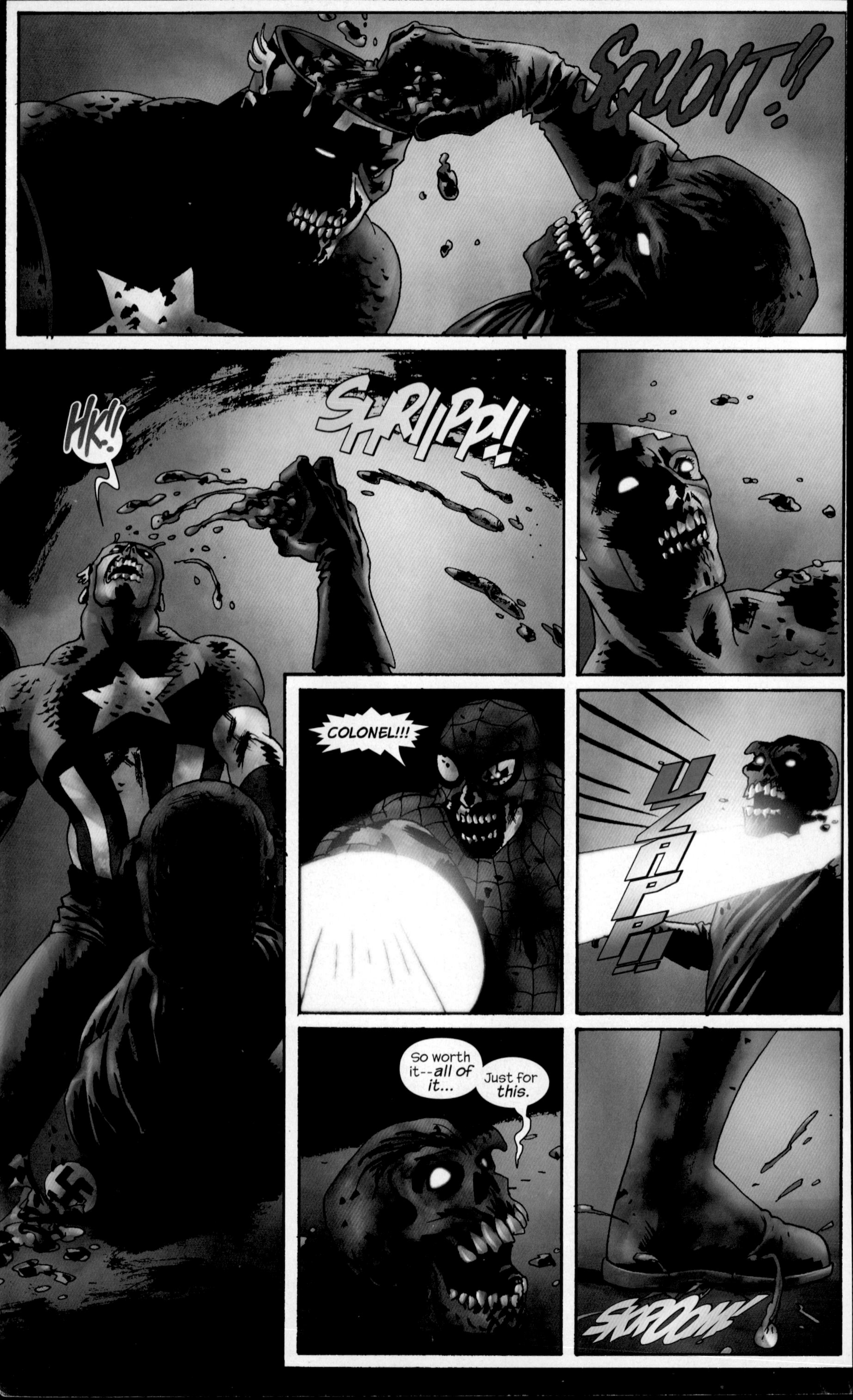
SQUIT!!
HK!!
SHRIPP!!
COLONEL!!!
VZAP!!
So worth it--*all of it*...
Just for *this.*
SKROOM!

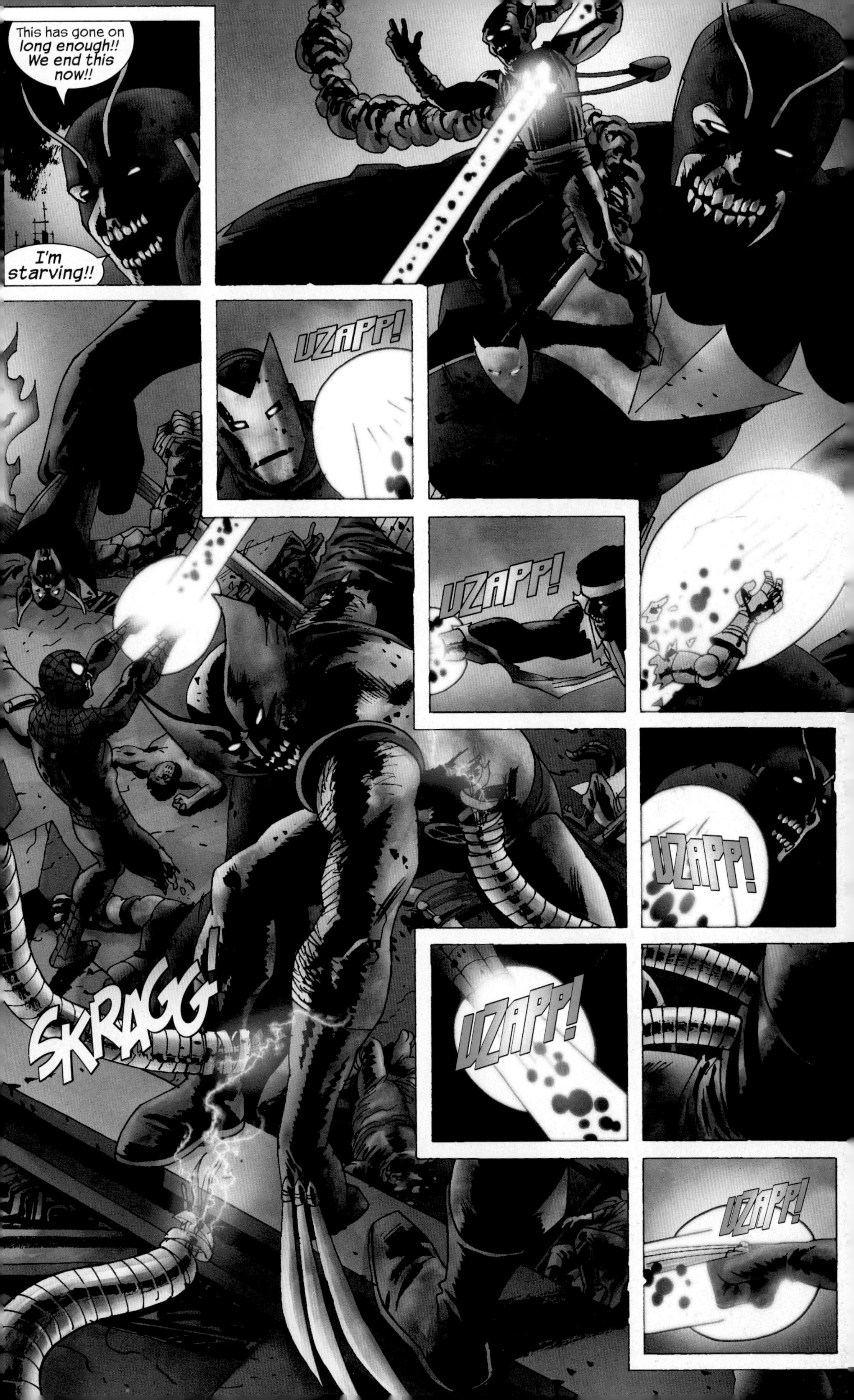
This has gone on long enough!! We end this now!!
I'm starving!!
UZAPP!
UZAPP!
UZAPP!
SKRAGG!
UZAPP!
UZAPP!

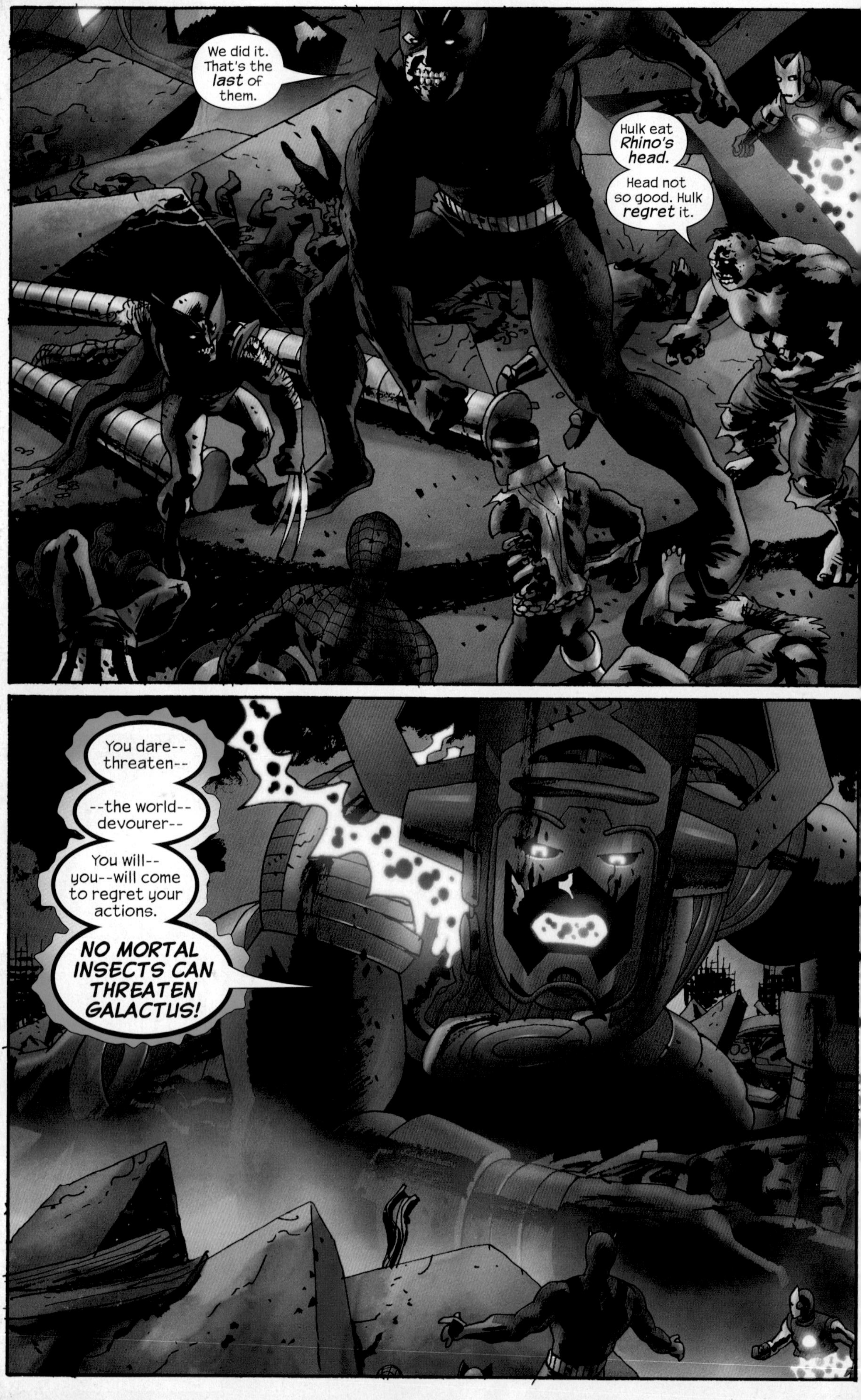
We did it. That's the *last* of them.
Hulk eat *Rhino's head.*
Head not so good. Hulk *regret* it.
You dare-- threaten--
--the world-- devourer--
You will-- you--will come to regret your actions.
NO MORTAL INSECTS CAN THREATEN GALACTUS!

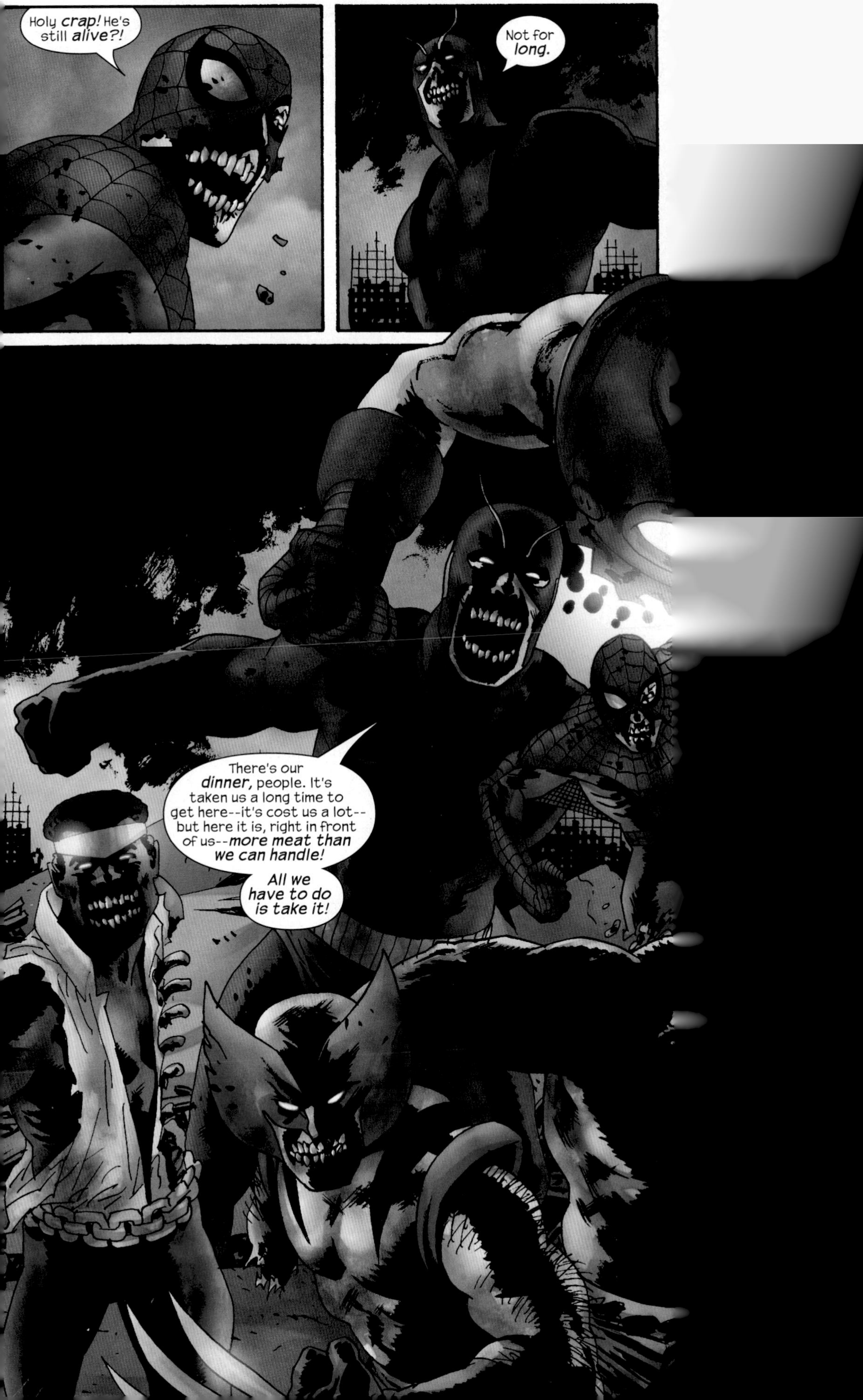
Holy crap! He's still alive?!
Not for long.
There's our dinner, people. It's taken us a long time to get here--it's cost us a lot--but here it is, right in front of us--more meat than we can handle!
All we have to do is take it!

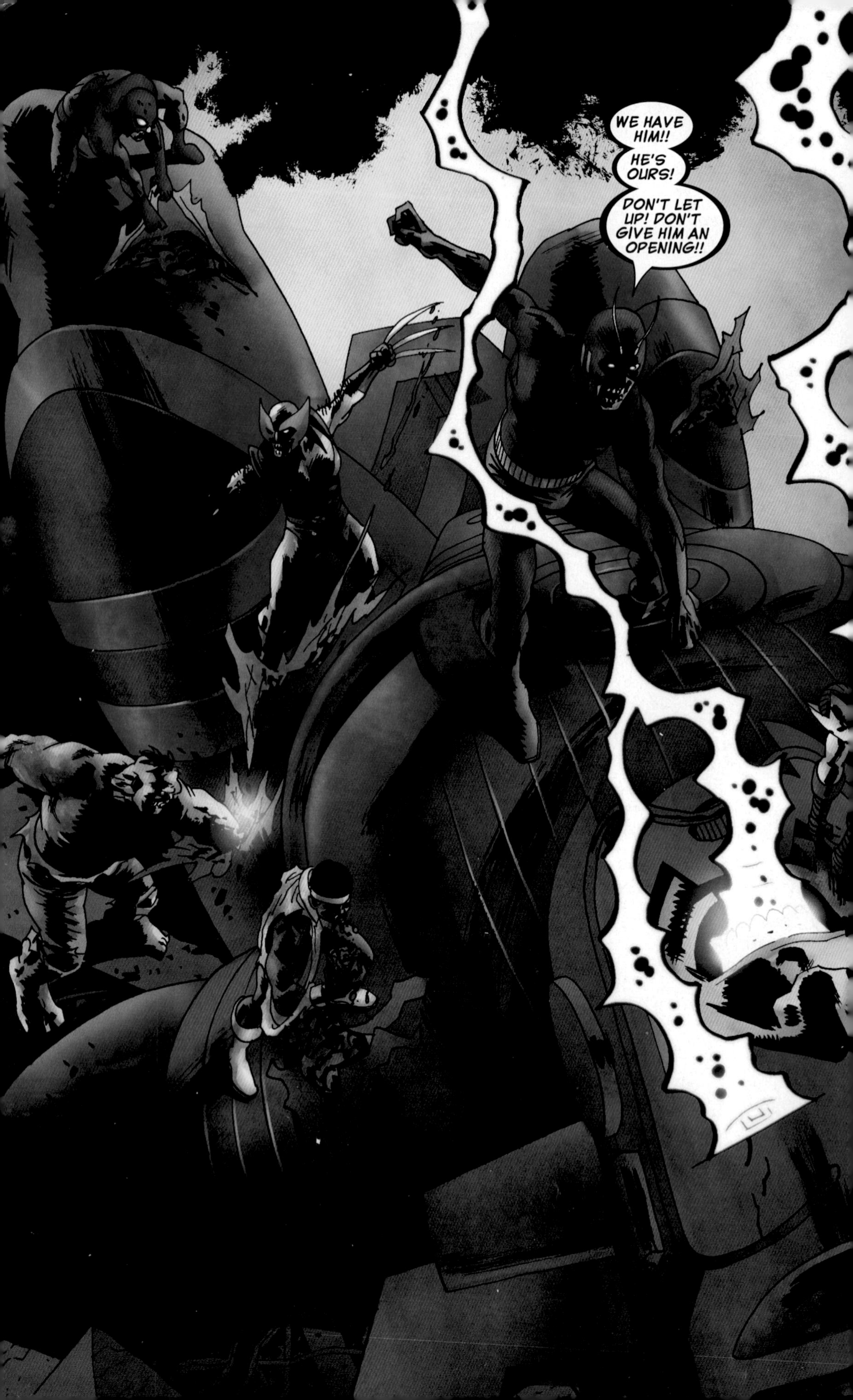
WE HAVE HIM!!
HE'S OURS!
DON'T LET UP! DON'T GIVE HIM AN OPENING!!

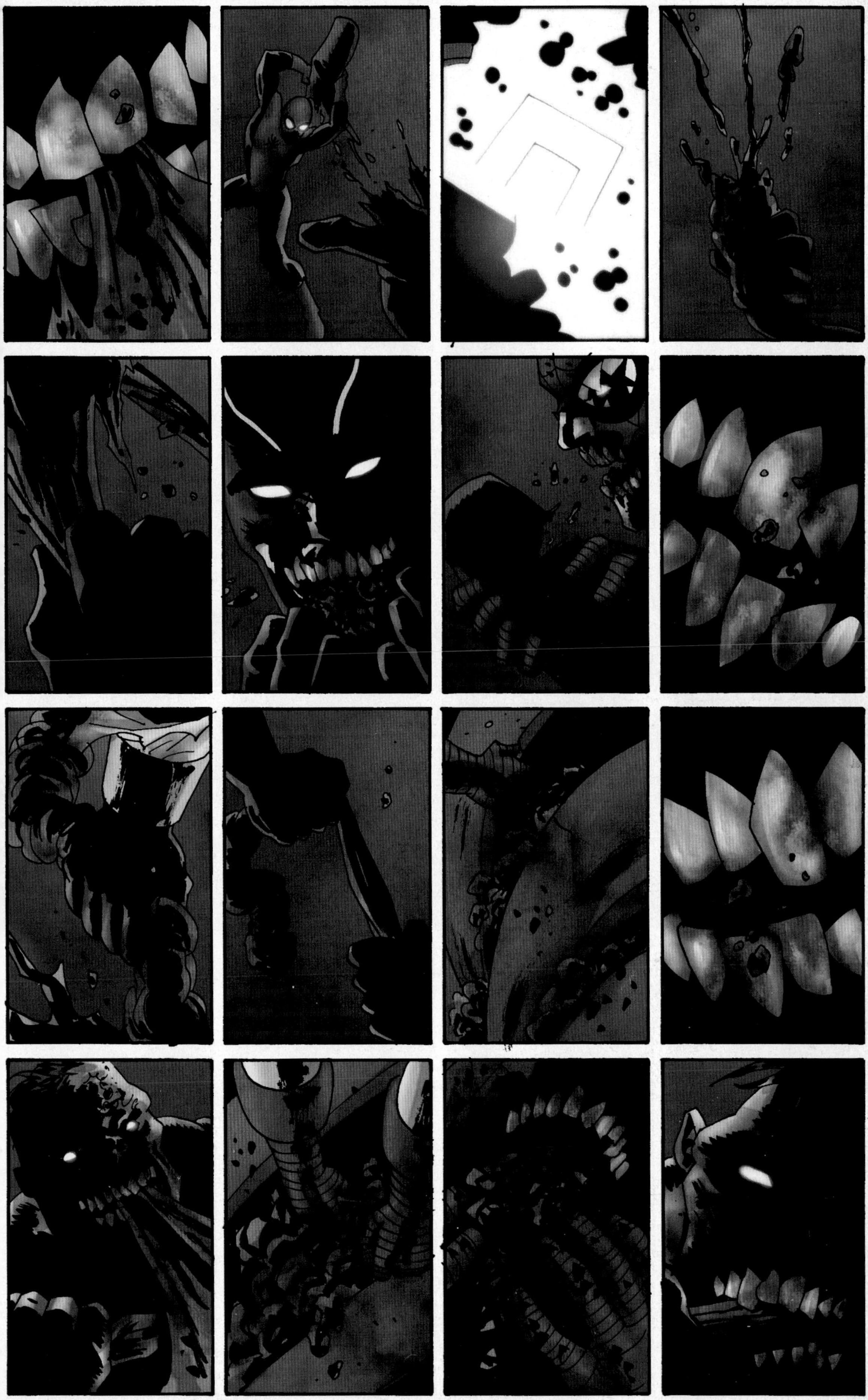

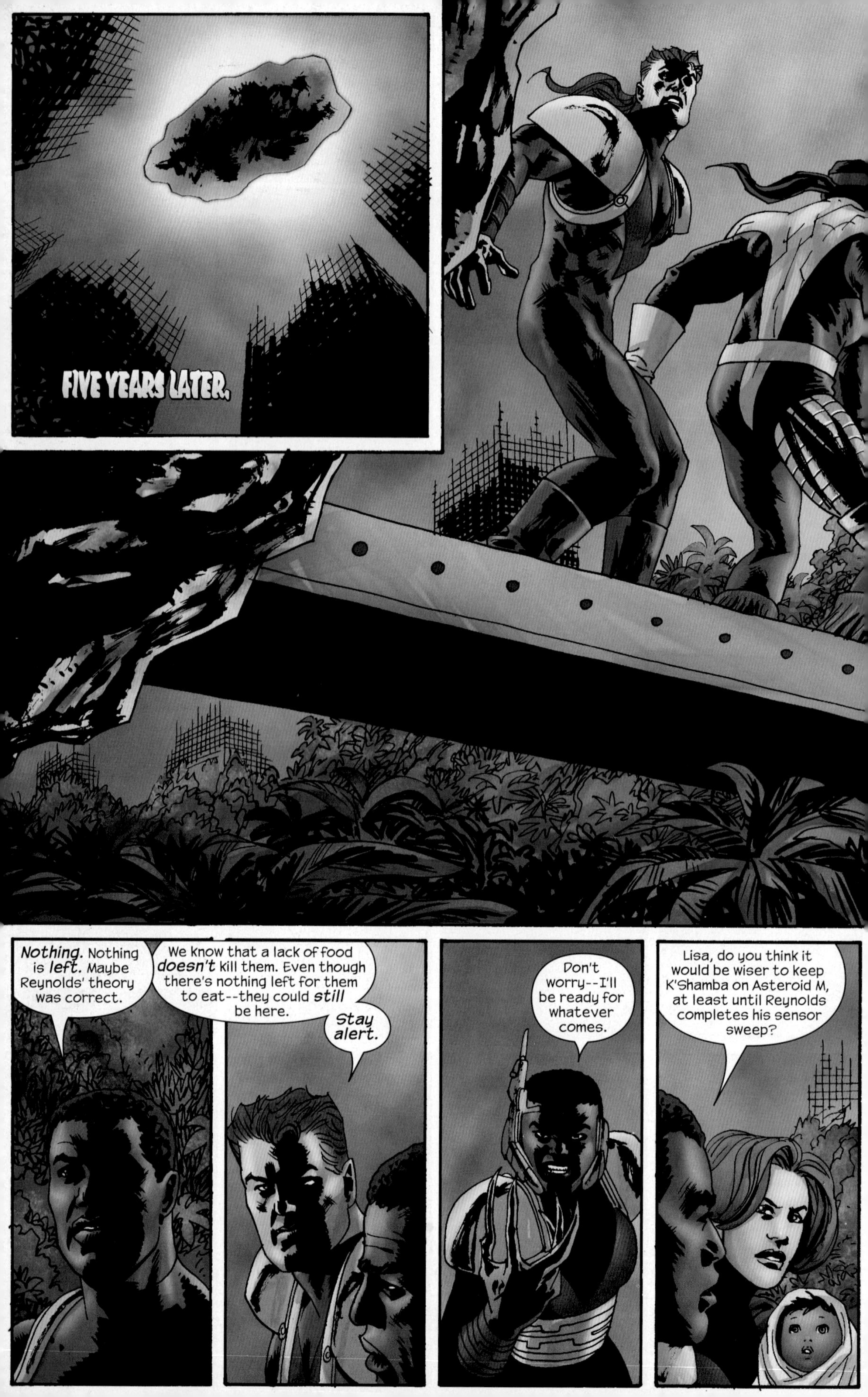
FIVE YEARS LATER.
Nothing. Nothing is left. Maybe Reynolds' theory was correct.
We know that a lack of food doesn't kill them. Even though there's nothing left for them to eat--they could still be here.
Stay alert.
Don't worry--I'll be ready for whatever comes.
Lisa, do you think it would be wiser to keep K'Shamba on Asteroid M, at least until Reynolds completes his sensor sweep?

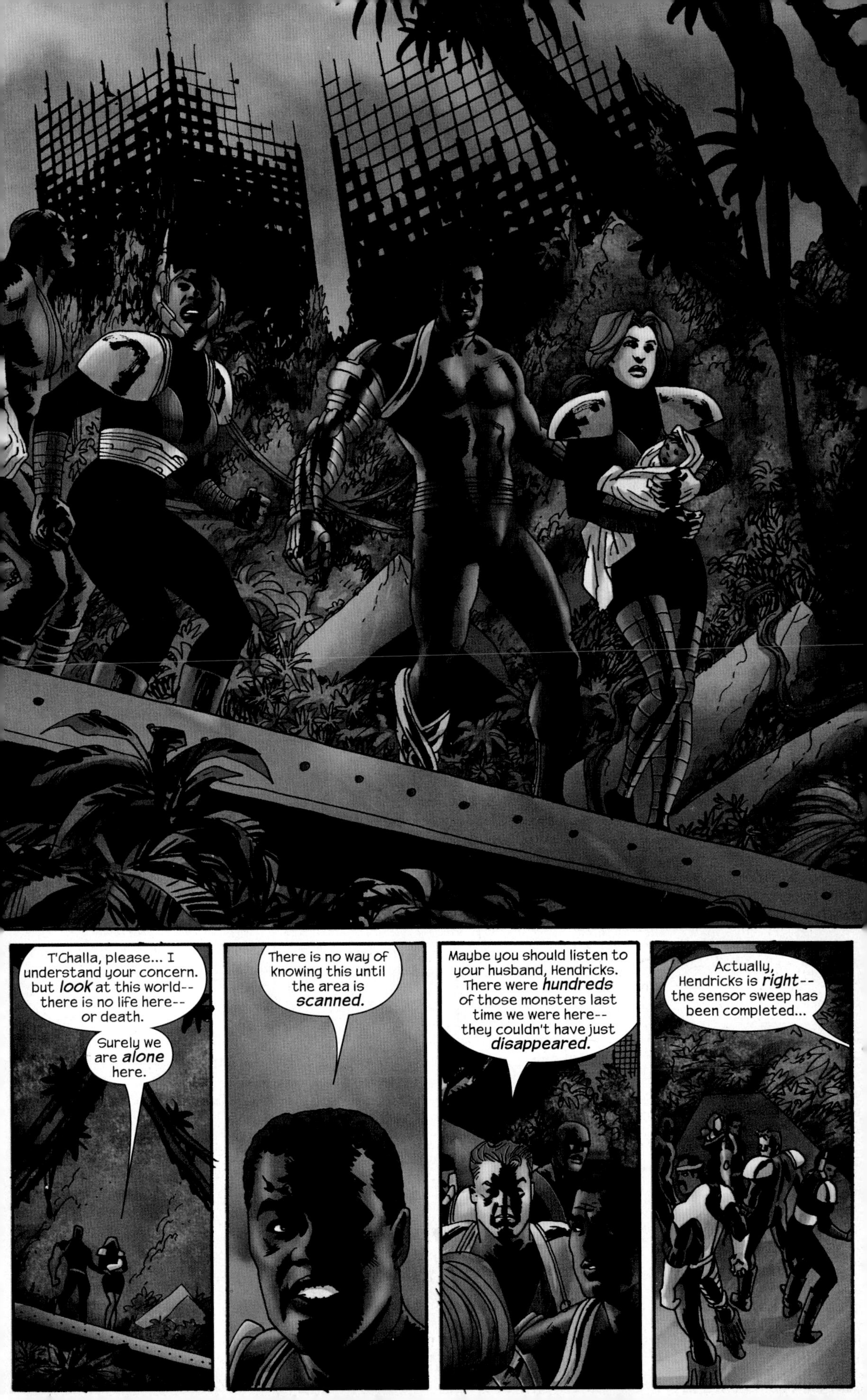
T'Challa, please... I understand your concern. but *look* at this world-- there is no life here-- or death.
Surely we are *alone* here.
There is no way of knowing this until the area is *scanned.*
Maybe you should listen to your husband, Hendricks. There were *hundreds* of those monsters last time we were here-- they couldn't have just *disappeared.*
Actually, Hendricks is *right*-- the sensor sweep has been completed...

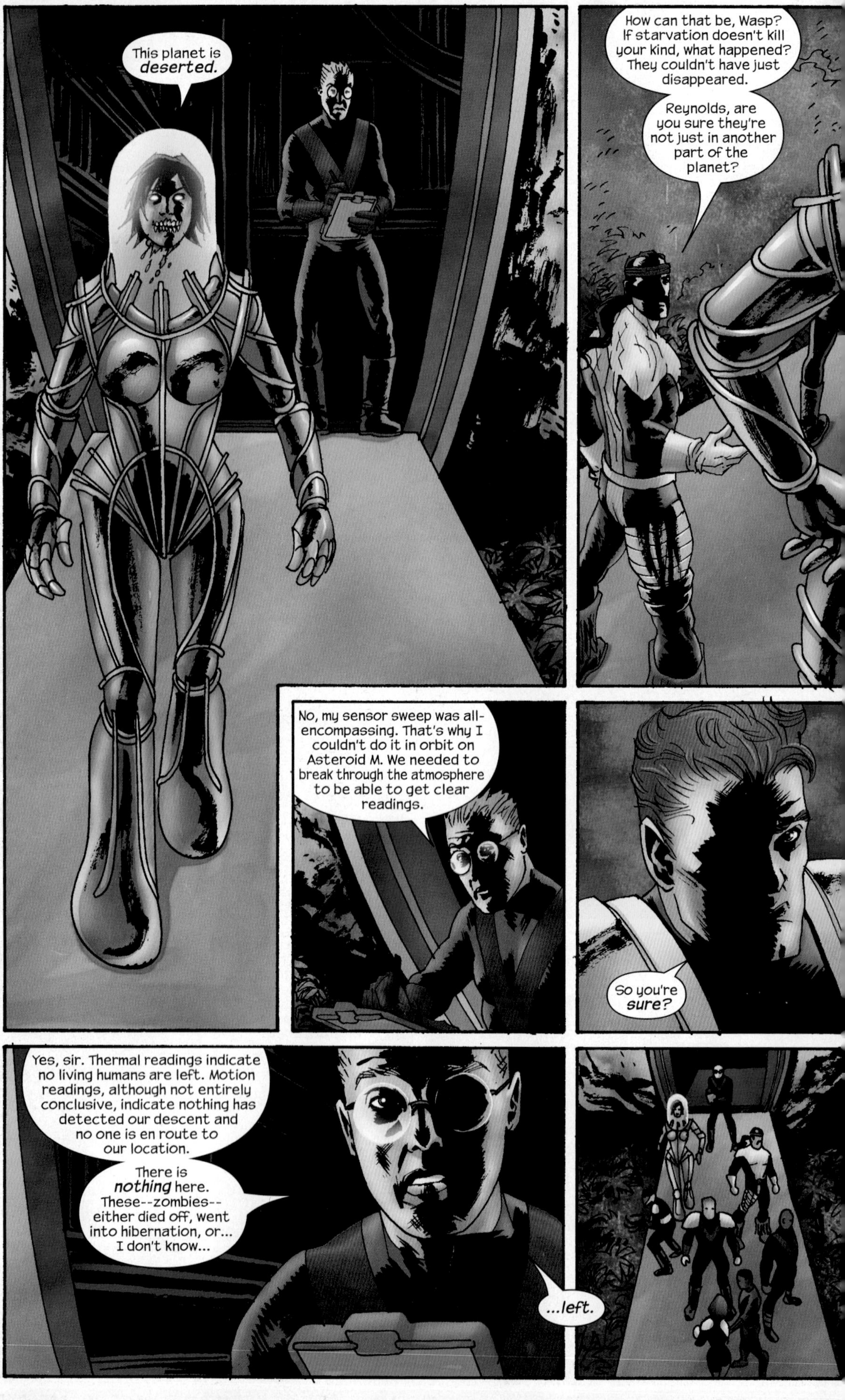
This planet is deserted.
How can that be, Wasp? If starvation doesn't kill your kind, what happened? They couldn't have just disappeared.
Reynolds, are you sure they're not just in another part of the planet?
No, my sensor sweep was all-encompassing. That's why I couldn't do it in orbit on Asteroid M. We needed to break through the atmosphere to be able to get clear readings.
So you're sure?
Yes, sir. Thermal readings indicate no living humans are left. Motion readings, although not entirely conclusive, indicate nothing has detected our descent and no one is en route to our location.
There is nothing here. These--zombies--either died off, went into hibernation, or... I don't know...
...left.

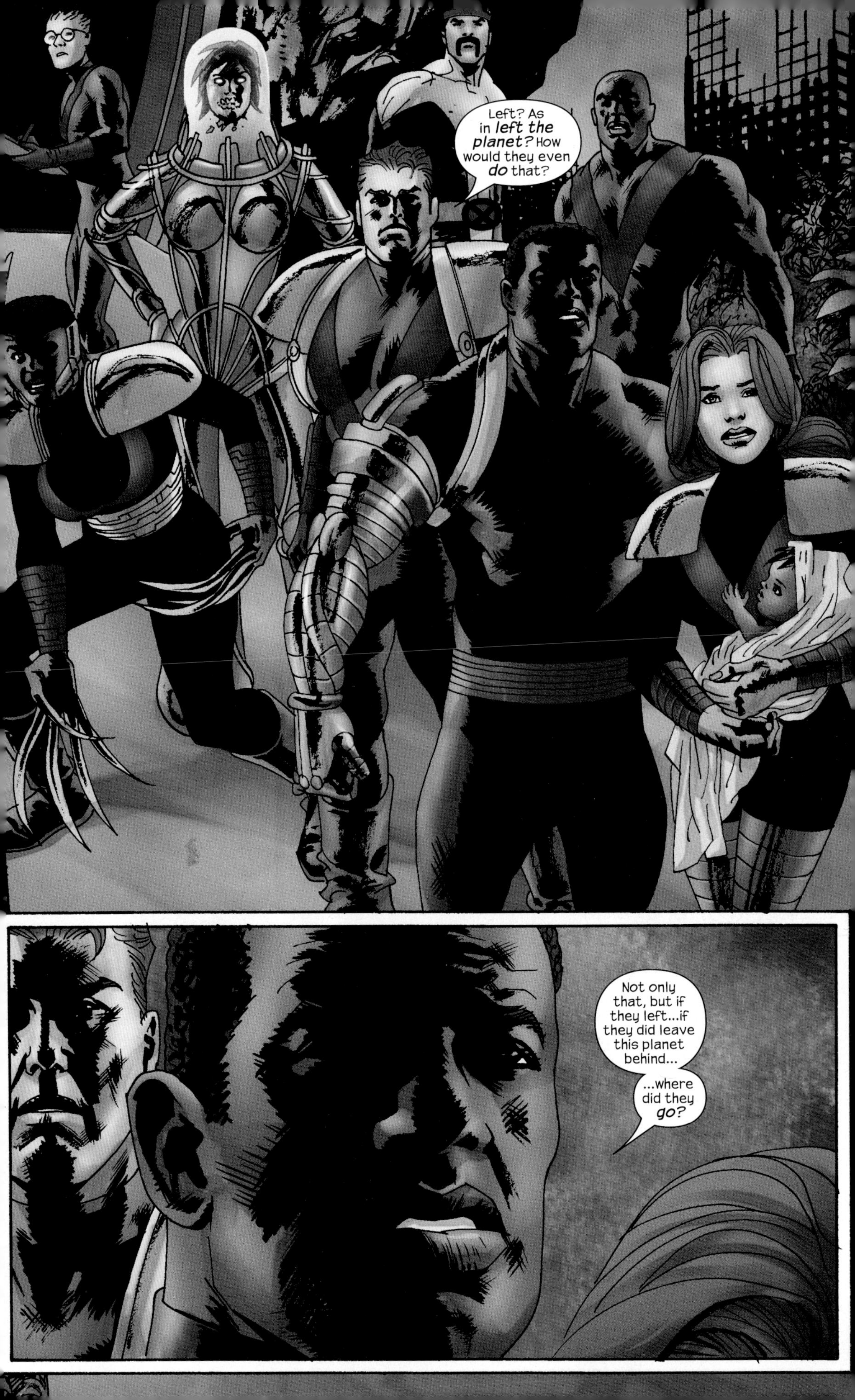
Left? As in *left the planet?* How would they even *do* that?
Not only that, but if they left...if they did leave this planet behind...
...where did they *go?*

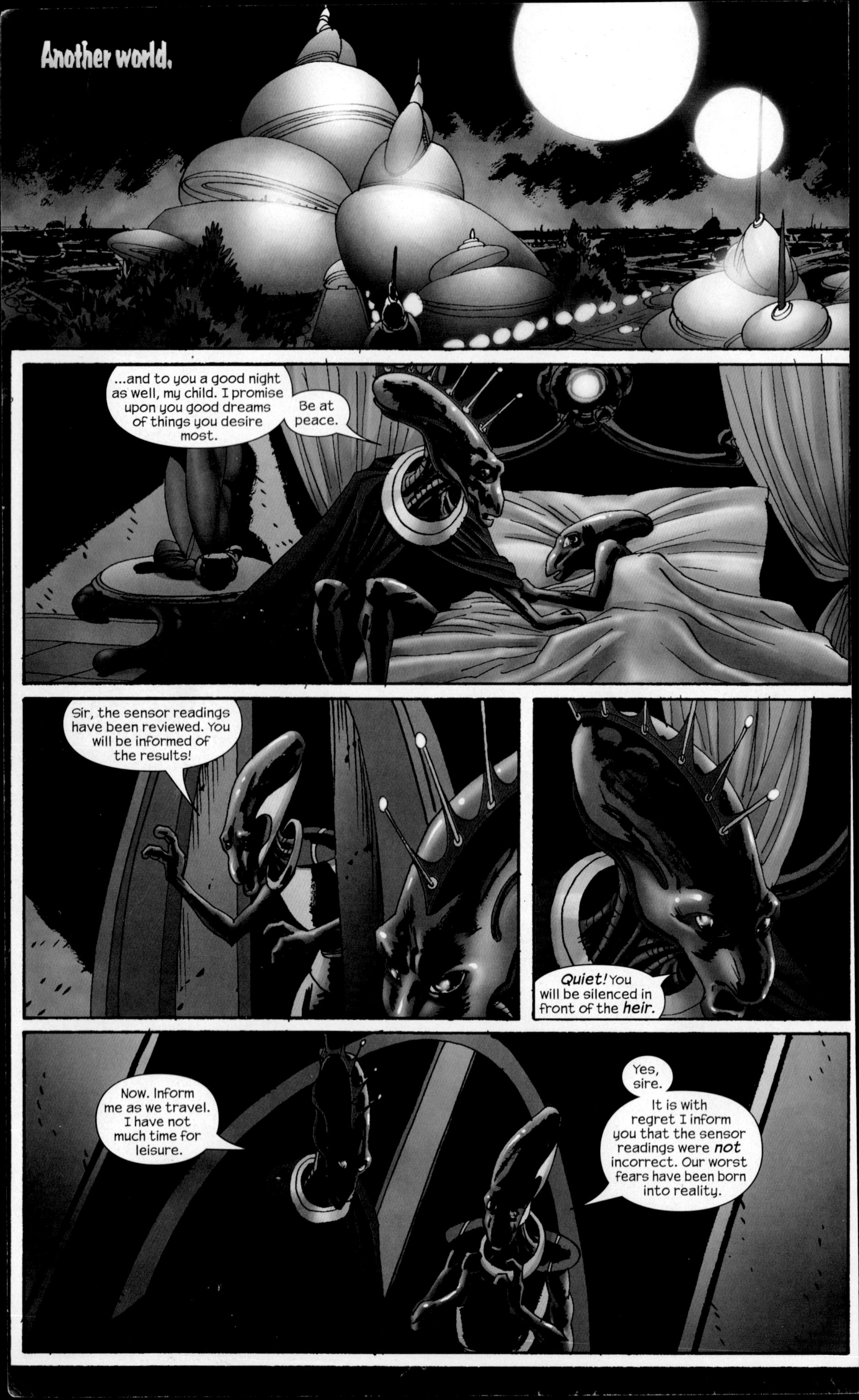
Another world.
...and to you a good night as well, my child. I promise upon you good dreams of things you desire most.
Be at peace.
Sir, the sensor readings have been reviewed. You will be informed of the results!
Quiet! You will be silenced in front of the heir.
Now. Inform me as we travel. I have not much time for leisure.
Yes, sire.
It is with regret I inform you that the sensor readings were not incorrect. Our worst fears have been born into reality.

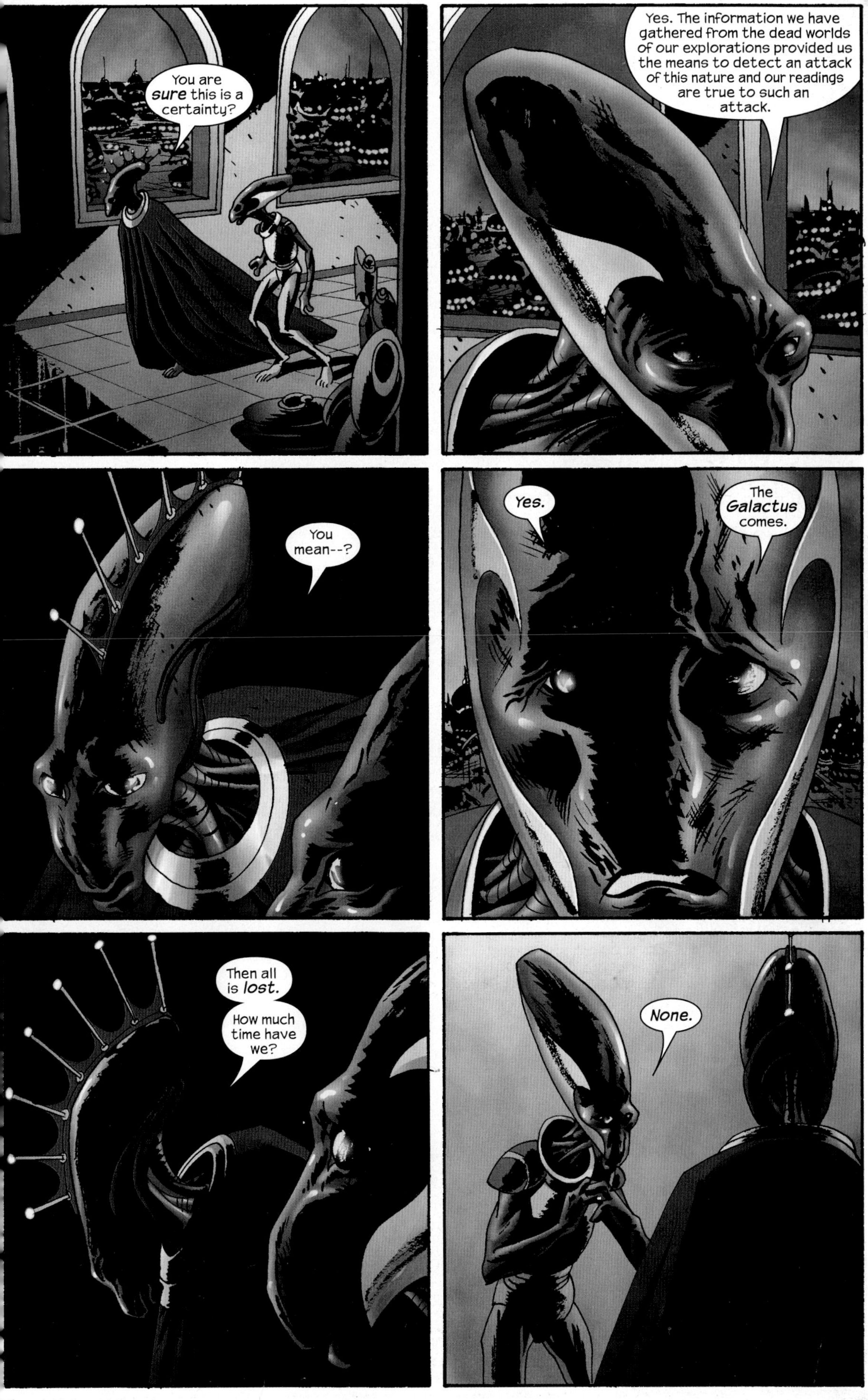
You are *sure* this is a certainty?
Yes. The information we have gathered from the dead worlds of our explorations provided us the means to detect an attack of this nature and our readings are true to such an attack.
You mean--?
Yes.
The *Galactus* comes.
Then all is *lost.*
How much time have we?
None.

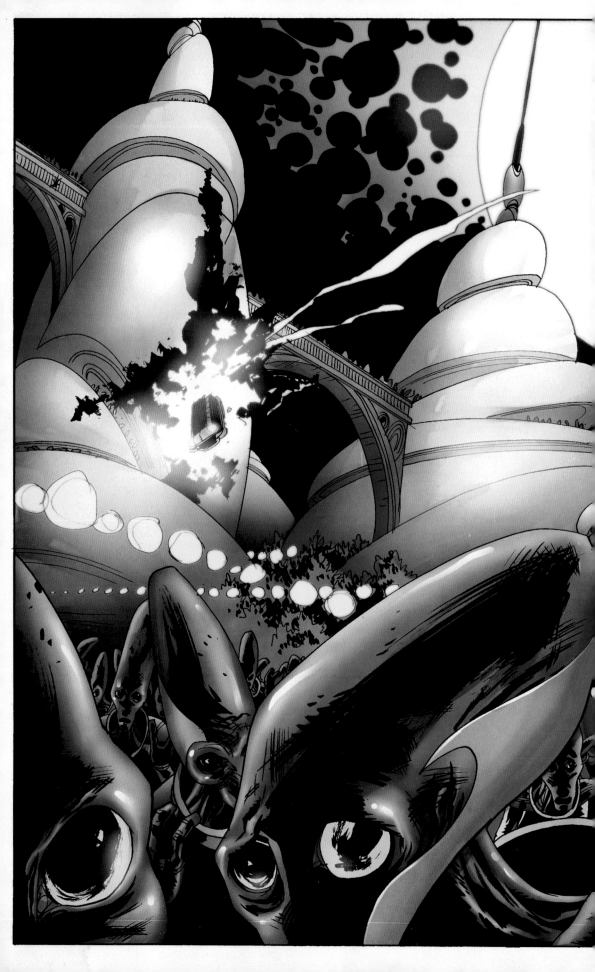

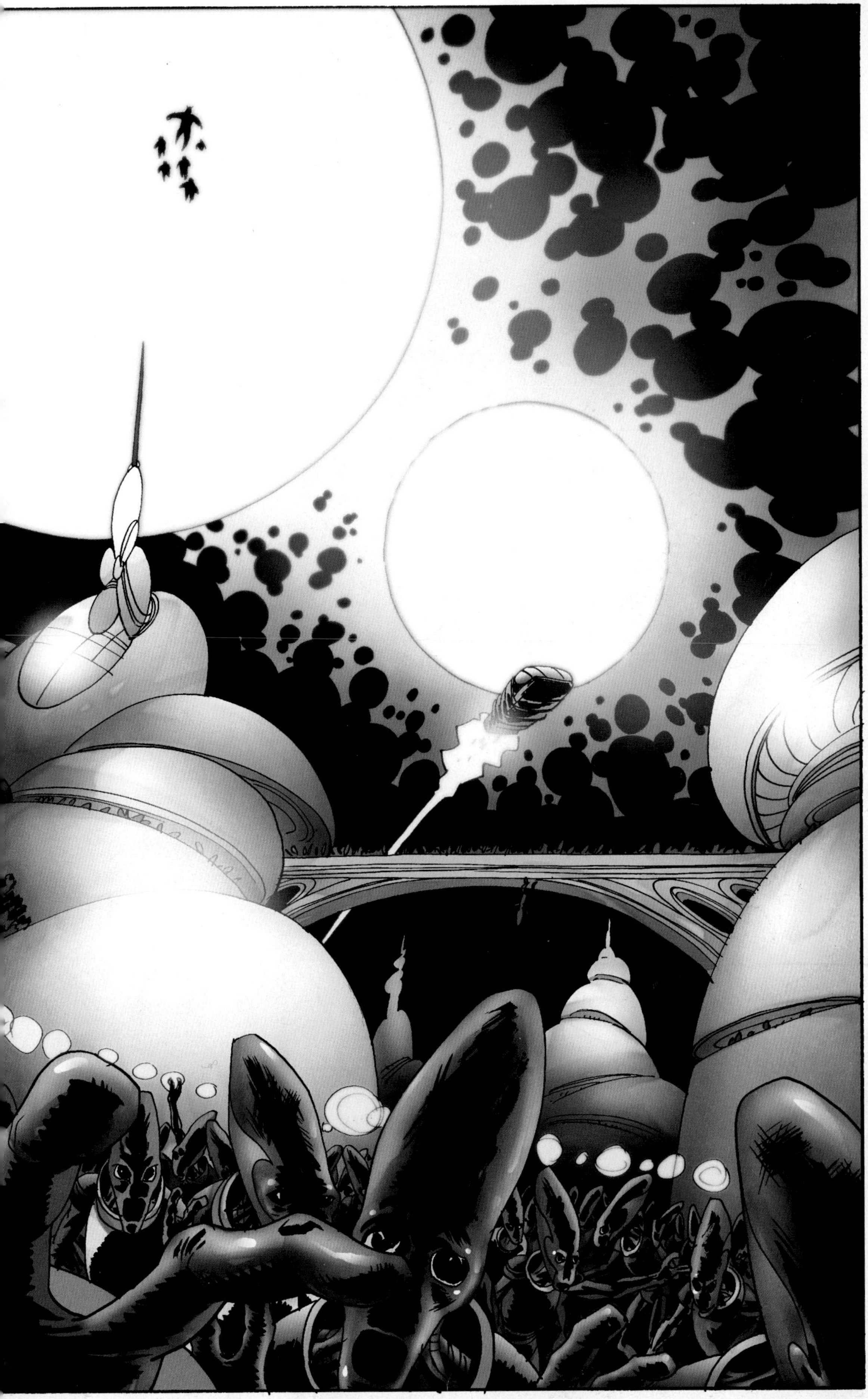

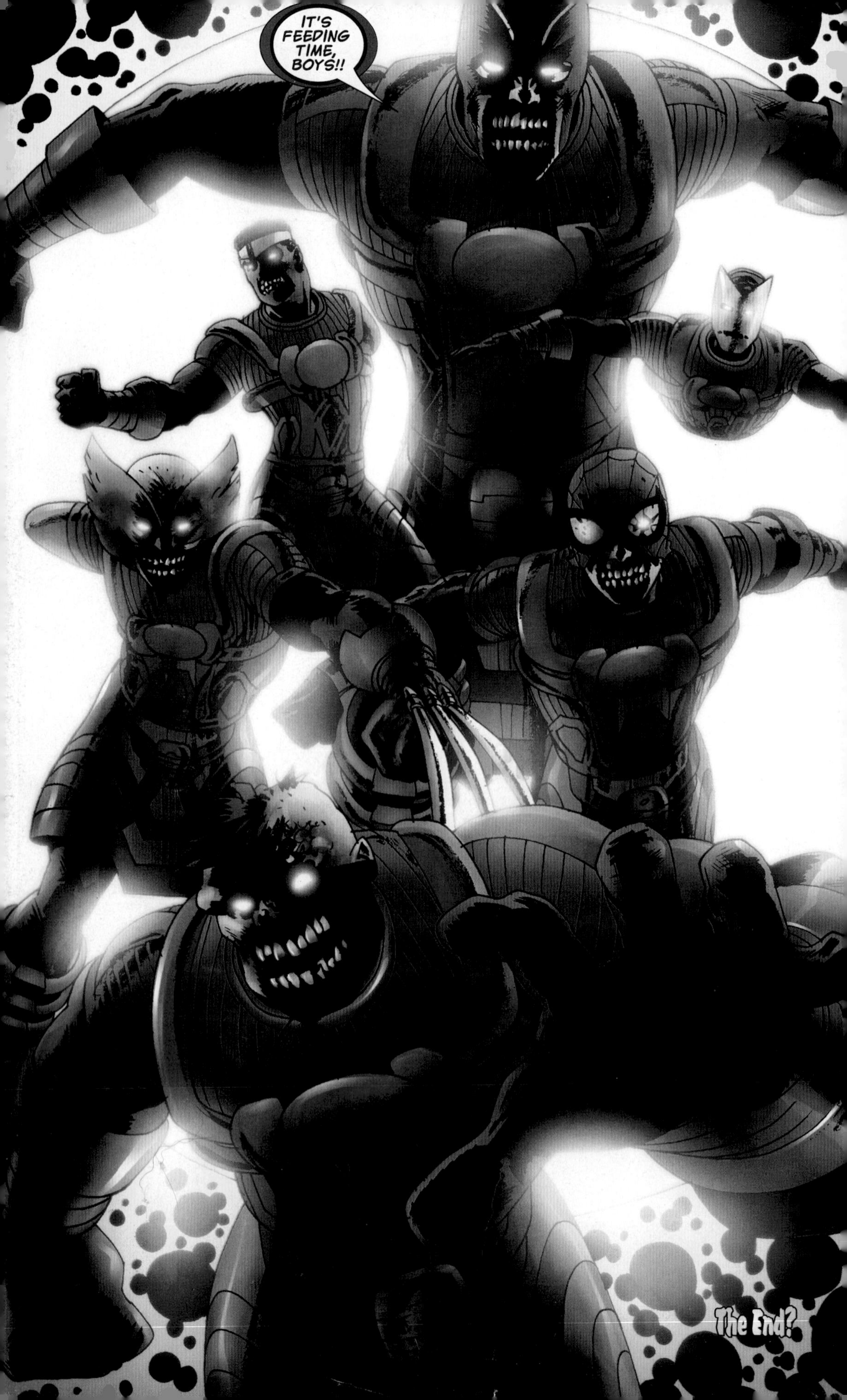
IT'S FEEDING TIME, BOYS!!
The End?

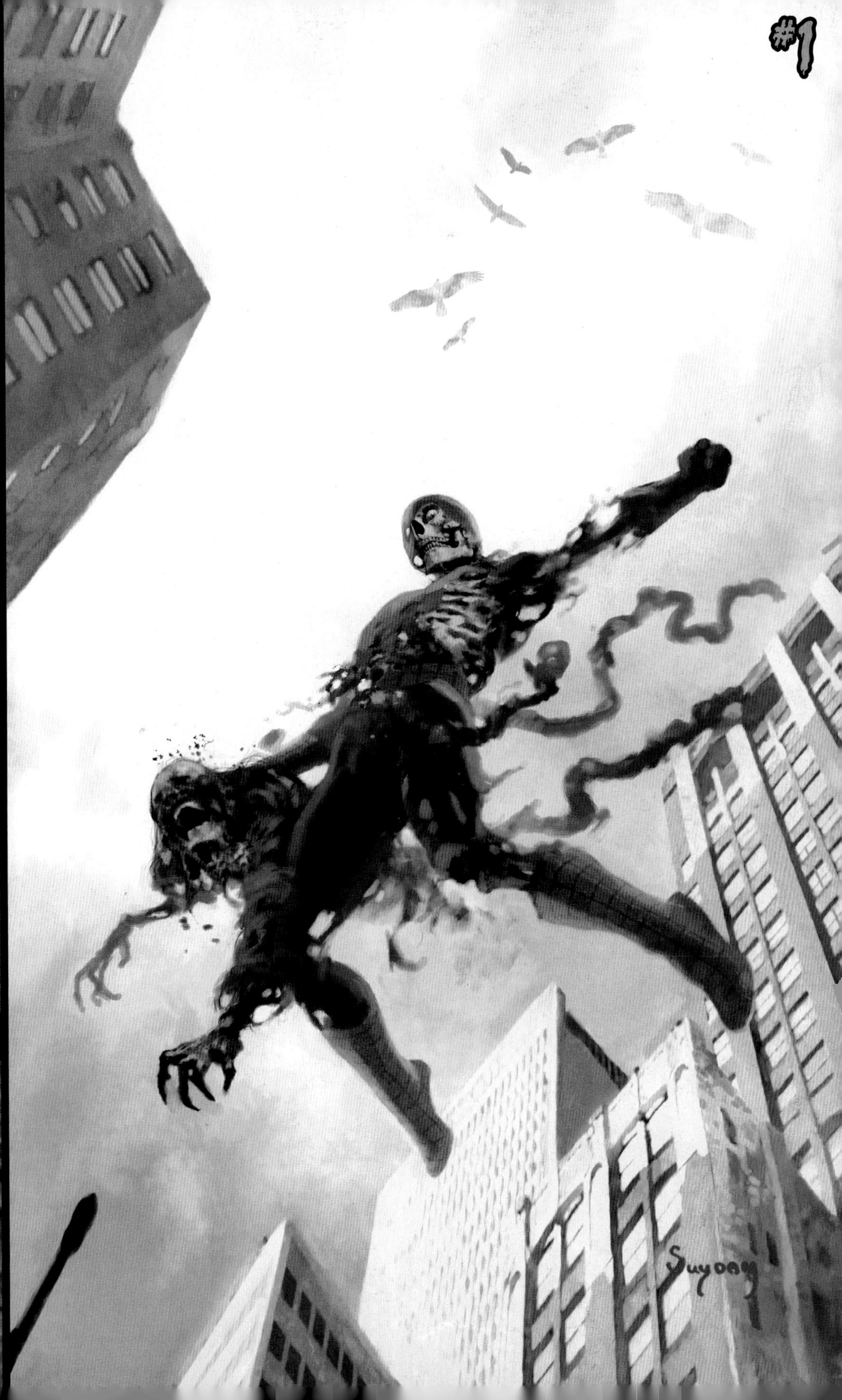
#1
Suydam

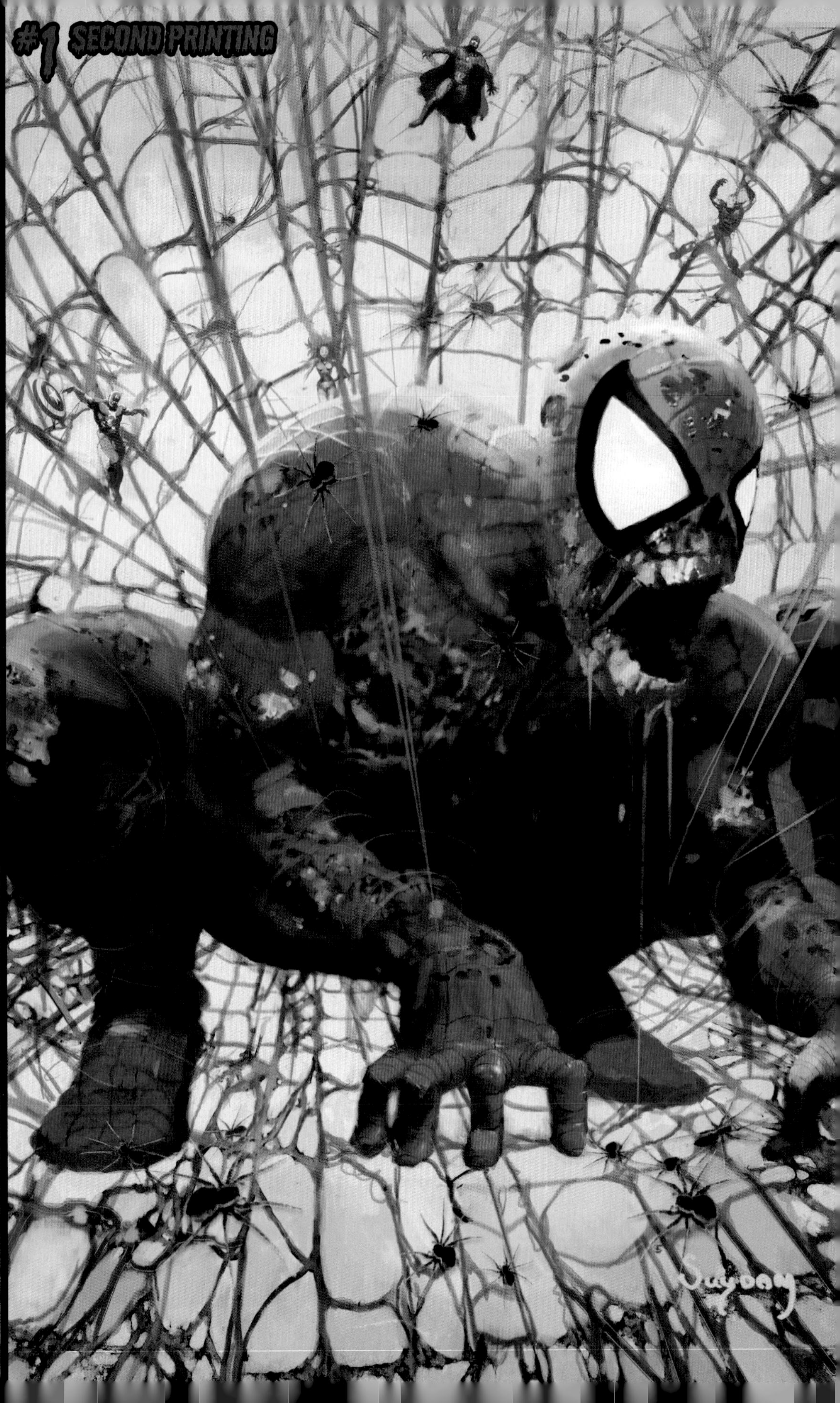
#1 SECOND PRINTING
Suydam

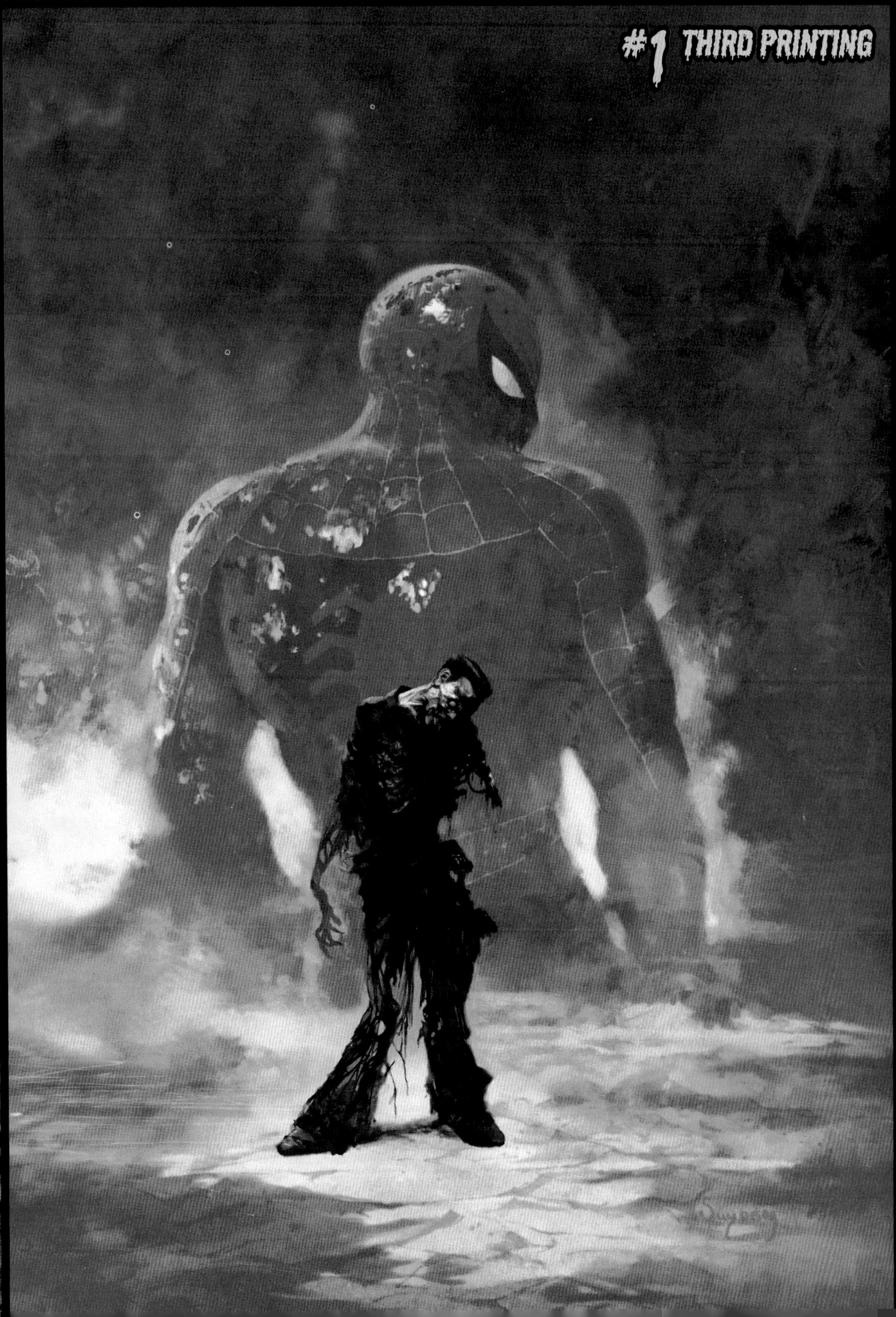
#1 THIRD PRINTING

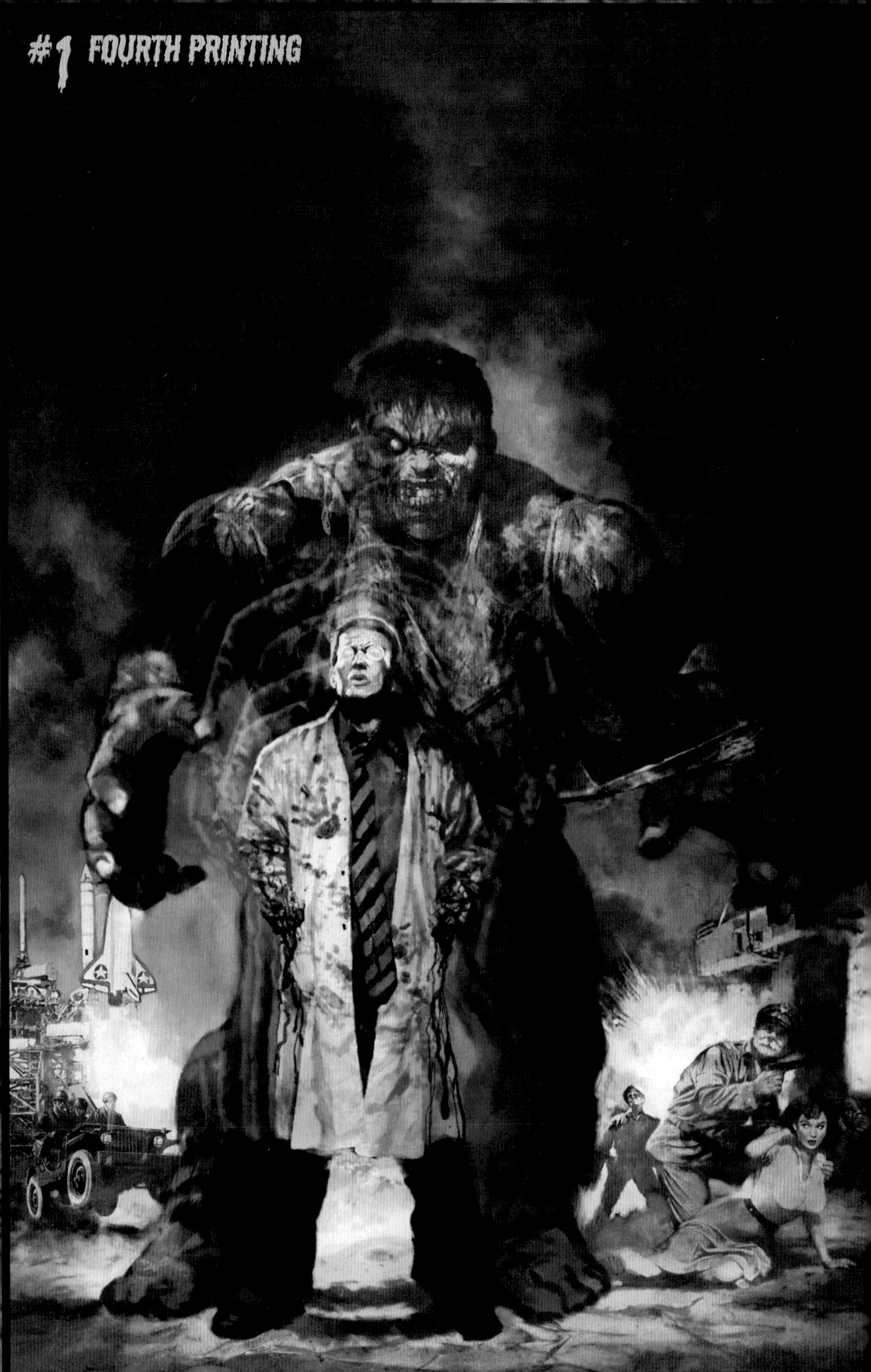
#1 FOURTH PRINTING

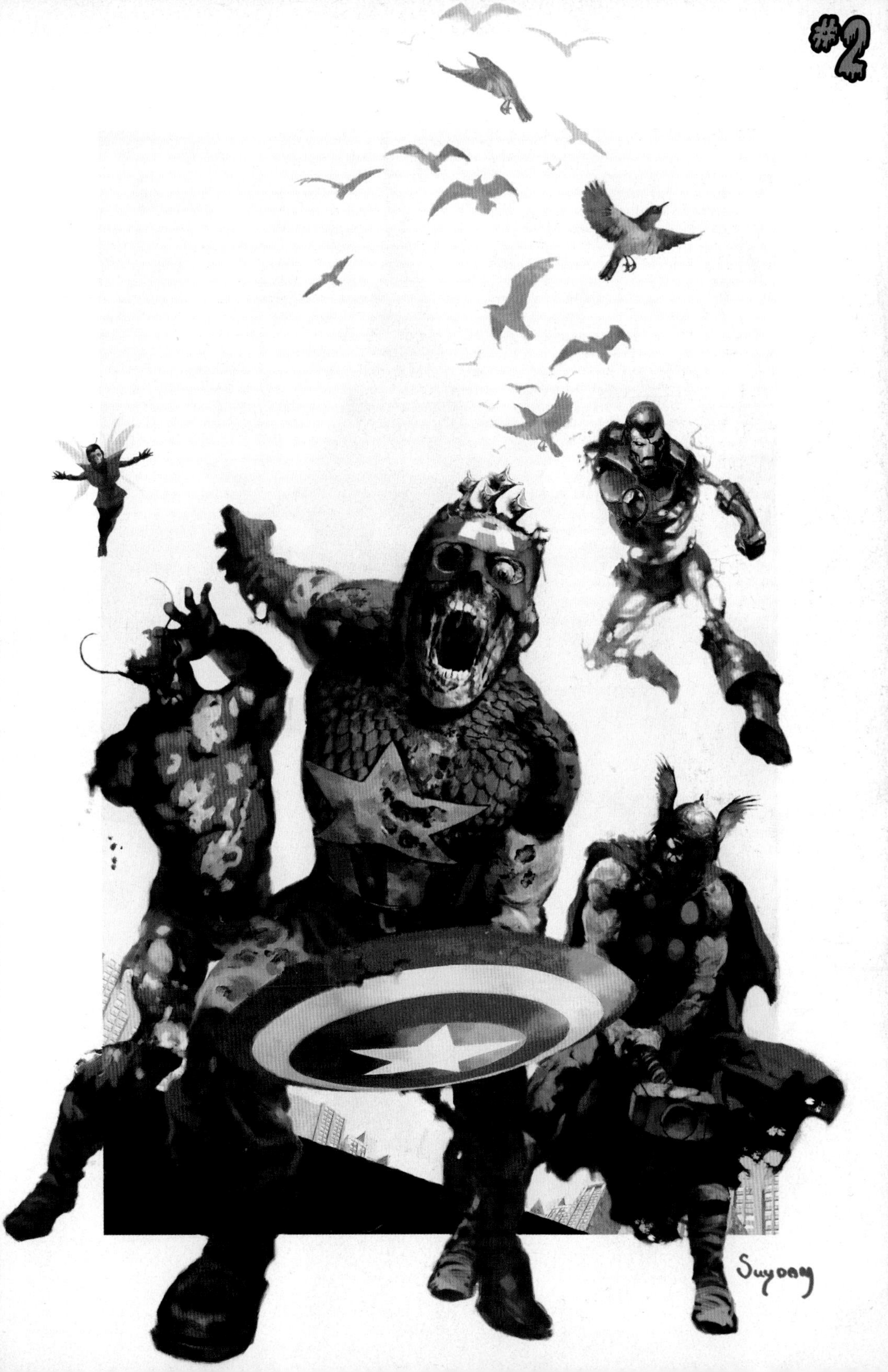
#2
Suydam

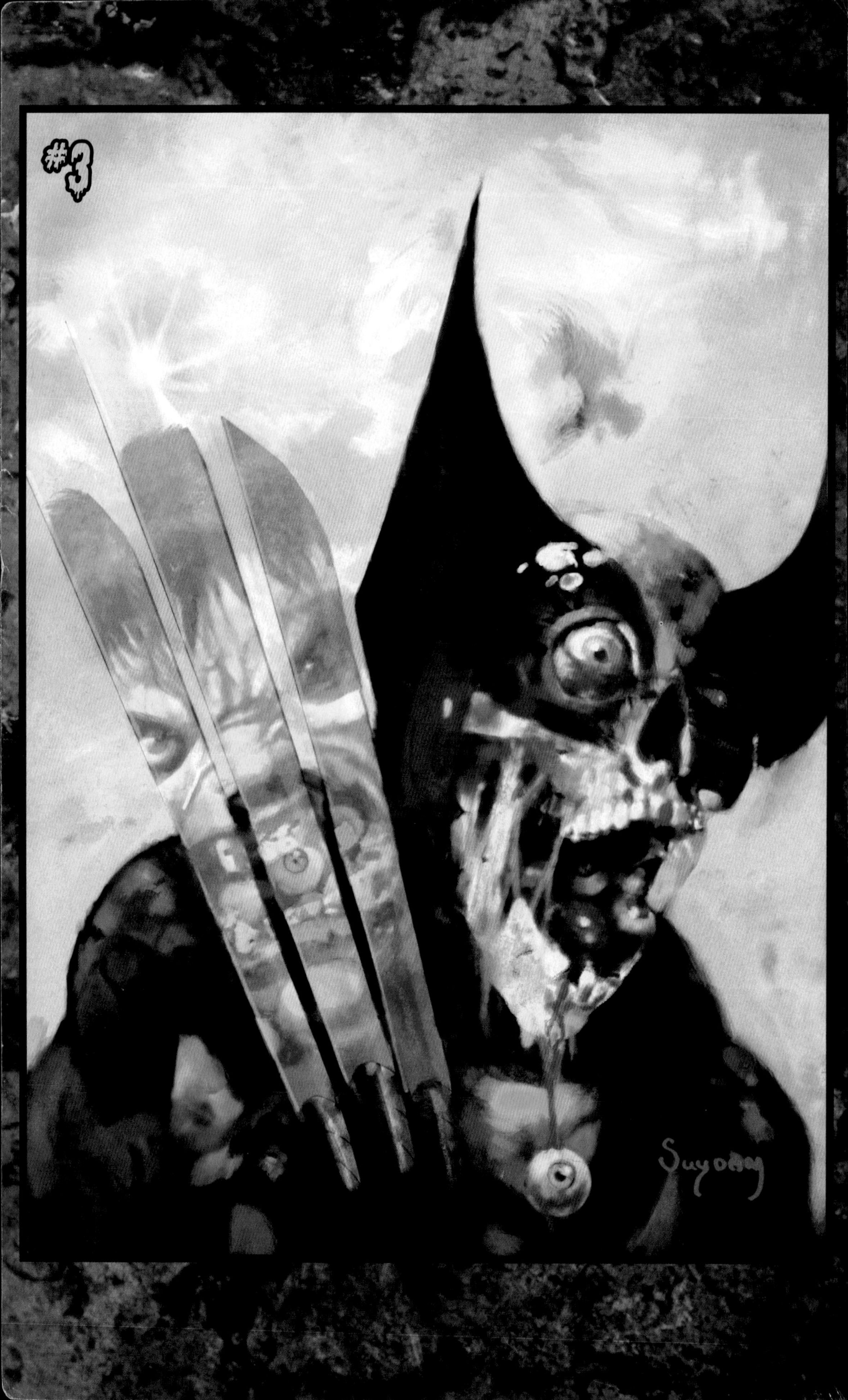
#3
Suydam

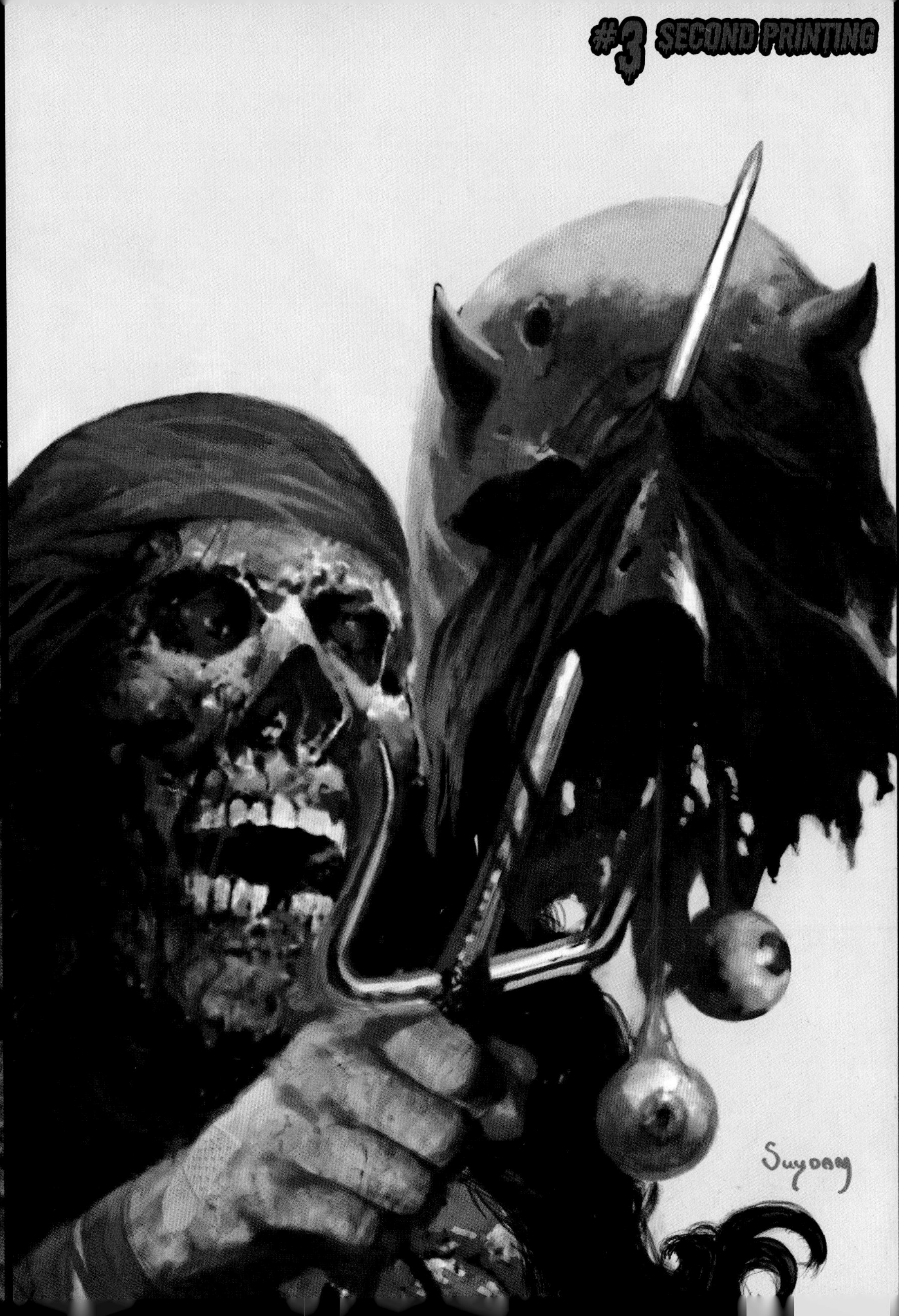
#3 SECOND PRINTING
Suydam

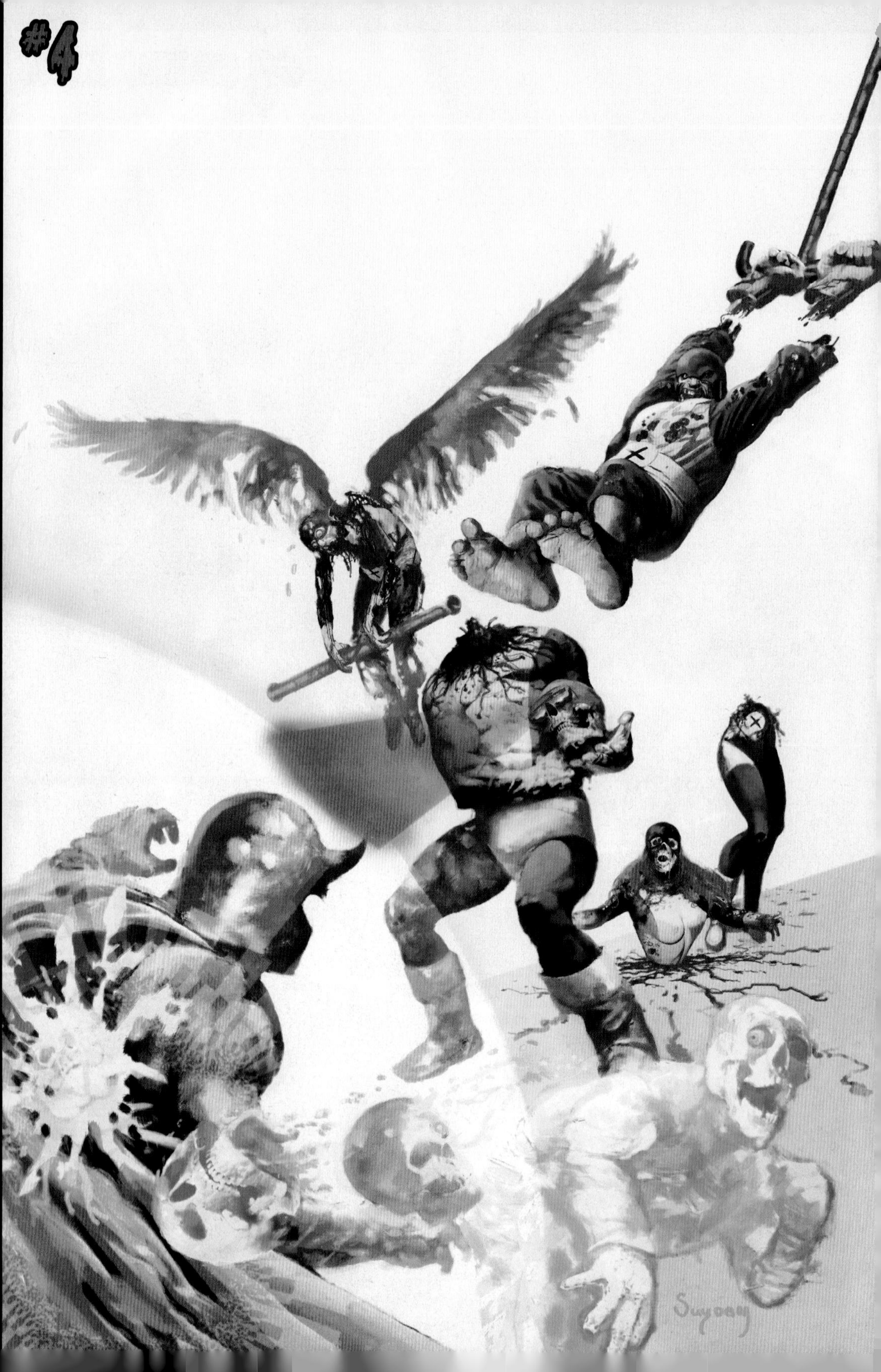
#4
Suydam

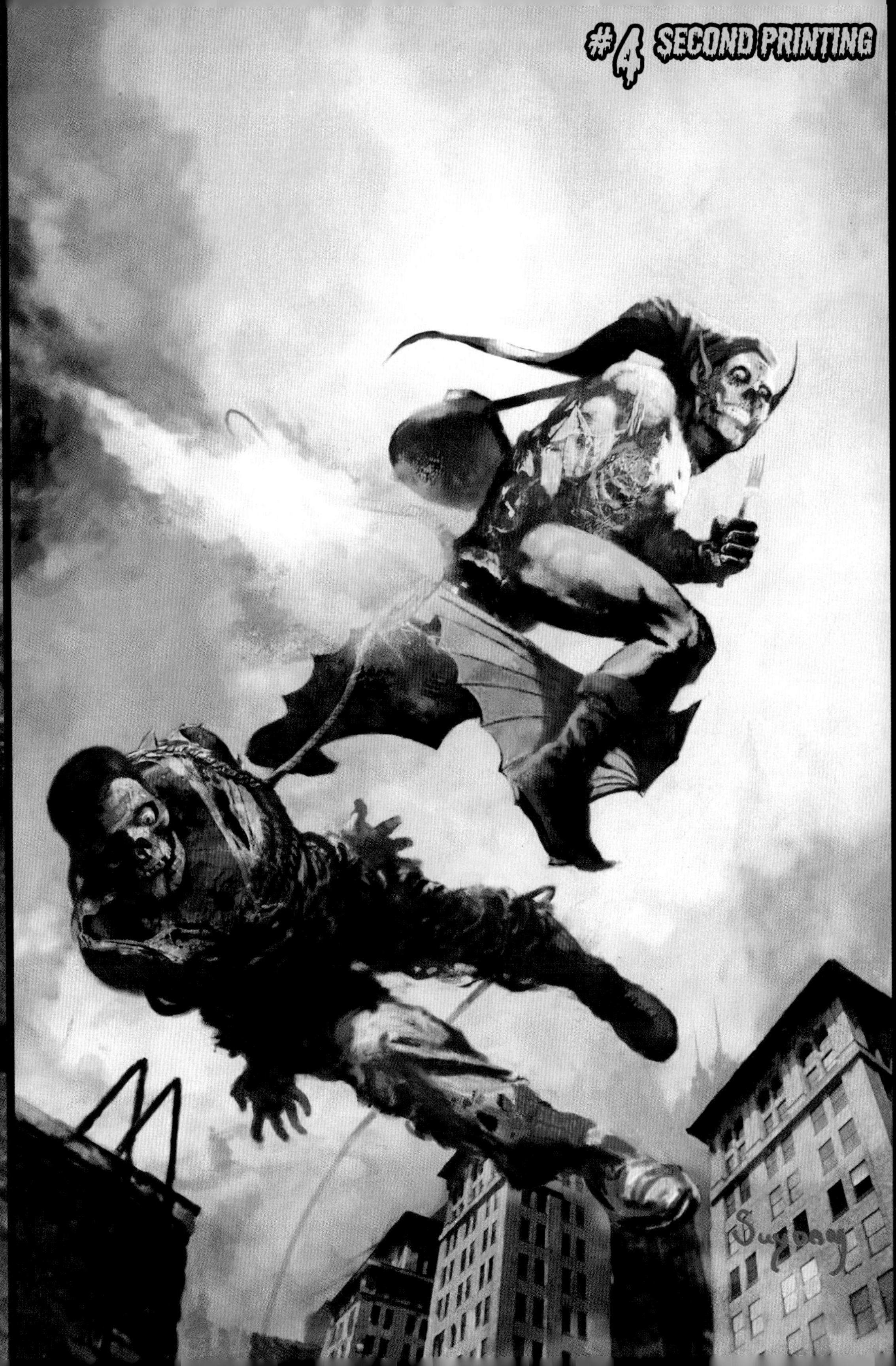
#4 SECOND PRINTING

#5

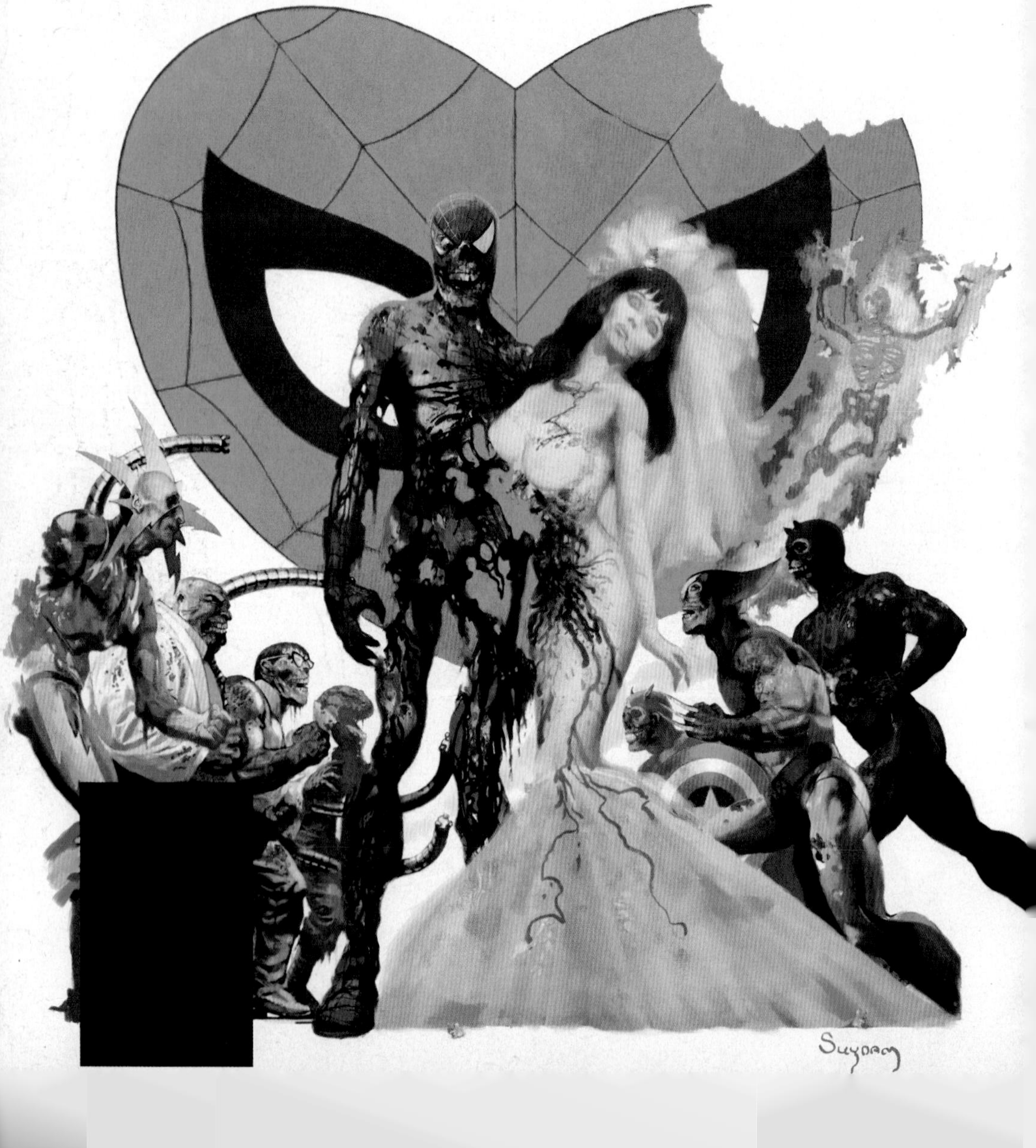
Suydam

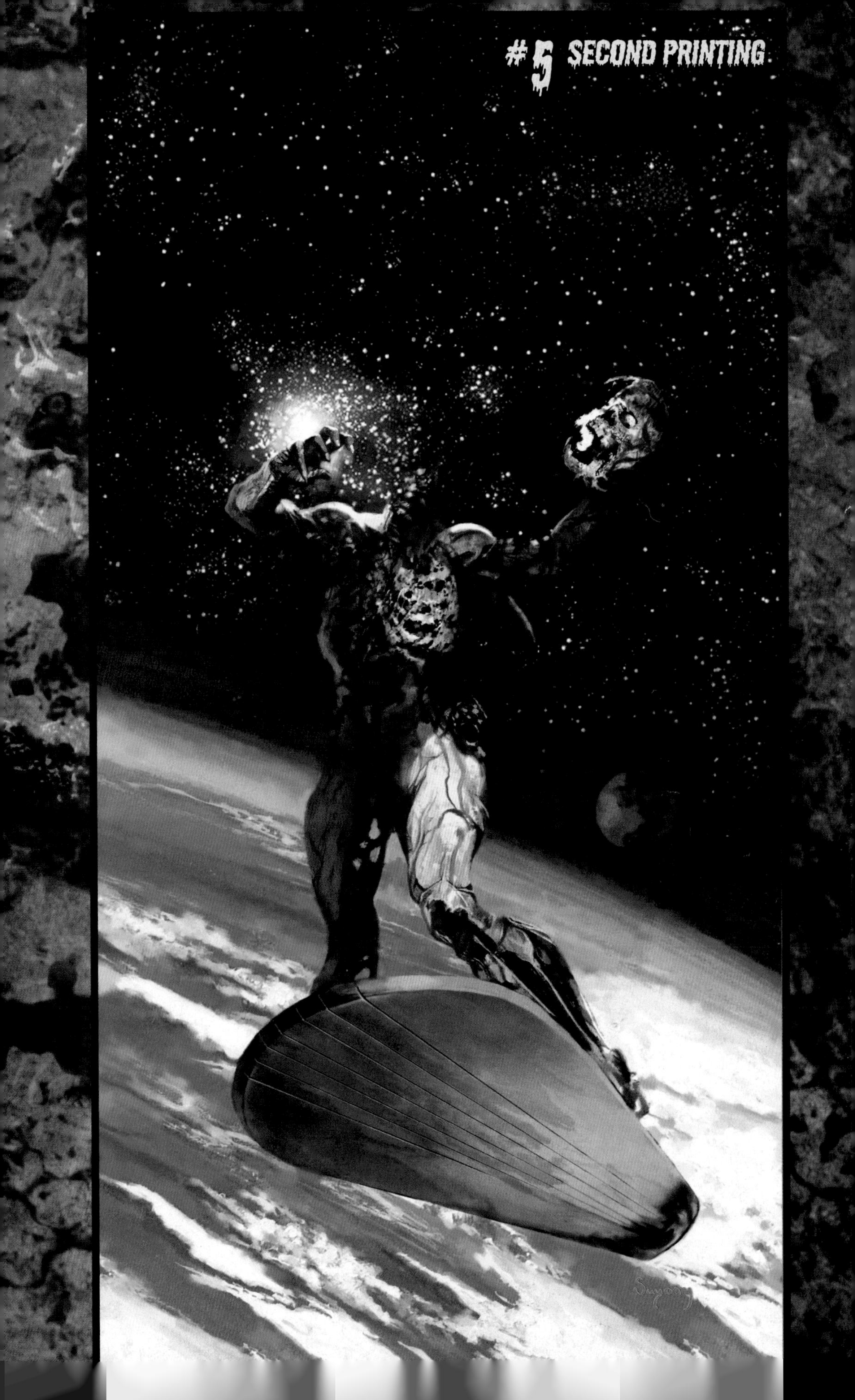
#5 SECOND PRINTING

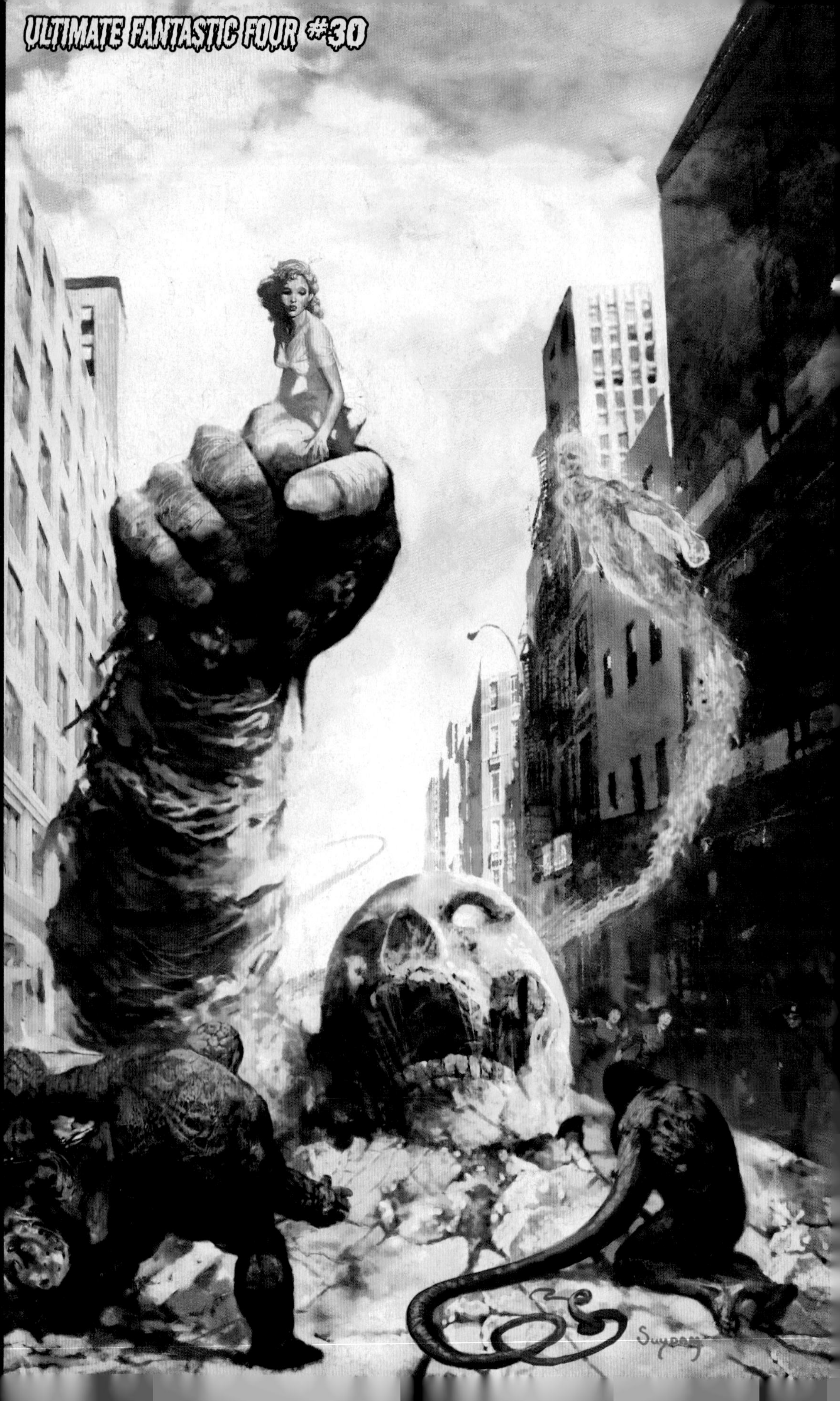
ULTIMATE FANTASTIC FOUR #30
Suydam

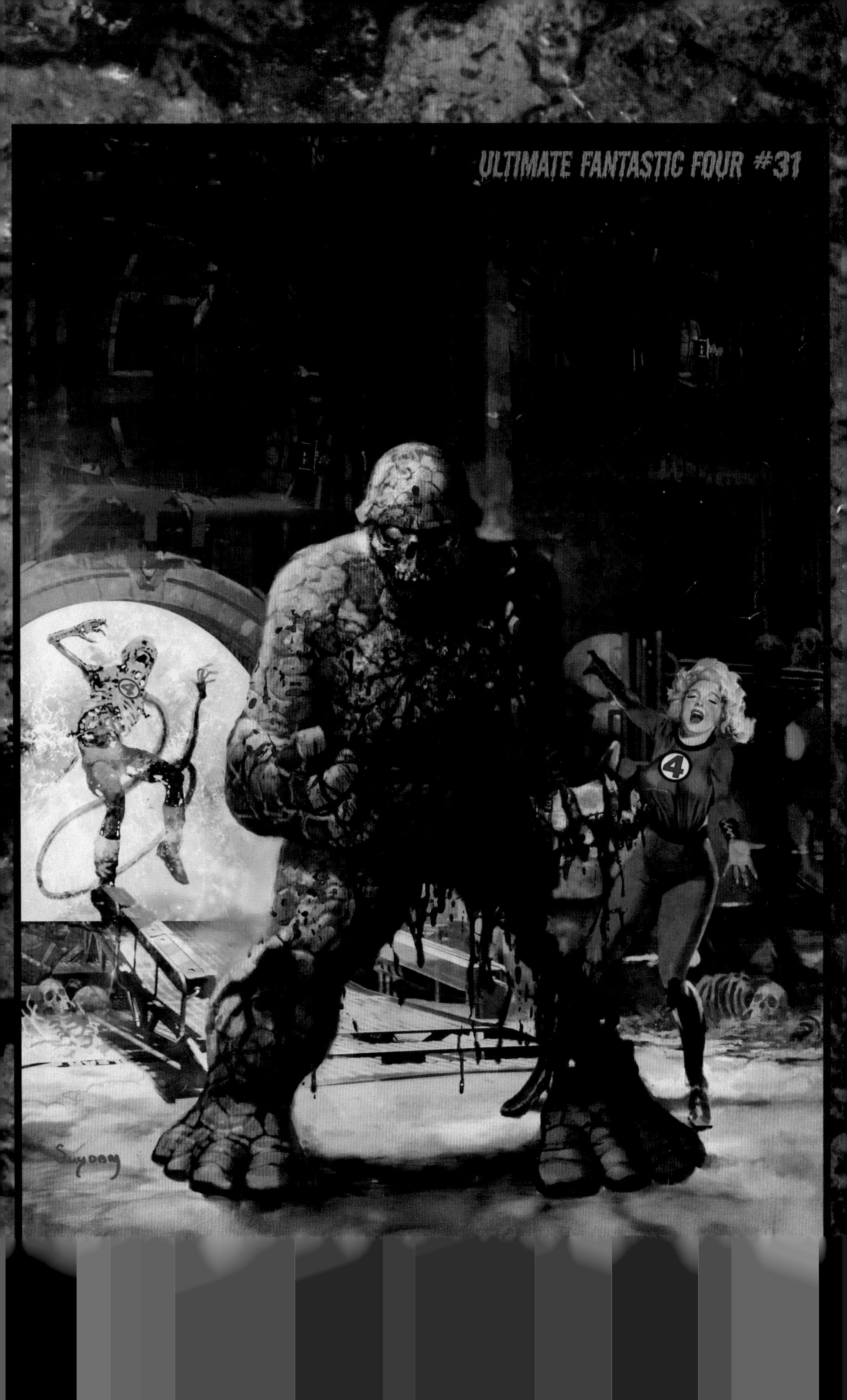
ULTIMATE FANTASTIC FOUR #31

ULTIMATE FANTASTIC FOUR #32

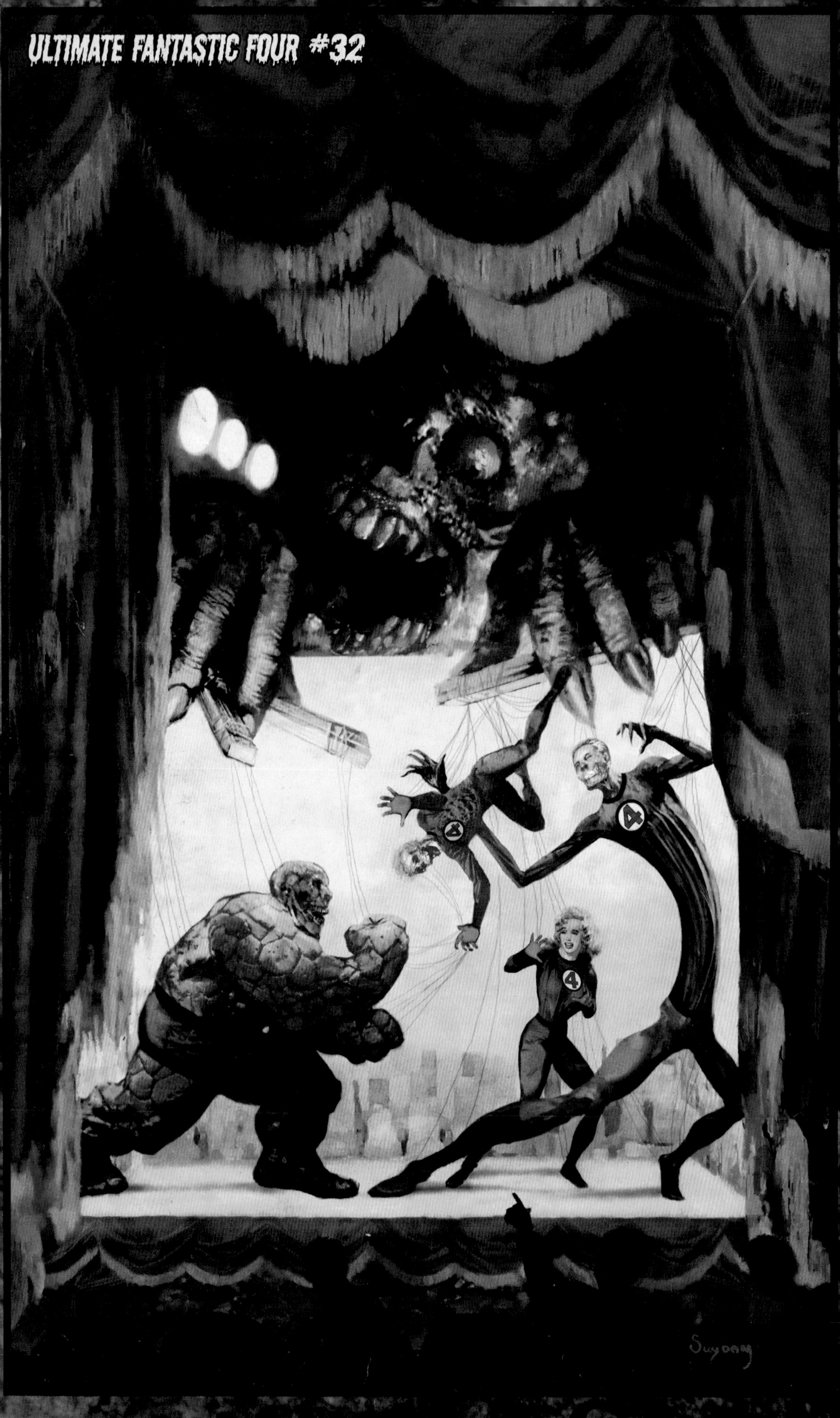
Suydam

REFERENCED COVERS

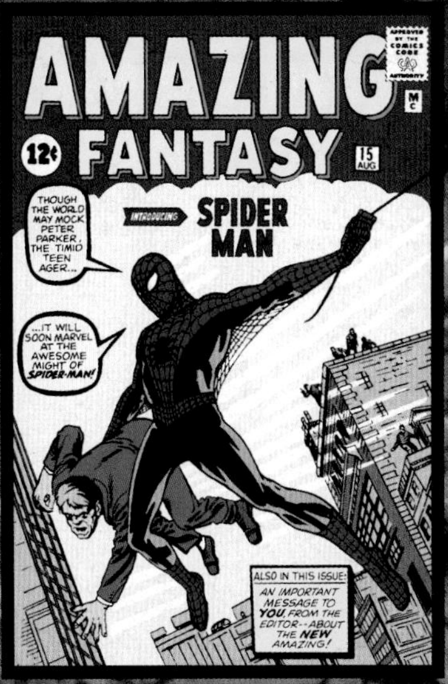

AMAZING
FANTASY
12¢
15 AUG
THOUGH THE WORLD MAY MOCK PETER PARKER, THE TIMID TEEN AGER...
INTRODUCING SPIDER MAN
...IT WILL SOON MARVEL AT THE AWESOME MIGHT OF SPIDER-MAN!
ALSO IN THIS ISSUE: AN IMPORTANT MESSAGE TO YOU, FROM THE EDITOR--ABOUT THE NEW AMAZING!

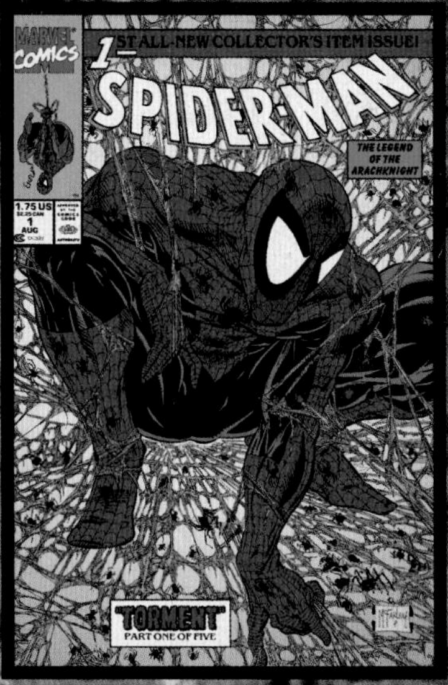

MARVEL COMICS
1ST ALL-NEW COLLECTOR'S ITEM ISSUE!
1 — SPIDER-MAN
THE LEGEND OF THE ARACHKNIGHT
1.75 US
1 AUG
"TORMENT"
PART ONE OF FIVE

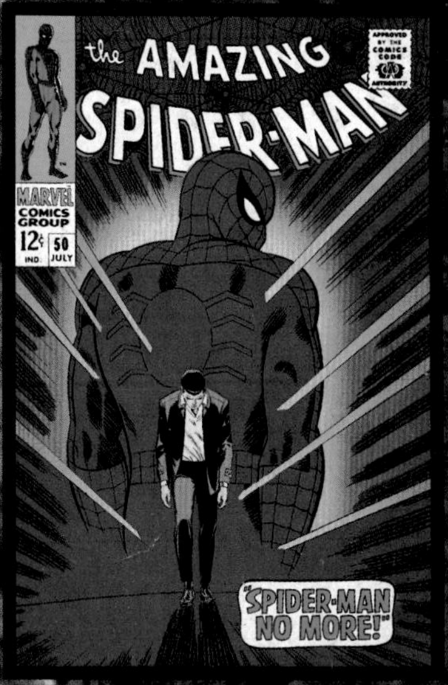

the AMAZING
SPIDER-MAN
MARVEL COMICS GROUP
12¢ 50 JULY
"SPIDER-MAN NO MORE!"

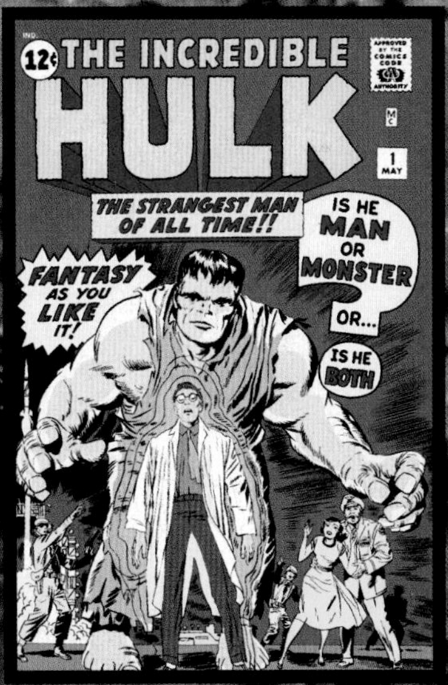

12¢ THE INCREDIBLE
HULK
1 MAY
THE STRANGEST MAN OF ALL TIME!!
IS HE MAN OR MONSTER OR... IS HE BOTH
FANTASY AS YOU LIKE IT!

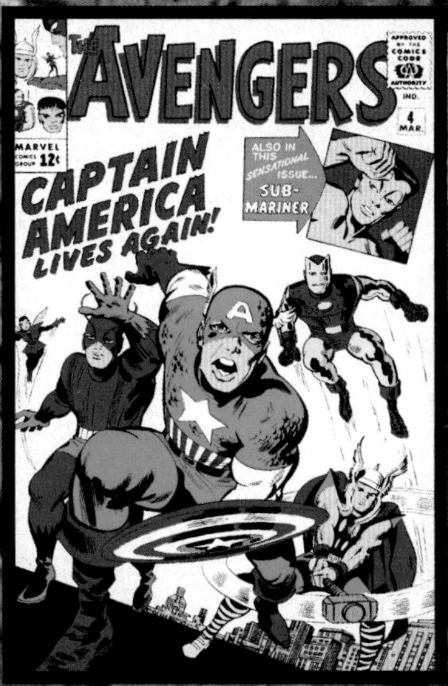

The AVENGERS
4 MAR.
MARVEL COMICS GROUP 12¢
CAPTAIN AMERICA LIVES AGAIN!
ALSO IN THIS SENSATIONAL ISSUE... SUB-MARINER

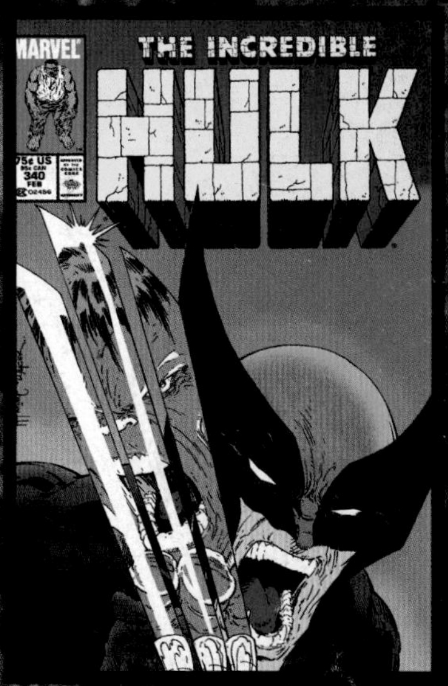

MARVEL
THE INCREDIBLE
HULK
75¢ US
340 FEB

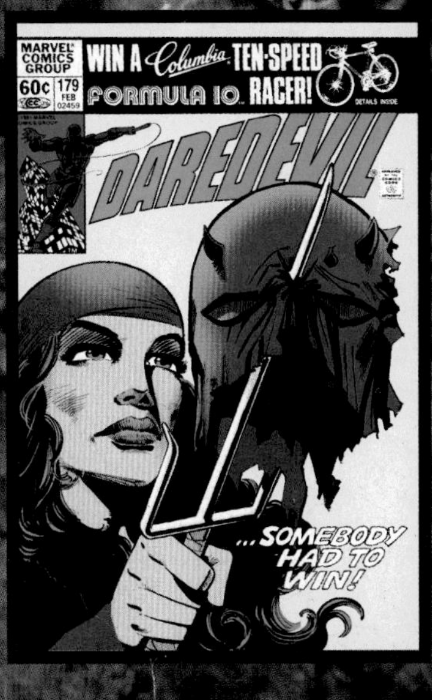

MARVEL COMICS GROUP
WIN A Columbia TEN-SPEED FORMULA 10 RACER!
60¢ 179 FEB
DETAILS INSIDE
DAREDEVIL
...SOMEBODY HAD TO WIN!

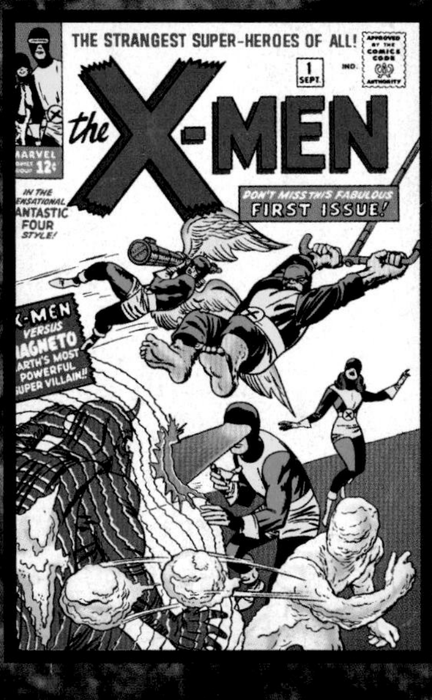

THE STRANGEST SUPER-HEROES OF ALL!
1 SEPT.
MARVEL 12¢
the X-MEN
DON'T MISS THIS FABULOUS FIRST ISSUE!
IN THE SENSATIONAL FANTASTIC FOUR STYLE!
X-MEN VERSUS MAGNETO EARTH'S MOST POWERFUL SUPER VILLAIN!!

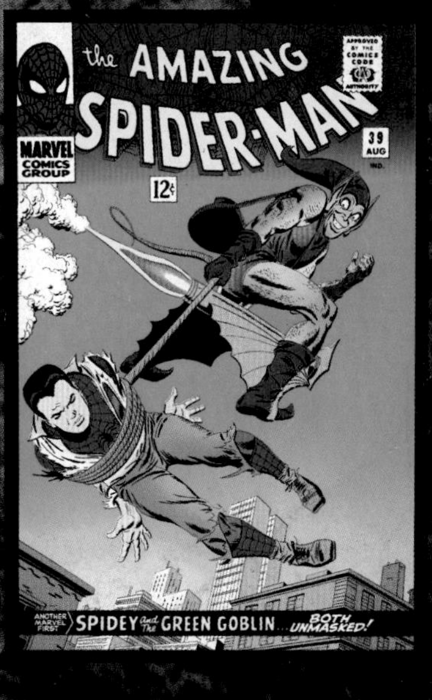

the AMAZING
SPIDER-MAN
39 AUG
MARVEL COMICS GROUP
12¢
ANOTHER MARVEL FIRST!
SPIDEY and the GREEN GOBLIN... BOTH UNMASKED!

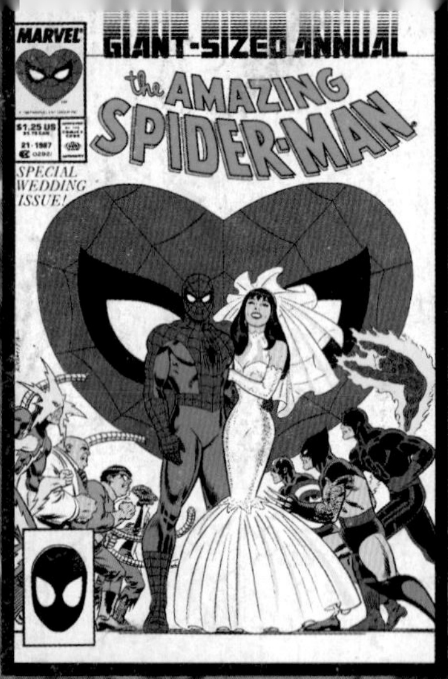
GIANT-SIZED ANNUAL
MARVEL
the AMAZING SPIDER-MAN
$1.25 US
21 1987
SPECIAL WEDDING ISSUE!

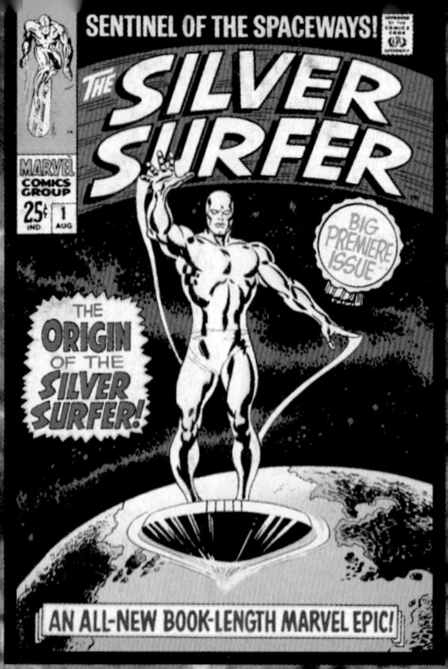
SENTINEL OF THE SPACEWAYS!
THE SILVER SURFER
MARVEL COMICS GROUP
25¢ 1 AUG
BIG PREMIERE ISSUE
THE ORIGIN OF THE SILVER SURFER!
AN ALL-NEW BOOK-LENGTH MARVEL EPIC!

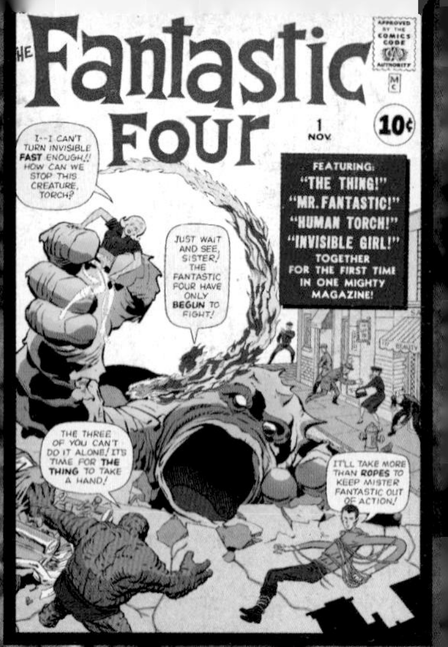
THE Fantastic FOUR
1 NOV.
10¢
FEATURING: "THE THING!" "MR. FANTASTIC!" "HUMAN TORCH!" "INVISIBLE GIRL!" TOGETHER FOR THE FIRST TIME IN ONE MIGHTY MAGAZINE!
I--I CAN'T TURN INVISIBLE FAST ENOUGH!! HOW CAN WE STOP THIS CREATURE, TORCH?
JUST WAIT AND SEE, SISTER! THE FANTASTIC FOUR HAVE ONLY BEGUN TO FIGHT!
THE THREE OF YOU CAN'T DO IT ALONE! IT'S TIME FOR THE THING TO TAKE A HAND!
IT'LL TAKE MORE THAN ROPES TO KEEP MISTER FANTASTIC OUT OF ACTION!

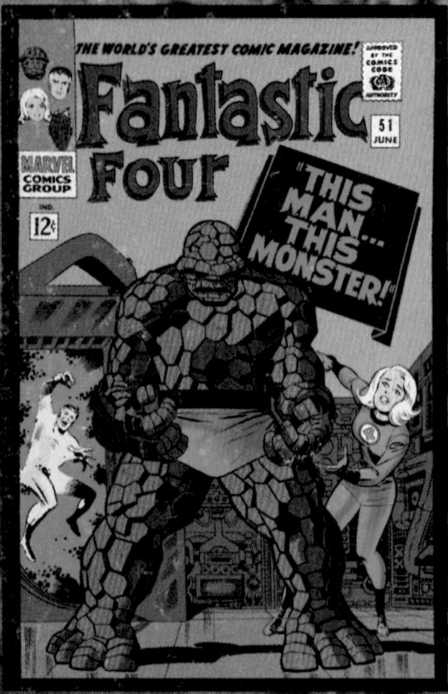
THE WORLD'S GREATEST COMIC MAGAZINE!
Fantastic FOUR
51 JUNE
MARVEL COMICS GROUP
12¢
"THIS MAN... THIS MONSTER!"

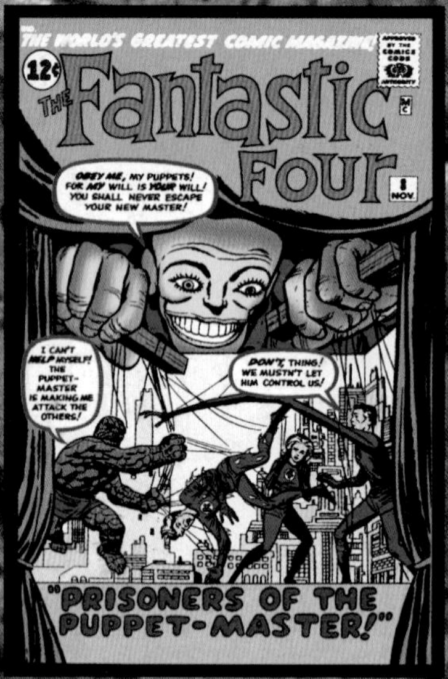
THE WORLD'S GREATEST COMIC MAGAZINE!
12¢
THE Fantastic FOUR
8 NOV.
OBEY ME, MY PUPPETS! FOR MY WILL IS YOUR WILL! YOU SHALL NEVER ESCAPE YOUR NEW MASTER!
I CAN'T HELP MYSELF! THE PUPPET-MASTER IS MAKING ME ATTACK THE OTHERS!
DON'T, THING! WE MUSTN'T LET HIM CONTROL US!
"PRISONERS OF THE PUPPET-MASTER!"

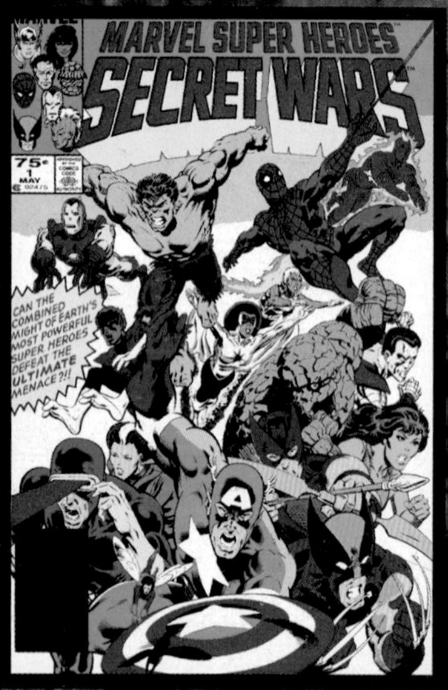
MARVEL SUPER HEROES SECRET WARS
75¢ 1 MAY
CAN THE COMBINED MIGHT OF EARTH'S MOST POWERFUL SUPER HEROES DEFEAT THE ULTIMATE MENACE?!!